Understanding Islām

A Comprehensive Guide

Immy Bloodworth Mahitab

ISBN: 979-8-9914768-0-5

Library of Congress Control Number: 2024920328

All translations of the Qur'ān within this book are based on the copyright free translation that was done by Maulana Wahiduddin Khan. The author of this book has edited certain instances of punctuation and wording.

Most translations of the ḥadīths within this book are either based on the translations published by Darussalam International Publishing & Distribution or based on translations by Abu Amina Elias. Copyrights of the ḥadīths within this book belong to the rightful owners.

Table of Contents

A Note on Pronunciation and Language

Throughout this book, I have spelled words with diacritical marks in order to represent the accurate pronunciation of words.

The macron (¯), the line over a vowel, indicates that the vowel is long, meaning that the sound is slightly stretched out when pronouncing it. In Arabic, the letter "a" is often pronounced as the "a" in "lamb." There are some exceptions to this. Any "a" following kh, r, ṣ ḍ, ṭ, ẓ, gh, and q is to be pronounced as the "a" in "father."

Additionally, in the name "Allāh," the second "a" is pronounced as the "a" in "father." The name Allāh is pronounced similar to "uh-l-LAH," with the "LAH" almost resembling the word "law."

The underdot (.) below a letter indicates that the letter is pronounced in a guttural manner.

The asper (') represents the Arabic letter 'ayn, which is made with a guttural sound from around the uvula. So " 'Abdullāh" would be pronounced with the guttural sound at the beginning of the name.

The apostrophe (') represents the Arabic sign hamzah, which is a short glottal stop.

The letters a, i, and u are generally pronounced as in "lamb," "feet," and "moon," respectively.

Kh is a raspy sound, similar to the Scottish word "loch," and gh is a guttural sound, somewhat like a "g" pronounced in the back of the throat.

Dh is pronounced as the "th" in "that," and not as the "th" in "teeth."

Ẓ is pronounced as the "th" as in "that" except with a guttural vowel following the consonant.

Q is pronounced similar to a "k" but from the back of the throat.

For those familiar with Arabic:

Th = ث ; Ḥ = ح ; Kh = خ ; Dh = ذ ; Ṣ = ص ; Ḍ = ض ; Ṭ = ط ; Ẓ = ظ ;
‘ = ع ; Gh = غ ; Q = ق ; ’ = ء

Finally, the word “ibn” means “son of,” and the word “bint” means “daughter of.”

A Note on Abbreviations

Throughout this book, there are abbreviations in superscript beside certain names. This is because, out of respect, Muslims often say a short prayer for certain individuals when they mention them. The abbreviation (saws) stands for *ṣallallāhu 'alayhi wa sallam*, which means "commendations and peace from God be upon him." It is said after the name of the Prophet Muḥammad (saws). The abbreviation (as) stands for *'alayhis-Salām*, which means "Peace be upon him." It is said after the names of prophets or angels. The abbreviation (ra) stands for *raḍiyallāhu 'anhu*, which means "may God be pleased with him." It is said after the names of the companions of Muḥammad (saws).

Part 1: The Message

A General Introduction to Islām

Chapter 1
General Questions

What is Islām?

The word *Islām* is derived from the Arabic trilateral root س ل م (S-L-M; *salima*). Salima means to be safe from defects, and Islām means "Submission (to the will of God)." This is the name of the religion, its proper name being *Al-Islām*, that was revealed in Arabic to the Prophet *Muḥammad* (saws) (570 – 632 C.E.), starting around the year 610 C.E. The word "Islām" is etymologically related to the Arabic word *salām*, which means "peace." A *Muslim* is, consequently, one who peacefully submits to the will of God (i.e., one who adheres to the religion of Islām). Although Muḥammad (saws) was an Arab and received revelation in Arabic, a Muslim is not required to be either an Arab or fluent in Arabic and may be a person of any nationality, race, ethnicity, or gender. There are currently about 1.9 billion Muslims around the globe, placing it second in demographics among the world's largest religions. Islām looks upon all races, Arab and non-Arab, as equal before God. It teaches that it is our faith and our deeds, not our social statuses, upon which God judges us.

Who is Allāh?

Allāh is the Arabic word for God, referring to the One God (that is, "God" with a capital "G"). It is *not* the Arabic word for god, as in "any god in general" (that is, "god" with a lowercase "g"); that word is *ilāh*. Indeed, "Allāh" is the actual Arabic *name* for the One God, the only God that truly exists, and even Arab Jews and Arab Christians refer to God as Allāh. The One that Christians call "the Father" is the same One that Muslims call "God," but Muslims believe that God prefers that humanity does not refer to Him as a Father. Instead of the concept of a Father and

His children, Muslims believe in the concept of a Creator and His creations.

Moreover, parts of the Bible are in Aramaic, the language that Jesus (as) spoke, and the Aramaic word for god is *Elah.* This word is related to the Hebrew words for god, *El* and *Eloah*, and it is also related to the Arabic word ilāh and the name Allāh, as Hebrew, Aramaic, and Arabic are all Semitic languages. Elah is used in the Bible in places such as Daniel 2:23 and Ezra 7:19, among other parts of the Bible.

English-speaking Muslims may refer to the Ultimate Being as "God," yet they often stick to calling Him "Allāh." This is because "Allāh" is the phonetic name with which God referred to Himself in His final revelation, and Muslims believe that every Arabic letter in Allāh's name has an etymological and spiritual significance. Nevertheless, the names "God" and "Allāh" will be used interchangeably in this book.

God is the One Who created us; there is no god other than Him. He is All-Powerful, All-Knowing, the Creator, the Sustainer, the Ruler, and the Owner of everything and everyone. He is the only One to Whom worship is due, He is the Source of all, the Most Loving, and the Absolute Reality. He does not need to rest or sleep, and He is the Infinitely Good and the Most Merciful. God is also referred to as *Rabb*, or "Lord." Muslims often say after mentioning Allāh's name: *subḥānahū wa ta'ālā*, which means "Glorified and Exalted is He," or *'azza wa jall*, which means "Mighty and Sublime." God's Throne is above the heavens and all creation, and God is above His Throne. God has revealed in the Qur'ān:

255God: there is no deity except for Him, the Ever-Living, the Eternal. Neither drowsiness nor sleep overtakes Him. To Him belong whatsoever is in the heavens and whatsoever is on the earth. Who can intercede with Him except by His permission? He knows all that is before them and all that is behind them. They can grasp only that part of His knowledge which He wills. His seat extends over the heavens and the earth, and their upholding does not weary Him. And He is the Most Exalted, the Absolute Greatest. (Qur'ān 2:255)

102This is God, your Lord, there is no god but Him, the Creator of all things, so worship Him. He is the Guardian of all things. (Qur'ān 6:102)

[1]*Everything in the heavens and earth glorifies God. He is the Almighty, the Most Wise.* [2]*He has sovereign control over the heavens and the earth. He gives life and brings death. He has power over all things.* [3]*He is the First and the Last, the Outward and the Inward. He has knowledge of all things. (Qur'ān 57:1-3)*

[22]*He is God: there is no deity save Him. He knows the unseen and the visible. He is the Most Compassionate, the Most Merciful.* [23]*He is God: there is no deity save Him, the Sovereign, the Most Pure, the Source of Peace, the Granter of Security, the Protector, the Almighty, the Subduer, the Supreme. Glory be to God, who is far above what they associate with Him.* [24]*He is God—the Creator, the Originator, the Giver of Form. His are the most excellent names. Everything in the heavens and earth declares His glory. He is the Almighty, the Most Wise. (Qur'ān 59:22-24)*

[14]*And He is the Most Forgiving and the Most Loving,* [15]*the Lord of the glorious Throne,* [16]*Doer of whatever He wills. (Qur'ān 85:14-16)*

[1]*Say [O Prophet], 'He is God, the One,* [2]*God, the Self-Sufficient, needed by all.* [3]*He does not have offspring, nor was He born,* [4]*and there is nothing like Him. (Qur'ān 112)*

These verses from the Qur'ān show that in Islām God is understood to be One, Infinite, Loving, the Creator, the Sustainer, the All-Powerful, and the All-Knowing. The concept of monotheism, the Oneness of God, is known in Arabic as *tawḥīd*. Muslim scholars have divided the concept of tawḥīd into three categories:

1. Tawḥīd Ar-Rubūbiyyah (Oneness of Lordship)
2. Tawḥīd Al-Ulūhiyyah (Oneness of Godhood)
3. Tawḥīd Al-Asmā' wa Aṣ-Ṣifāt (Oneness of the Names and Attributes)

Oneness of Lordship refers to the belief that God is the only Creator, Ruler, and Sustainer of all things. Oneness of Godhood refers to the belief that there is no god except for Allāh, meaning that there is none worthy of worship except for God alone. And Oneness of the Names and Attributes refers to the belief in all of the names and attributes of God that have been described in the religion and that they all attest to His perfect glory. The meanings of His names and attributes should not be changed, ignored, or twisted. An authentic narration states that God has 99 names.

When did Islām begin?

Some people say that Islām began with the Prophet Muḥammad (saws), but according to Muslims this is not true. As Islām means "Submission (to the will of God)," it was the religion adhered to, albeit perhaps in differing ritual practices, by all of the prophets of God, commencing with Adam (as). Noah (as), Abraham (as), Ishmael (as), Isaac (as), Jacob (Israel) (as), Moses (as), John (the Baptist) (as), and Jesus Christ (as), amongst others, were all Muslim prophets who preached of peace and submission. Muḥammad (saws) was the last in the line of these humans to be bestowed with a Scripture from God and the rank of prophethood.

What are the sources of Islām?

There are only two primary sources to which Muslims look for guidance: the *Qur'ān* and the *Sunnah*:

- The Qur'ān (sometimes spelled: "Koran") is the holy book of Islām, and the word "Qur'ān" literally means "Recitation." Muslims believe the Qur'ān to be the literal word of God, which was revealed to Muḥammad (saws) through the Angel Gabriel (as), who in Arabic is called *Jibrīl* (as), over the course of 23 years. The book consists of 114 *sūrahs* (i.e., chapters of the Qur'ān), and each sūrah contains a number of verses. The word used for a verse of the Qur'ān is *āyah*, which literally means "sign," and the Arabic plural is *āyāt*. The Qur'ān is the last in a series of scriptural revelations that included the Torah and the Gospel. The Qur'ān has been preserved in its entirety since its revelation. During the life of the Prophet Muḥammad (saws), followers of his memorized it and wrote it down, and there was never a widespread suppression or rejection of the Qur'ān in the overall Muslim community throughout history. There is, and always has been, only one Qur'ān in all sects of Islām.

- The Sunnah (literally: "Example") refers to the example and teachings of the Prophet Muḥammad (saws). It is the precedent by which Muslims model every aspect of life – from how to clean oneself, to how to maintain a family, to judicial matters. The Sunnah is primarily recorded in the *ḥadīths* (Arabic plural:

aḥādīth), or "narrations," which, in the context of Islām, are usually narrations that contain the sayings, actions, and approvals of the Prophet Muḥammad (saws).

There are two primary sources of ḥadīths that are widely considered to be the most *ṣaḥīḥ*, or "authentic," and they are the books that are popularly known as *Ṣaḥīḥ Al-Bukhārī* and *Ṣaḥīḥ Muslim*. Ṣaḥīḥ Al-Bukhārī is widely held to be first in authenticity between the two and was compiled by Imām Muḥammad ibn Ismā'īl Al-Bukhārī (810 – 870 C.E.). Ṣaḥīḥ Muslim was compiled by Imām Muslim ibn Al-Ḥajjāj (820 – 875 C.E.). These are the first two books of what most Muslims view to be the six canonical books of aḥādīth. These six canonical books are known as *Al-Kutub As-Sittah (the Six Books)*, and they are commonly associated with their compilers, the names of whom are presented in bold:

- Ṣaḥīḥ **Al-Bukhārī**
- Ṣaḥīḥ **Muslim**
- Sunan **Abū Dāwūd**
- Sunan **An-Nasā'ī**
- Jāmi' **At-Tirmidhī**
- Sunan **Ibn Mājah**

Ad-Dārimī's Sunan was sometimes included in this collection. It is important to note that only the books of Al-Bukhārī and Muslim are authentic in their near entirety. The other books also have ḥadīths that are less authentic or not authentic. The levels of ḥadīth authenticity are ṣaḥīḥ (authentic), ḥasan (good), ḍa'īf (weak), and mawḍū' (fabricated). There is a complex methodology used in discerning a ḥadīth's authenticity, and it involves analyzing a ḥadīth's *matn* (text) and *isnād* (chain of narrators between the ḥadīth collector and the Prophet (saws)). Additionally, a ḥadīth that contains a saying of God that is not in the Qur'ān is called a ḥadīth qudsī (sacred ḥadīth). Also note that in many English ḥadīth translations, the full isnād is not translated, and this is to maintain brevity.

There are also many other books of aḥādīth, and many other scholars of aḥādīth, some of whom include Mālik ibn Anas, Aḥmad ibn Ḥanbal, An-Nawawī, Ibn Ḥajar Al-'Asqalānī, and Nāṣiruddīn Al-Albānī, to name a few. Some noteworthy compilations of aḥādīth that draw from the original compilations include the Forty Aḥādīth of An-Nawawī, Riyāḍ Aṣ-Ṣāliḥīn

(Gardens of the Righteous) by An-Nawawī, and Bulūgh Al-Marām (Attainment of the Objective) by Ibn Ḥajar Al-ʻAsqalānī. It may additionally be noted that biographical narratives about the Prophet (saws) are recorded in a historical genre of literature known as *sīrah.*

What is the "royal we"?

It should perhaps be noted that in the Qur'ān, God often refers to Himself alone in the plural (We, Us, Our, etc.). This concept is known as the "royal we," and it is used by figures of authority to refer to themselves alone. There is only one God, and He often uses this literary technique while referring to Himself alone.

What is tafsīr?

Tafsīr is a type of literature that explains the Qur'ān. There have been many tafsīrs throughout history, but one of the most popular is the tafsīr written by Ibn Kathīr.

What is Sharīʻah?

All of the rulings derived from the Qur'ān and the Sunnah that are to be implemented in a believer's life are called *Sharīʻah.* Muslim scholars also derive rulings based on *ijmāʻ* (consensus) and *qiyās* (analogy). While Sharīʻah can simply be described as "Law," it actually encompasses much more than judicial commandments, and its scope includes the entire religion. Essentially, the Sharīʻah is simply the Islāmic way of life, and its goal is peace, justice, and the Pleasure of God. The science of law is called jurisprudence, and the Arabic word for jurisprudence is *fiqh*. The word *ḥalāl* means "lawful" or "permissible," and the word *ḥarām* means "unlawful" or "impermissible."

Where do Muslims congregate?

The place of worship for Muslims is called a *mosque* (Arabic: *masjid*). The person who leads Muslims in prayer is called an *imām*. "Imām" also refers to the spiritual leader of a Muslim community, and it can also refer to a scholar.

What is the weekly day of congregation in Islām?

The most significant day of the week in Islām is Friday, the 6th day. It is called *Al-Jumu'ah*, and on that day, Muslims gather at the masjid in the early afternoon to listen to the imām give a sermon (Arabic: *khuṭbah*) and to perform a short congregational prayer. One reason that Friday is sacred is because Adam (as) was created on that day.

What are the Pillars of Īmān (Faith)?

Islām belongs to a group of faiths known as the "Abrahamic Religions" (usually known to be Judaism, Christianity, and Islām), as they all have ties to a Semitic prophet named Abraham (as) who lived a few thousand years ago. As such, Muslims share many of the same beliefs held by Jews and Christians. According to the example of the Prophet Muḥammad (saws), Islāmic beliefs are usually summarized in 6 "Pillars of Īmān (Faith)":

1. Belief in God (in Arabic: Allāh)
2. Belief in God's Angels
3. Belief in God's Books
4. Belief in God's Messengers
5. Belief in the Last Day
6. Belief in God's Decree

Angels

The Arabic word for angel is *malak*, the plural being *malā'ikah*. Angels are beings of light that carry out orders from God and worship Him. They do not disobey God, so there is no concept in Islām of "fallen angels."

Every person has two guardian angels and two angels that record one's good deeds and bad deeds. Three particularly important angels in Islām are Gabriel (Jibrīl) (as), the angel in charge of revelation; Michael (Mīkāl) (as), the angel in charge of rain and plants; and Isrāfīl (as), the angel in charge of blowing the horn that will signal the Last Day. In fact, Gabriel (as) is the Holy Spirit (Arabic: *Rūḥ Al-Qudus*), who was sent to both Jesus (as) and Muḥammad (saws). Contrary to Christianity, Islām does not have the concept of a "Trinity." In other words, there are not three beings (i.e., the Father, the Son, and the Holy Spirit) in one Godhead. Islām establishes clearly that God is one, not three in one, and that Gabriel (as), being the Holy Spirit, is distinct from God and a creation of His.

Additionally, angels are not to be confused with *jinns*, which are also not generally perceptible to humans but have free will and live in this world as we do. Muslims believe that Satan (Arabic: *Shayṭān*), whose name is Iblīs, was not a fallen angel but rather a jinn who had been amongst the angels, and he chose evil. Iblīs is also the forefather of all jinns as Adam (as) was the forefather of all humans. As God created Adam (as) from clay and angels from light, jinns were created from a smokeless flame of fire. The word "jinn" is also sometimes spelled "djinn." Also note that in certain literature, the plural of "jinn" is the same as the singular.

Books

The Arabic word for book is *kitāb*, and the plural is *kutub*. Books of God are Scriptures that were revealed by Him through prophets to inform, guide, and warn humanity. The last book from God is the Qur'ān, which confirms that the Torah (Arabic: *Tawrāh*) and the Gospel (Arabic: *Injīl*) were also from God. However, Muslims believe that the Torah and the Gospel were altered by people, whereas the Qur'ān is, and will remain, unaltered. Consequently, Muslims neither affirm nor disaffirm certain stories and laws that are in the Bible but not addressed in Islām, as long as they do not contradict Islām.

If the Qur'ān and the authentic ḥadīths approve something, Muslims approve it; if the Qur'ān and the authentic ḥadīths rejects something, Muslims reject it; and if the Qur'ān and the authentic ḥadīths neither approve nor reject something, Muslims leave it alone. To give examples, Muslims accept that God parted the sea for Moses (as) and the Israelites to cross and then drowned Pharaoh and his forces because that story is in both the Bible and the Qur'ān. Muslims do not accept the Biblical story that Solomon (as) worshipped idols later in his life because the Qur'ān says that Solomon (as) was not a disbeliever. And Muslims neither accept nor reject the stories about certain Biblical kings after Solomon (as) because they are not mentioned in the Qur'ān or the authentic ḥadīths.

The Qur'ān refers to the Jews, Christians, and Sabians (a monotheistic religious group that has become ambiguous to history) as "People of the Book" (Arabic: *Ahlul-Kitāb*). The "Book" in the phrase "People of the Book" refers to scriptural revelation.

The content of the Qur'ān is summarized within the brevity of the seven verses of its first sūrah, *Al-Fātiḥah* (The Opening). Al-Fātiḥah is also the most significant part of the formal prayer in Islām, and it is translated as follows:

In the name of God, the Most Compassionate, the Most Merciful.

[1]All praise is due to God, the Lord of all worlds, [2]the Most Compassionate, the Most Merciful, [3]Master of the Day of Judgement. [4]You alone we worship, and to You alone we turn for help. [5]Guide us to the straight path, [6]the path of those You have blessed, [7]not of those who have incurred wrath, nor of those who have gone astray.

Messengers

The Arabic word for prophet is *nabī*, and the plural can be *nabiyyūn* or *anbiyā'*. The Arabic word for messenger is *rasūl*, and the plural is *rusul*, so the term *Rasūlullāh* means "Messenger of God." A "prophet" was one who received some sort of clear revelation from God and had to convey it. Among the prophets were men known as "messengers," and these were prophets who were sent to disbelieving peoples. Therefore, every messenger was a prophet, but not every prophet was a messenger. Five of the most significant messengers were Noah (as), Abraham (as), Moses (as), Jesus (as), and Muḥammad (saws). In order to attain full faith, a Muslim must believe in *all* of the Messengers of God that have been mentioned in the Qur'ān, not just a few.

The Last Day

The Arabic term for the Last Day is *Yawm Al-Ākhir*. It is also known as the Day of Judgement (*Yawm Ad-Dīn*), the Day of Resurrection (*Yawm Al-Qiyāmah*), and other names. The Last Day is the Day on which humans, jinns, and all of God's creations will perish. Then the world will be recreated, and everyone will be physically resurrected. On that Day we will be judged by God based on our faith and our deeds, and thereafter we will be sent either to Hell or to Heaven. The Arabic word *Jahannam* refers to Hell. The Arabic word *Al-Jannah* means the Garden, and it refers to Paradise, which is Heaven.

The Decree

The Arabic word for decree is *qadar*. The Decree of God is the notion that Allāh has already decreed everything, good and bad, in the past, present, and future. This does not contradict the notion of humans and jinns having free will. Allāh, being the All-Knowing, already knew what people's choices and actions in their lives would be, and He recorded them all and ordained them. We must still strive to do good deeds that are within our capacity.

What are the Pillars of Islām?

According to the Sunnah, significant Islāmic ritual practices are often summarized in the form of the 5 "Pillars of Islām":

Shahādah: To bear witness: "I testify that there is no god except Allāh, and I testify that Muḥammad is the Messenger of Allāh" (in Arabic: "*Ash-hadu an lā ilāha illallāh, wa ash-hadu anna Muḥammadar-rasūlullāh*").

Ṣalāh: To perform 5 daily formal prayers. The prayers are *Fajr* (during dawn), *Ẓuhr* (during the early afternoon), *'Aṣr* (during the late afternoon), *Maghrib* (during sunset), and *'Ishā'* (during the early night). On Fridays, Ẓuhr is replaced by *Jumu'ah*, when Muslims gather at the mosque to listen to the imām give a sermon and then perform a congregational prayer.

Zakāh: To give in charity 2.5% of one's savings (and a certain portion of one's livestock, merchandise, and harvest, if applicable), provided they reach a certain amount after one lunar year. Zakāh is different from regular charity, which is called *ṣadaqah*.

Ṣawm: To fast (abstaining from water, food, sexual activity, and anything else that breaks the fast) every day, from dawn to sunset, during the lunar month of Ramaḍān. Ramaḍān is holy because it is the month in which the Qur'ān was first revealed. Another word for Ṣawm is Ṣiyām.

Ḥajj: To perform a pilgrimage to certain sites in Mecca and surrounding areas at least once in one's life if one is able to. Ḥajj can only be performed during a certain time of the year. There is also a minor pilgrimage to Mecca called 'Umrah, which is not obligatory, and it can be performed throughout the year, but Ḥajj is the one that is obligatory.

What is iḥsān?

The word *iḥsān* means "excellence," and in practice it means to worship God as if you see Him, for even though you do not see Him, He sees you. There is a very significant ḥadīth called *Ḥadīth Jibrīl (the Gabriel Narration)*, in which the Angel Gabriel (as) reviewed the *deen*, or religion, with the Prophet Muḥammad (saws) in front of some of the Prophet's (saws) companions. According to the Gabriel Ḥadīth, there are three fundamental aspects of the religion: Islām (Submission), Īmān (Faith), and Iḥsān (Excellence). It is important to be familiar with the 5 arkān (pillars) of Al-Islām, the 6 arkān (pillars) of Al-Īmān, and Iḥsān.

What is the status of Jesus in Islām?

Muslims believe that Jesus (as) was among the most significant Messengers of Allāh, the Christ / Messiah (Arabic: *Al-Masīḥ*), a word which He conveyed to Mary, and a spirit from Him. The Qur'ān teaches that Mary was a virgin when she gave birth to Jesus (as), but God is not his Father. Instead, God is his Creator, and He created Jesus (as) without a father similarly to how He created Adam (as) without a father or a mother. Jesus (as) was a human messenger whom God supported with miracles, and Islām rejects the notion of Jesus (as) having been God or a literal son of God. Such notions are results of humans having tampered with the original Gospel that was given to Jesus (as).

253 *Of these messengers, We have favored some over others. There are some to whom God spoke directly and others He exalted in rank. We gave Jesus son of Mary clear signs and strengthened him with the Holy Spirit. Had God pleased, those who succeeded them would not have fought against one another after the clear signs had come to them. But they*

disagreed among themselves; some believed, while others did not. Yet had God willed, they would not have fought against one another; but God does whatever He wills. (Qur'ān 2:253)

Islām also teaches that Jesus (as) was neither crucified, nor did he die. Instead, God raised him up to Heaven, and a disciple of Jesus (as) was crucified in his stead. The Muslim perspective is that a crucifixion did not lead to salvation for humanity, but God's mercy leads to salvation because God's mercy is greater than anyone can comprehend.

Islām teaches that Jesus (as) will come back before the Last Day and will kill the Antichrist (in Arabic: *Al-Masīḥ Ad-Dajjāl*). Jesus (as) will guide the Jews and Christians to Islām and live as a prominent Muslim leader until he dies.

How does Islām view the concept of original sin?

Islām rejects the concept of original sin. Muslims believe that when Adam (as) and Eve ate from the forbidden tree, they regretted their decision and turned to God in repentance, so God forgave them.

37*Then Adam received some words [of prayer] from his Lord and He accepted his repentance. He is the Accepter of repentance, the Most Merciful. (Qur'ān 2:37)*

23*They replied, 'Our Lord, we have wronged our souls. If You do not forgive us and have mercy on us, we shall be among the lost.' (Qur'ān 7:23)*

Islām teaches that every soul is born with a clean record and that no soul can take on the sins of another soul. It is up to every individual to do good deeds, avoid bad deeds, and rely on the mercy of God.

15*Whoever chooses to follow the right path, follows it for his own good; and whoever goes astray, goes astray at his own peril. No bearer of burdens shall bear the burdens of another. Nor do We punish until We have sent forth a messenger to forewarn them. (Qur'ān 17:15)*

18*No bearer of burden shall bear another's burden, and if some over-laden soul should call out for someone else to carry his load, not the least portion of it will be borne for him, even though he were a near relative. You can only warn those who fear their Lord in the unseen, and* *pray regularly. Anyone who purifies himself will benefit greatly from doing so. To God all shall return. (Qur'ān 35:18)*

What is the significance of Mecca, Medina, and Jerusalem?

Mecca (also spelled *Makkah*) is the holiest city for Muslims. It contains the Kaaba (also spelled *Ka'bah*), which was the first house of worship that God appointed, and it was built by Abraham (as) and his son, Ishmael (as). Surrounding the Kaaba is the holiest mosque, Al-Masjid Al-Ḥarām. Makkah is also the birthplace of the Prophet Muḥammad (saws). Medina (also spelled *Al-Madīnah*) is the second holiest city for Muslims. It contains the mosque of the Prophet Muḥammad (saws), Al-Masjid An-Nabawī, and it was the city to which he migrated and spent the later years of his life. Jerusalem (in Arabic: *Al-Quds*) is the third holiest city for Muslims. It was a city of importance for Israelite prophets and the Israelite believers who followed them, and Muslims believe that one night Muḥammad (saws) ascended with Gabriel (as) into Heaven from Jerusalem and descended back to the world on the same night. The Dome of the Rock marks where this event occurred. Jerusalem also contains Al-Masjid Al-Aqṣā, rebuilt by Solomon (as) thousands of years ago and rebuilt more times over the years.

What is the purpose of life according to Islām?

The purpose of life for sane adult human beings is to serve God, believing in His messages, adhering to what He has enjoined and avoiding what He has forbidden. Life in this world, and the good and the bad with it, is a test. Sin and hardships surround us, and we must strive to remain steadfast in our service to God. Islām is about forming the closest relationship that one may have with their Creator, the Absolute Reality. One should understand God with the correct belief (inasmuch as a human can). When one does their part in striving towards Allāh out of love, peace, and devotion, then the mercy of Allāh is the ultimate, incomparable, infinite mercy. However, He does not wrong any soul in the least, so one should not behave towards God with indifference, arrogance, or hatred. Out of His mercy, He has provided us with all that we have, and He asks of us so little. What prevents the finite from humbling itself to the Infinite? What prevents the many from striving towards the One? Indeed, we would not be real without the Absolute Reality, the Most Holy, the Most Loving, so when one seeks Allāh with their truest compassion, then, if Allāh wills, they will be requited with His compassion, and that is the best compassion.

56 I created the jinn and humans only so that they might worship Me. 57 I seek no sustenance from them, nor do I want them to feed Me. 58 It is God who is the great Sustainer, the Mighty One, the Invincible. (Qur'ān 51:56-58)

1 I swear by the passage of time 2 that the human is surely in a state of loss, 3 except for those who believe and do good deeds and exhort one another to hold fast to the truth and exhort one another to patience. (Qur'ān 103)

What do Muslims believe about the afterlife?

The word *dunyā* refers to this world, and the word *ākhirah* refers to the afterlife. When a person is about to die, the Angel of Death comes with other angels to remove the soul, or *nafs*. If the individual was good, then the process will be smooth and pleasurable. There are seven levels of Heaven, and the soul ascends to the seventh level, and God commands that the soul's book of deeds be recorded in a record of the righteous, then the soul is brought back to earth. Two angels, Al-Munkar and An-Nakīr, question the soul about its faith, and the believer, or *mu'min*, answers the questions correctly. Thereafter, the soul is allowed to experience some of Paradise.

If the individual was bad, then the process of removing the soul will be painful and miserable. The soul ascends but is denied access to the first level of Heaven, God commands that the soul's book of deeds be recorded in a record of the wicked, then the soul is brought back to earth. Al-Munkar and An-Nakīr question the soul about its faith, but the disbeliever, or *kāfir*, will not be able to answer the questions correctly. Thereafter, the soul is exposed to a portion of Hell.

The questioning takes place in the grave, or whatever is the resting place of the body, and the realm of existence inhabited by the souls of the dead is called *Al-Barzakh*. Souls remain in this state until the Day of Resurrection, when all of humanity will be recreated in body, and everyone will be gathered together in a reddish white land with no landmarks. The sun will be brought a mile away, and people will be afflicted by its heat. However, the best among humankind will be provided with shade. The Day of Resurrection will last for 50,000 years, but for the believers it will feel like a shorter time. God will then judge every individual based on their faith and deeds. Whoever was not adequately exposed to Islām in the dunyā (such as the deaf person, the insane person, the senile person, or the person born between the time of Jesus (as) and Muhammad (saws)) will have their own test on the Day of Judgment.

Those who disbelieved will be cast into Hell, also known as *An-Nār*, the Fire. The believers will then have to cross the bridge called Aṣ-Ṣirāṭ, and some will fall into Hell on account of bad deeds. Others will make it into Paradise. Then God will allow the prophets, the angels, and the believers to intercede for those in Hell so that some will be taken out and allowed into Heaven. Finally God Himself, in His mercy, will take individuals out of Hell. The tortures of Hell and the joys of Paradise are described vividly in the Qur'ān and the Sunnah, although they transcend our worldly comprehension. Although there are physical rewards in Heaven, such as beautiful landscapes, homes, and spouses, the greatest reward is the eternal Pleasure of God, and those in Heaven will be able to see Him.

What is the Muslim greeting?

The standard way that Muslims greet each other is to say, "As-Salāmu 'alaykum," and the reply is, "Wa 'alaykum As-Salām." This translates to, "Peace be upon you," and the reply is, "And upon you be Peace." Note that *As-Salām*, which means *The Ultimate Peace*, is also a name of God. Muslims may also add, "wa raḥmatullāhi wa barakātuhū," which means, "and the mercy of God and His blessings."

What are the Muslim holidays?

Islām has two holidays, both called *'Īd*: *'Īd Al-Fiṭr*, which is a celebration after the month of Ramaḍān, and *'Īd Al-Aḍḥā*, which is a celebration during the days of Ḥajj. 'Īd may also be spelled as 'Eid, and a common greeting on the occasion is "'Eid Mubārak!" which means "Blessed 'Eid!" The days of 'Eid are specifically for celebration, and there are other sacred days in the religion.

What are some other holy times in Islām?

There are other sacred times in Islām, including *Laylah Al-Qadr* (pronounced "Laylatul-Qadr"; the Night of Power). It is the night on which the Qur'ān was first revealed, it is worth more than one thousand months, and praying during it can lead to the forgiveness of one's minor sins. It is on one of the odd nights of the last ten nights of Ramaḍān (i.e., the 21st, 23rd, 25th, 27th, or 29th), and the exact night is not known for certain. The first ten days of the Islāmic month of Dhul-Ḥijjah are the best of the year, and the 9th day, *Yawm 'Arafah* (the Day of 'Arafah), is the best day in Islām. God completed the religion on this day, and fasting on this day can lead to the forgiveness of two years of minor sins. Another holy day is *Yawm 'Āshūrā'* which is the day on which God saved Moses and his people from Pharaoh, and fasting on this day can lead to the forgiveness of minor sins from the previous year. Yawm 'Āshūrā' is on the 10th of the month of Muḥarram. Also on this day, the grandson of the Prophet, Al-Ḥusayn, was martyred, so Shī'ahs mourn on this day.

What is du'ā'?

The word *du'ā'* means "supplication" or "call," and it refers to calling on God about whatever one wishes to. Muslims often slightly raise their hands with their palms up when making 'du'ā', and while this is preferred, it is not required.

What is dhikr?

The word *dhikr* means "remembrance," and the plural in Arabic is *adhkār*. It refers to remembering Allāh by saying phrases of praise to Him, such as *Subḥānallāh* ("Glory be to God"), *Alḥamdulillāh* ("All praise is for God"), *Allāhu Akbar* ("God is Greater"), *Lā ilāha illallāh* ("There is no god except for Allāh"), or *Lā ḥawla walā quwwata illā billāh* ("There is no might and no strength except with God"). There are other phrases of dhikr too.

Additionally, saying "Subḥānallāh" is called *tasbīḥ*, "Alḥamdulillāh" is *taḥmīd*, "Allāhu Akbar" is *takbīr*, and "Lā ilāha illallāh" is *tahlīl*.

What does in shā Allāh mean?

In shā Allāh means "if God wills," or "God-willing." Muslims often say this phrase after mentioning future plans, as the Qur'ān says:

[23]Never say of anything, 'I shall certainly do this tomorrow,' [24]without [adding], 'if God so wills.' Remember your Lord whenever you might forget and say, 'I trust my Lord will guide me to that which is even nearer to the right path than this.' (Qur'ān 18:23-24)

Conversely, *mā shā Allāh* means "what God willed," and it is used to refer to something that has already happened.

What does Bismillāh mean?

The phrase *Bismillāh* means "In the name of God," and Muslims are encouraged to say it before doing things. An elongated version of it is *Bismillāhir-Raḥmānir-Raḥīm*, which means "In the name of God, the Infinitely Good, the Most Merciful."

What does Jazākallāhu khayran mean?

The phrase *Jazākallāhu khayran* means "May God reward you with good," and it is said as thanks to someone when they do good. The common response is *wa iyyāk*, which means "and you."

What does Astaghfirullāh mean?

Astaghfirullāh is a commonly said phrase that means "I seek God's forgiveness." To ask God for forgiveness is called *istighfār*.

What does Innā lillāhi wa innā ilayhi rāji'ūn mean?

Innā lillāhi wa innā ilayhi rāji'ūn means "Indeed, we belong to God, and indeed, to Him we shall return." Muslims say this when some sort of hardship happens, such as the death of a person. God says in the Qur'ān:

[155]We shall certainly test you with fear and hunger, and loss of property, lives and crops. Give good news to those who endure with fortitude. [156]Those who say, when afflicted with a calamity, 'We belong to God and to Him we shall return,' [157]are the ones who will have blessings and mercy from their Lord. It is they who are on the right path! (Qur'ān 2:155-157)

What is the symbol of Islām?

While many people use the crescent moon and star as the symbol for Islām, this is not actually something that is prescribed in the religion. It originated from the Turks during World War II as a symbol for Islāmic relief efforts just as the red cross was a symbol for Christian relief efforts. The symbol became culturally tied to Islām. A significance of the moon in Islām is that the religion goes by a lunar calendar, but neither the Prophet Muḥammad (saws) nor his companions ever designated this to be the symbol of Islām. Moreover, there is no official symbol that the religion of Islām designated for itself.

What is the difference between Sunnī and Shī'ah Muslims?

As with other religions, people have divided Islām into different sects. The largest sect in Islām by far is known as the *Sunnī* sect, although its proper name is *Ahlus-Sunnah wal-Jamā'ah* (the People of the Sunnah and the Community). At least 85% of all Muslims in the world are Sunnīs. The second largest sect in Islām is the *Shī'ah* sect, which is short for *Shī'atu 'Alī* (the Partisans of 'Alī). About 13% of all Muslims are Shī'ahs. Note that these labels of Sunnī and Shī'ah did not exist at the time of the Prophet (saws).

The difference between the two sects is not theological but political. Sunnīs believe that the rightful successors to the Prophet Muḥammad (saws) were his four closest companions: Abū Bakr, ‘Umar, ‘Uthmān, and ‘Alī, in that order. Shī‘ahs believe that the rightful successor to the Prophet Muḥammad (saws) was his cousin ‘Alī and that the right to lead the Muslim community was strictly to remain within the Prophet’s (saws) family through ‘Alī’s descendants, and they refer to each leader from ‘Alī’s descendants as an Imām. Within the Shī‘ah sect are different denominations, including the *Imāmiyyah*, or *Twelver Shī‘ah*, which is the largest Shī‘ah denomination. They believe that 12 Imāms succeeded the Prophet Muḥammad (saws), starting with ‘Alī.

Because of the difference of opinion regarding the successorship to Prophet Muḥammad (saws), Sunnīs trust all of the companions of the Prophet (saws), whereas Shī‘ahs only trust certain companions of his. This has led to the two sects having different books of aḥādīth, which in turn has led to different practices between the two sects. In other words, Sunnīs and Shī‘ahs do not do everything the same way, although the theological foundation of the two sects is the same, and both sects have the same Qur’ān. As a side note, Shī‘ahs have four main books of aḥādīth, known as *Al-Kutub Al-Ar’ba‘ah (the Four Books)*, and they are: Kitāb Al-Kāfī (by Al-Kulaynī), Man Lā Yaḥḍuruhul-Faqīh (by Ibn Bābawayh), Tahdhīb Al-Aḥkām (by Aṭ-Ṭūsī), and Al-Istibṣār (by Aṭ-Ṭūsī).

Lastly, it should be known that the Qur’ān warns against dividing into sects:

153[He has enjoined], ‘This is My straight path, so follow it, and do not follow other ways. That will lead you away from His path.’ That is what He enjoins upon you, so that you may guard yourselves. (Qur’ān 6:153)

159Have nothing to do with those who have split up their religion into sects. Their case rests with God. He will tell them about what they used to do. (Qur’ān 6:159)

10Surely all believers are brothers. So make peace between your brothers, and fear God, so that mercy may be shown to you. (Qur’ān 49:10)

What is a madhhab?

A *madhhab* (Arabic plural: *madhāhib*) is a school of thought that has its own unique interpretations of fiqh. It is not a sect of Islām. A madhhab is only a way of interpreting and practicing matters of religious jurisprudence. There are currently four major Sunnī madhhabs in the world, and they are named after the four imāms whose teachings form the basis for each madhhab: the Ḥanafī madhhab, named after Imām Abū Ḥanīfah; the Mālikī madhhab, named after Imām Mālik ibn Anas; the Shāfi'ī madhhab, named after Imām Ash-Shāfi'ī; and the Ḥanbalī madhhab, named after Imām Aḥmad ibn Ḥanbal. There are also two major Shī'ah madhhabs: the Ja'farī madhhab, named after Imām Ja'far Aṣ-Ṣādiq; and the Zaydī madhhab, named after Imām Zayd ibn 'Alī. Muslims of different cultures follow different madhhabs, and not every Muslim associates with a madhhab.

What is the Islāmic calendar?

In Islām, years are recorded using the Islāmic calendar, known as the *Hijrī* calendar. It is a lunar calendar, meaning that it changes based on the revolutions of the moon. It is named the Hijrī calendar after the *Hijrah*, which was when the Prophet Muḥammad (saws) migrated from Mecca to Medina. This event is discussed later in this book. The Hijrah took place in the Gregorian year of 622 C.E., and it marks the first year of the Hijrī calendar. Dates of the Hijrī calendar are followed in English with the letters "A.H.," which stand for "After the Hijrah." Dates before 1 A.H. may be followed by the letters "B.H.," which stand for "Before the Hijrah." Because the calendar is lunar, each month has 29 or 30 days, and the Hijrī dates change each year on the Gregorian calendar, which is solar. For example, Ramaḍān may start in May one year and then in April the next, and years later it would even be in December. There are 12 months in the Hijrī calendar:

1. Muḥarram
2. Ṣafar
3. Rabī' Al-Awwal
4. Rabī' Ath-Thānī
5. Jumādā Al-Awwal
6. Jumādā Ath-Thānī
7. Rajab
8. Sha'bān
9. Ramaḍān
10. Shawwāl
11. Dhūl-Qa'dah
12. Dhūl-Ḥijjah

Chapter 2

Conduct, Virtues, and Sins

The Qur'ān and the Sunnah enjoin the believers to be good to people. This includes incorporating into one's life the qualities of mercy, forgiveness, kindness, anger management, peace, love, patience, humility, tolerance, and justice towards humanity in general – believers and disbelievers, men and women. The virtue of showing gratitude to God will also be mentioned herein as well as passages about critical thinking and education.

General Conduct

[177]Virtue does not consist in whether you face towards the East or the West. Virtue means believing in God, the Last Day, the angels, the Book and the prophets. The virtuous are those who, despite their love for it, give away their wealth to their relatives and to orphans and the very poor, and to travelers and those who ask [for charity], and to set slaves free, and who attend to their prayers and pay the alms, and who keep their pledges when they make them, and show patience in hardship and adversity, and in times of distress. Such are the true believers, and such are the God-fearing. (Qur'ān 2:177)

[102]Believers, fear God as is His due, and when death comes, be in a state of complete submission to Him. [103]Hold fast to the rope of God and let nothing divide you. Remember the blessings He has bestowed upon you. You were enemies, and then He united your hearts, and by His grace you became brothers. You were on the brink of an abyss of Fire, and He rescued you from it. Thus God makes His signs clear to you, so that you may find guidance. [104]Let there be a group among you who call others to good, and enjoin what is right, and forbid what is wrong. Those who do this shall be successful. [105]Do not be like those who, after they had been

given clear evidence, split into factions and differed among themselves. A terrible punishment awaits such people. (Qur'ān 3:102-105)

133And hasten to your Lord's forgiveness and for a Paradise as vast as the heavens and the earth, which has been prepared for the God-fearing, 134for those who spend (in charity), both in prosperity and adversity, who restrain their anger and are forgiving towards their fellow humans—God loves those who do good works. 135And who, when they have committed an indecency or have wronged their souls, remember God and pray that their sins be forgiven—for who but God can forgive sins?—and do not knowingly persist in their misdeeds. 136Their recompense is forgiveness from their Lord, and gardens with rivers flowing through them, where they will abide forever. How excellent will be the reward of those who do good works. (Qur'ān 3:133-136)

36Whatever you have been given is only a temporary provision of this life, but that which is with God is better and more lasting for those who believe and put their trust in their Lord, 37who refrain from heinous sins and gross indecencies, who forgive when they are angry, 38who respond to their Lord and attend to their prayers, who conduct their affairs by mutual consultation and spend out of what We have provided for them, 39who, when they are attacked, defend themselves. 40Let harm be requited by an equal recompense. But whoever pardons and amends will find his reward with God. He does not love the wrongdoers. 41Those who defend themselves after they have been wronged cannot be held blameworthy, 42blame falls only on those who wrong people and transgress on this earth without justification—such will have a painful punishment— 43whoever is patient and forgiving, acts with great courage and resolution. (Qur'ān 42:36-43)

Abū Hurayrah (ra) narrated: The Messenger of God (saws) said, "Charity does not decrease wealth, no one forgives another except that God increases his honor, and no one humbles himself for the sake of God except that God raises his status." (Ṣaḥīḥ Muslim, Ḥadīth 2588)

Anger Management

Abū Hurayrah (ra) narrated: A man said to the Prophet (saws), "Advise me." The Prophet (saws) said, "Do not become angry." The man repeated his request several times, and the Prophet (saws) replied, "Do not become angry." (Ṣaḥīḥ Al-Bukhārī, Ḥadīth 6116; Riyāḍ Aṣ-Ṣāliḥīn, Ḥadīth 48)

Abū Hurayrah [(ra)] narrated: The Messenger of God [(saws)] said, "The strong man is not one who is good at wrestling, but the strong man is one who controls himself in a fit of rage." (Ṣaḥīḥ Al-Bukhārī, Ḥadīth 6114; Ṣaḥīḥ Muslim, Ḥadīth 2609; Riyāḍ Aṣ-Ṣāliḥīn, Ḥadīth 45)

Attitude Towards Believers

[10]Surely all believers are brothers. So make peace between your brothers, and fear God, so that mercy may be shown to you. (Qur'ān 49:10)

Anas [(ra)] narrated: The Prophet [(saws)] said, "None of you will have faith till he wishes for his brother what he likes for himself." (Ṣaḥīḥ Al-Bukhārī, Ḥadīth 13; Ṣaḥīḥ Muslim, Ḥadīth 45)

Attitude Towards Disbelievers

[256]There shall be no compulsion in religion. True guidance has become distinct from error. Whoever refuses to be led by false gods and believes in God has grasped the strong handhold that will never break. God is All-Hearing and All-Knowing. (Qur'ān 2:256)

[7]It may well be that God will create goodwill between you and those of them with whom you are now at enmity—for God is All-Powerful, Most Forgiving and Most Merciful. [8]He does not forbid you to deal kindly and justly with anyone who has not fought you on account of your faith or driven you out of your homes. God loves the just. [9]God only forbids you to make friends with those who have fought against you on account of your faith and driven you out of your homes or helped others to do so. Any of you who turn towards them in friendship will truly be transgressors. (Qur'ān 60:7-9)

Diversity and Equality

[22]Another of His signs is that He created the heavens and earth, and the diversity of your languages and colors. There truly are signs in this for those who know. (Qur'ān 30:22)

[13]Humanity! We have created you from a male and female, and made you into peoples and tribes, so that you might come to know each other. The

noblest of you in God's sight is the one who fears God most. God is All-Knowing and All-Aware. (Qur'ān 49:13)

Jundab ibn 'Abdullāh Al-Bajalī (ra) narrated: The Messenger of God (saws) said, "Anyone who dies while blindly following tribalism or supporting it has passed away in ignorance." (Ṣaḥīḥ Muslim, Ḥadīth 1850)

Abū Naḍrah (ra) reported: The Messenger of God (saws) said during the middle of the day at the end of the pilgrimage, "O people, your Lord is one and your father Adam is one. There is no favor of an Arab over a foreigner, nor a foreigner over an Arab, and neither white skin over black skin, nor black skin over white skin, except by righteousness. Have I not delivered the message?" They said, "The Messenger of God has delivered the message." (Musnad Aḥmad, Ḥadīth 23489; Al-Arnā'ūṭ graded it ṣaḥīḥ.)

Jābir ibn 'Abdullāh (ra) narrated: The Messenger of God (saws) addressed us during the middle of the day at the end of the pilgrimage in the Farewell Sermon. (The Prophet (saws)) said, "O people, your Lord is one and your father Adam is one. There is no virtue of an Arab over a foreigner, nor a foreigner over an Arab, and neither white over black nor black over white, except by righteousness. Have I not delivered the message?" They said, "Of course, O Messenger of God." The Prophet (saws) said, "Let the witness inform those who are absent." (Shu'ab Al-Īmān by Al-Bayhaqī, Ḥadīth 4706; Al-Albānī graded it ṣaḥīḥ.)

Education

Islām encourages people to use the gift of intellect that God gave them. This will lead to progress amongst humanity, and Islām encourages both males and females to seek knowledge. There have also been many Muslim scientists throughout history.

[1]Read [O Prophet] in the name of your Lord, Who created. [2]He created man from a clot. [3]Read! Your Lord is the Most Bountiful [4]Who taught by the pen, [5]taught man what he did not know. (Qur'ān 96:1-5)

[29]This is a blessed Book which We sent down to you [O Prophet], for people to ponder over its messages, and for those with understanding to take heed. (Qur'ān 38:29)

[36]Do not follow what you do not know, for the ear and the eye and the heart shall all be called to account. (Qur'ān 17:36)

Anas ibn Mālik narrated: The Messenger of God (saws) said, "Seeking knowledge is an obligation upon every Muslim." (Sunan Ibn Mājah, Ḥadīth 224; Al-Albānī graded it ṣaḥīḥ.)

Forgiveness

[22]Let not those who are possessed of means and plenty among you resolve to withhold their bounty from their kindred and the needy and those who have migrated from their homes in the cause of God. Let them forgive and overlook. Do you not wish God to forgive you? God is Forgiving and Merciful. (Qur'ān 24:22)

[14]Tell the believers to forgive those who do not believe in the coming of the days of God. He will requite people for what they have done. (Qur'ān 45:14)

Gratitude

[145]No soul shall die except with God's permission and at an appointed time. And if one desires the rewards of this world, We shall grant it to him. And if one desires the rewards of the life to come, We shall grant it to him. We will reward the grateful. (Qur'ān 3:145)

[7]Remember also the time when your Lord declared, "If you are grateful, I will surely bestow more favors on you; but if you are ungrateful, then know that My punishment is severe indeed." (Qur'ān 14:7)

Abū Hurayrah (ra) narrated: the Messenger of God (saws) said, "Whoever is not grateful to people, he is not grateful to God." (Jāmi' At-Tirmidhī, Ḥadīth 1954; Zubayr 'Alī Za'ī graded it ṣaḥīḥ.)

Abū Sa'īd Al-Khudrī (ra) narrated: the Messenger of God (saws) said, "Whoever is not grateful to people, he is not grateful to God." (Jāmi' At-Tirmidhī, Ḥadīth 1955; Zubayr 'Alī Za'ī graded it ṣaḥīḥ.)

Humility

[63]The true servants of the Most Compassionate are those who walk upon the earth with humility and when they are addressed by the ignorant ones, their response is, 'Peace.' (Qur'ān 25:63)

Justice

[135]Believers, be strict in upholding justice and bear witness for the sake of God, even though it be against yourselves, your parents, or your kindred. Be they rich or poor, God knows better about them both. Do not, then, follow your own desires, lest you swerve from justice. If you conceal the truth or evade it, then remember that God is well aware of all that you do. (Qur'ān 4:135)

[8]Believers, be steadfast in the cause of God and bear witness with justice. Do not let your enmity for others turn you away from justice. Deal justly; that is nearer to being God-fearing. Fear God. God is aware of all that you do. (Qur'ān 5:8)

Kindness and Mercy

[36]Worship God, and do not associate partners with Him. Be good to your parents, to relatives, to orphans, to the needy, and the neighbor who is a kinsman, and the neighbor who is not related to you and your companions and the travelers and those whom you rightfully possess. God does not like arrogant, boastful people. (Qur'ān 4:36)

Jarīr ibn 'Abdullāh (ra) narrated: The Messenger of God (saws) said, "God will not be merciful to those who are not merciful to humanity." (Ṣaḥīḥ Al-Bukhārī, Ḥadīth 7376)

'Abdullāh ibn 'Amr ibn Al-'Āṣ (ra) narrated: The Messenger of God (saws) said, "He who desires to be rescued from the Fire and enter the Garden should die in a state of complete belief in God and the Last Day and should do unto others what he wishes to be done unto him." (Ṣaḥīḥ Muslim, Ḥadīth 1844; Riyāḍ Aṣ-Ṣāliḥīn, Ḥadīth 1566)

'Ā'ishah (ra) narrated: The Prophet (saws) said, "God is Gentle and loves gentleness in all things." (Ṣaḥīḥ Al-Bukhārī, Ḥadīth 6927; Riyāḍ Aṣ-Ṣāliḥīn, Ḥadīth 632)

'Ā'ishah (ra) narrated: The Messenger of God (saws) said, "Indeed, by his good character a believer will attain the degree of one who prays during the night and fasts during the day." (Sunan Abū Dāwūd, Ḥadīth 4798; Riyāḍ Aṣ-Ṣāliḥīn, Ḥadīth 628; Al-Albānī graded it ṣaḥīḥ.)

Abū Ad-Dardā' (ra) narrated: The Prophet (saws) said, "There is nothing heavier than good character put in the scale of a believer (on the Day of Resurrection)." (Sunan Abū Dāwūd, Ḥadīth 4799; Al-Albānī graded it ṣaḥīḥ.)

'Ubādah ibn Aṣ-Ṣāmit (ra) narrated: The Messenger of God (saws) decreed, "Do not cause harm or return harm." (Sunan Ibn Mājah, Ḥadīth 2340; Al-Albānī graded it ṣaḥīḥ.)

Abū Dharr (ra) narrated: The Messenger of God (saws) said, "Refrain from harming people, for it is your charity due upon yourself." (Aṣ-Ṣamt by Ibn Abū Dunyā, Ḥadīth 68; Al-Albānī graded it ṣaḥīḥ.)

Abū Al-Muntafiq (ra) narrated: I said, "O Messenger of God, teach me what will save me from the punishment of God and admit me into Paradise." He (the Messenger of God (saws)) said, "Worship God and do not associate anything with Him, establish the prescribed prayers, give the obligatory charity, perform the Ḥajj and 'Umrah pilgrimages, and fast the month of Ramaḍān. Look at the way you would love people to treat you and do so to them, and whatever you would hate for them to do to you, spare them of it." (Al-Mu'jam Al-Kabīr by Aṭ-Ṭabarānī, 19/210; Al-Albānī graded it ṣaḥīḥ.)

Love

Abū Hurayrah (ra) narrated: The Messenger of God (saws) said, "You will not enter Paradise until you believe, and you will not believe until you love one another. Should I not direct you to a thing which, if you do it, you will foster love amongst you? Give (the greeting of) peace amongst you." (Ṣaḥīḥ Muslim, Ḥadīth 54; Riyāḍ Aṣ-Ṣāliḥīn, Ḥadīth 378)

Patience

[45]Seek help with patience and prayer. This is indeed a burden, but not to the humble. (Qur'ān 2:45)

[200]O you who believe, be patient, compete in being patient, be on guard, and fear God, so that you may be successful. (Qur'ān 3:200)

Some Forbidden Actions

Islam forbids many actions that the religion labels as sinful, including: idolatry, murdering innocents, disrespecting one's parents, theft, adultery, fornication, bearing false witness, consuming intoxicants, gambling, magic, slander, dealing with interest payments, and consuming forbidden meat such as pork. These prohibitions are intended to protect individuals and to raise their spiritual statuses. This is not a complete list of forbidden actions, but many are listed herein.

[151]Say [O Prophet], 'Come! I will tell you what your Lord has really forbidden you! Do not associate anything with Him; be good to your parents; and do not kill your children for fear of poverty—We shall provide sustenance for you as well as for them; refrain from committing indecent deeds, whether openly or in secret; and do not take life, which God has made sacred, save by [legal] right. That is what He has enjoined upon you, so that you may understand. [152]Stay well away from an orphan's property, except with the best intentions, before they come of age. Give full measure and weight, according to justice. We never charge a soul with more than it can bear. When you speak, observe justice, even though it concerns a close relative. And fulfil the covenants of God. That is what He has enjoined upon you so that you may take heed. [153][He has enjoined], 'This is My straight path, so follow it, and do not follow other ways. That will lead you away from His path.' That is what He enjoins upon you, so that you may guard yourselves. (Qur'ān 6:151-153)

[73]They worship, instead of God, things that have no control over their provision from the heavens or the earth in any way, nor do they have any power [to do so]. [74]Do not compare God with anyone. God has knowledge, but you have not. (Qur'ān 16:73-74)

[69]Say [O Prophet], 'Those who lie about God shall not prosper.' [70]Their portion is short-lived enjoyment in this world, but to Us they shall return.

Then We shall make them taste a severe punishment because of their denial of truth. (Qur'ān 10:69-70)

90Believers, intoxicants, gambling, idols, and making decisions by drawing lots are abominations devised by Satan. Avoid them, so that you may prosper. 91Satan seeks to sow enmity and hatred among you by means of intoxicants and gambling, and to keep you from the remembrance of God and from your prayers. Will you not then abstain? (Qur'ān 5:90-91)

32Do not go near adultery, for it is an indecent thing and an evil course. (Qur'ān 17:32)

2Believers! Why do you say one thing and do another? 3It is most despicable to God that you do not practice what you preach. (Qur'ān 61:2-3)

'Abdullāh ibn 'Amr (ra) narrated: The Prophet (saws) said, "The biggest sins are: To join others in worship with God; to be undutiful to one's parents; to kill somebody unlawfully; and to take a false oath. (Ṣaḥīḥ Al-Bukhārī, Ḥadīth 6675)

Abū Hurayrah (ra) narrated: The Messenger of God (saws) said, "Avoid the seven great destructive sins." It was said, "O Messenger of God, what are they?" He said, "Associating others with God; magic; killing a soul whom God has forbidden killing, except in a just cause; consuming interest; consuming the property of the orphan; fleeing on the day of the march (to the battlefield); and slandering chaste women who never even think of anything touching their chastity and are good believers." (Ṣaḥīḥ Al-Bukhārī, Ḥadīth 6857)

Ibn 'Umar (ra) narrated: The Messenger of God (saws) said, "Among the greatest of sins to God is that a man marries a woman and, when he fulfills his needs with her, he divorces her and leaves with her dowry; and that a man employs another man and leaves without paying him; and finally one who kills an animal for fun. (As-Sunan Al-Kubrā by Al-Bayhaqī, Ḥadīth 14395; Al-Albānī graded it ḥasan.)

Abū Ad-Dardā' (ra) narrated: My close friend (the Prophet (saws)) advised me, "Do not associate anything with God, even if you are slashed and burned. Do not leave the obligatory prayers on purpose, for whoever leaves them on purpose has forfeited the protection of God. Do not drink wine, for it is the key to every evil." (Sunan Ibn Mājah, Ḥadīth 4034; Al-Albānī graded it ṣaḥīḥ.)

Abū Hurayrah (ra) narrated: The Messenger of God (saws) said, "God does not like for you to waste wealth, nor ask many unnecessary questions, nor spread gossip." (Musnad Al-Bazzār, Ḥadīth 8463; Al-Albānī graded it ṣaḥīḥ.)

Abū Hurayrah (ra) narrated: The Messenger of God (saws) said, "Do not envy one another. Do not inflate prices by overbidding against one another. Do not hate one another. Do not harbor malice against one another. And do not enter into a commercial transaction when others have entered into that (transaction). And be brothers (to one another), O servants of God. A Muslim is the brother of another Muslim. He neither oppresses him, nor does he look down upon him, nor does he humiliate him. Piety is here," (and he pointed to his chest three times). "It is enough evil for a Muslim to hold his Muslim brother in contempt. All things of a Muslim are inviolable for his brother-in-faith: his blood, his property, and his honor." (Ṣaḥīḥ Muslim, Ḥadīth 2564; Riyāḍ Aṣ-Ṣāliḥīn, Ḥadīth 235; Bulūgh Al-Marām, Ḥadīth 1292)

Avoid judging others

11Believers, let not some men ridicule others. It may be that the latter are better than the former. Nor should some women ridicule others: it may be that the latter are better than the former. Do not defame each other or call each other by [offensive] nicknames. How bad it is to earn an evil reputation after accepting the faith! Those who do not repent are doers of evil. 12Believers, avoid much suspicion. Indeed some suspicion is a sin. And do not spy on one another and do not backbite. Would any of you like to eat his dead brother's flesh? No, you would hate it. Fear God. God is the Accepter of repentance and Most Merciful. (Qur'ān 49:11-12)

Sahl ibn Sa'd As-Sā'idī (ra) narrated: The Messenger of God (saws) said, "Verily, a man may appear to people as doing the deeds of the people of Paradise, yet he is among the people of Hellfire. Verily, a man may appear to people as doing the deeds of the people of Hellfire, yet he is among the people of Paradise." (Ṣaḥīḥ Al-Bukhārī, Ḥadīth 2898; Ṣaḥīḥ Muslim, Ḥadīth 112)

Anas [ra] narrated: The Messenger of God [saws] said, "Ṭūbā (a tree in Paradise) will be for he who is too occupied with his own defects to mention the defects of other people." [Al-Bazzār reported it with a ḥasan chain of narrators.] (Bulūgh Al-Marām, Ḥadīth 1305; Musnad Al-Bazzār, Ḥadīth 6237)

Abū Hurayrah [ra] narrated: The Messenger of God [saws] said, "One of you sees the speck in his brother's eye while he forgets the log in his own eye." (Ṣaḥīḥ Ibn Ḥibbān, Ḥadīth 5761; Al-Albānī graded it ṣaḥīḥ.)

Do not take God's name in vain

180 God has the Most Excellent Names. Call on Him by His Names and keep away from those who abuse them. They shall be requited for what they do. (Qur'ān 7:180)

Note that abusing God's name, or names, does not mean only to say cuss words with His name (although it does refer to that too). Nor does it only involve making fun of God's names, although that is also prohibited. Abusing God's name, or taking it in vain, also refers to doing violent actions and proclaiming His name in praise. Or it may refer to openly having bad character yet giving praise to God. This has nothing to do with Islām or humanity. And God knows best.

Do not backbite or slander

Abū Hurayrah [ra] narrated: The Messenger of God [saws] said, "Do you know what backbiting is?" They (the companions) said, "God and His Messenger know better." He (the Prophet [saws]) said, "Backbiting is talking about your brother in a manner which he dislikes." It was said to him, "What if my brother is as I say?" He (the Prophet [saws]) said, "If he is actually as you say, then that is backbiting; but if that is not in him, that is slandering." (Ṣaḥīḥ Muslim, Ḥadīth 2589; Riyāḍ Aṣ-Ṣāliḥīn, Ḥadīth 1523)

Do not consume intoxicants

Ibn 'Umar (ra) narrated: The Messenger of God (saws) said, "Every intoxicant is khamr (i.e., wine), and every intoxicant is forbidden. He who drinks wine in this world and dies while he is addicted to it, not having repented, will not drink it in the Hereafter." (Ṣaḥīḥ Muslim, Ḥadīth 2003)

Jābir (ra) narrated: The Prophet (saws) said, "Whoever believes in God and the Last Day, then he is not to sit at a spread in which wine (or any intoxicant) is circulated." (Jāmi' At-Tirmidhī, Ḥadīth 2801; Zubayr 'Alī Za'ī graded it ḥasan.)

Avoid Astrology

Ibn 'Abbās (ra) narrated: The Messenger of God (saws) said, "If anyone acquires any knowledge of astrology, he acquires a branch of magic of which he gets more as long as he continues to do so." (Sunan Abū Dāwūd, Ḥadīth 3905; Al-Albānī graded it ḥasan.)

Avoid Fortune Tellers

'Ā'ishah (ra) narrated: Some people asked the Messenger of God (saws) about soothsayers. The Messenger of God (saws) said to them, "They are upon nothing." They said, "O Messenger of God, sometimes they speak about things that come true." The Messenger of God (saws) said, "That is the word snatched by the jinn, who whisper it into the ears of their friends (i.e., the soothsayers), and it is mixed with more than one hundred lies." (Ṣaḥīḥ Al-Bukhārī, Ḥadīth 6213; Ṣaḥīḥ Muslim, Ḥadīth 2228)

Do not cheat

Abū Hurayrah (ra) narrated: The Messenger of God (saws) said, "He who takes up arms against us is not of us. And he who cheats us is not of us." (Ṣaḥīḥ Muslim, Ḥadīth 101; Riyāḍ Aṣ-Ṣāliḥīn, Ḥadīth 1579)

Abū Hurayrah (ra) narrated: The Messenger of God (saws) passed by a heap of food. He put his hand in that (heap), and his fingers felt moisture. He said, "What is this, O owner of the food?" The owner replied: "These have been drenched by rainfall, O Messenger of God." The Prophet (saws) said, "Why did you not place this (i.e., the drenched part of the heap) over the food so that people might see it? He who deceives is not my follower." (Ṣaḥīḥ Muslim, Ḥadīth 102)

Can Muslims have boyfriends and girlfriends?

Islām discourages pre-marital relations between people of the opposite sex, and it encourages single people to lower their gaze from the opposite sex. A man and a woman may meet in a public place to talk, preferably with friends or guardians, but Islām encourages individuals to get married rather than to be boyfriend and girlfriend.

32 Marry those among you who are single, and those of your male and female slaves who are righteous. If they are poor, God will provide for them from His bounty, for God is All-Bountiful, All-Knowing. (Qur'ān 24:32)

Avoid Smoking

Smoking has been proven to cause cancer and other serious health problems. The Qur'ān clearly states:

29 And do not kill yourselves. (Qur'ān 4:29)

And recall the following ḥadīth:

'Ubādah ibn Aṣ-Ṣāmit (ra) narrated: The Messenger of God (saws) decreed, "Do not cause harm or return harm." (Sunan Ibn Mājah, Ḥadīth 2340; Al-Albānī graded it ṣaḥīḥ.)

"Causing harm" includes harming oneself, and because smoking undoubtedly causes harm, many consider it to be forbidden.

Tattoos and Hair Extensions are Forbidden

Ibn 'Umar (ra) narrated: The Messenger of God (saws) said, "God has cursed such a woman as lengthens hair artificially or gets it lengthened, and also a woman who tattoos or gets herself tattooed." (Ṣaḥīḥ Al-Bukhārī, Ḥadīth 5937; Ṣaḥīḥ Muslim, Ḥadīth 2124)

Abū Hurayrah (ra) narrated: The Messenger of God (saws) forbade tattooing. (Ṣaḥīḥ Al-Bukhārī, Ḥadīth 5740)

Do not shave only part of the head

Nāfi' narrated: Ibn 'Umar (ra) narrated: The Messenger of God (saws) prohibited partial shaving. It was said to Nāfi', "What is partial shaving?" Nāfi' said, "It is to shave part of a boy's head and leave the rest." (Ṣaḥīḥ Al-Bukhārī, Ḥadīth 5920; Ṣaḥīḥ Muslim, Ḥadīth 2120)

An-Nawawī said, "The scholars agreed upon the disapproval of partial shaving if it is done in different places, unless it is done for medical treatment and so on." (Sharḥ of An-Nawawī on Ṣaḥīḥ Muslim 2120)

Men Wearing Gold and Silk

Abū Mūsā Al-Ash'arī (ra) narrated: The Messenger of God (saws) said, "The wearing of silk and gold has been made unlawful for the males of my nation (i.e., all Muslims) and lawful for the females. (Jāmi' At-Tirmidhī, Ḥadīth 1720; Zubayr 'Alī Za'ī graded it ṣaḥīḥ.)

Plates and Vessels of Gold and Silver

Ḥudhayfah ibn Al-Yamān (ra) narrated: The Messenger of God (saws) said, "Do not drink from gold or silver vessels, and do not eat from plates made from them. Verily, these are for disbelievers in this world and for us in the Hereafter." (Ṣaḥīḥ Al-Bukhārī, Ḥadīth 5426; Ṣaḥīḥ Muslim, Ḥadīth 2067)

Do not help others to commit sin

In Islām, one should not only avoid sins, but one should also avoid helping others to sin. This includes avoiding dealing with ḥarām (unlawful) substances. So, for example, one should avoid jobs in which one must deal with pork, alcohol, interest, or jobs in which one generally has trouble practicing Islām.

[2]Help one another in goodness and in piety. Do not help one another in sin and transgression. Fear God! God is severe in punishment. (Qur'ān 5:2)

Jābir (ra) narrated: The Messenger of God (saws) cursed the one who accepts interest, and the one who pays it, and the one who records it, and the two witnesses, and he said, "They are all equal." (Ṣaḥīḥ Muslim, Ḥadīth 1598)

Ibn 'Umar (ra) narrated: The Messenger of God (saws) said, "Wine is cursed from ten angles: the wine itself, the one who squeezes (the grapes, etc.), the one for whom it is squeezed, the one who sells it, the one who buys it, the one who carries it, the one to whom it is carried, the one who consumes its price, the one who drinks it and the one who pours it." (Sunan Ibn Mājah, Ḥadīth 3380; Zubayr 'Alī Za'ī graded it ḥasan.)

'Alī (ra) narrated: The Prophet (saws) said, "There is no obedience to anyone if it is disobedience to God. Indeed, obedience is only in good conduct." (Ṣaḥīḥ Al-Bukhārī, Ḥadīth 7257; Ṣaḥīḥ Muslim, Ḥadīth 1840)

The Characteristics of a Munāfiq (Hypocrite)

A *munāfiq* is one who outwardly professes Islām but inwardly disbelieves, and they may even seek to work against the religion privately.

[8]And there are some who say, "We believe in God and the Last Day," yet they are not ˹true˺ believers. [9]They seek to deceive God and the believers, yet they only deceive themselves, but they fail to perceive it. (Qur'ān 2:8-9)

[120]When you ˹believers˺ are touched with good, they grieve; but when you are afflicted with evil, they rejoice. ˹Yet,˺ if you are patient and mindful ˹of God˺, their schemes will not harm you in the least. Surely God is Fully Aware of what they do. (Qur'ān 3:120)

'Abdullāh ibn 'Amr (ra) narrated: The Prophet (saws) said, "Whoever has the following four characteristics will be a pure hypocrite, and whoever

has one of the following four characteristics will have one characteristic of hypocrisy unless and until he gives it up.

- *Whenever he is entrusted, he betrays.*
- *Whenever he speaks, he lies.*
- *Whenever he makes a covenant, he proves treacherous.*
- *Whenever he quarrels, he behaves in a very rash, evil, and insulting manner.*

(Ṣaḥīḥ Al-Bukhārī, Ḥadīth 34; Ṣaḥīḥ Muslim, Ḥadīth 58; Riyāḍ Aṣ-Ṣāliḥīn, Ḥadīth 689)

Chapter 3
Islāmic Dietary Laws

In Islām, several types of food are forbidden (ḥarām) including:

- Pork
- Carrion (meat from an animal that was found dead)
- Blood
- Meat slaughtered in the name of false deities
- Meat that was slaughtered improperly
- Meat sacrificed on altars
- Meat taken from an animal that was still alive
- Carnivorous animals with canine teeth or fangs (including cats, dogs, alligators, and crocodiles)
- Carnivorous birds with talons
- The meat of domesticated donkeys
- Ants
- Bees
- Hoopoes
- Shrikes
- Hedgehogs
- Frogs
- Animals that feed on filth

However, any animal from the sea, that is not harmful when eaten, is lawful to eat.

[3]*You are forbidden carrion; blood; pork; and any flesh over which the name of any other than God is invoked; and any creature which has been strangled, or killed by a blow or in a fall, or has been gored to death; or partially eaten by a wild animal, except that which you make lawful [by slaughtering properly while it was still alive] and what has been slaughtered at an altar. You are forbidden to draw lots for decisions. That is sinful conduct. Those who deny the truth have this day despaired*

of ever harming your religion. So do not fear them. Fear Me. Today I have completed your religion for you and completed My blessing upon you. I have chosen for you Islām as your religion. But if anyone is forced by hunger to eat something which is forbidden, not intending to commit a sin, he will find God Forgiving and Merciful. [4]*If they ask you what has been made lawful for them, say, 'All good things have been made lawful for you;' and what you have taught your birds and beasts of prey to catch, training them as God has taught you. So eat what they catch for you, but first pronounce God's name over it. Fear God, for God is swift in taking account. (Qur'ān 5:3-4)*

Abū Hurayrah [(ra)] *narrated: The Prophet* [(saws)] *said, "Every wild animal that has fangs, eating it is unlawful." (Ṣaḥīḥ Muslim, Ḥadīth 1933)*

Abū Hurayrah [(ra)] *narrated: A man asked the Prophet* [(saws)]*, "O Messenger of God! We travel on the sea and take a small quantity of water with us. If we use this for ablution, we will suffer from thirst. Can we perform ablution with sea water?" The Messenger of God* [(saws)] *replied, "Its water is pure and what dies in it is lawful food." (Sunan Abū Dāwūd, Ḥadīth 83; Al-Albānī graded it ṣaḥīḥ.)*

Note that any meat that a Muslim is allowed to eat is called *ḥalāl*, which is a word that refers to anything permissible. The method of slaughtering an animal is called *dhabīḥah* (also spelled: *zabihah*), and Islāmically it involves mentioning God's name and then slicing the animal's jugular veins in its throat. The Qur'ān states:

[5]*Today, all good things have been made lawful to you. The food of the People of the Book is lawful to you, and your food is lawful to them. (Qur'ān 5:5)*

[118]*Eat then, only that over which God's name has been pronounced, if you truly believe in His revelations. (Qur'ān 6:118)*

And the following ḥadīths state:

Rāfi' ibn Khadīj [(ra)] *narrated: The Prophet* [(saws)] *said, "Eat what is slaughtered (with any instrument) that makes blood flow out, except what is slaughtered with a tooth or a nail." (Ṣaḥīḥ Al-Bukhārī, Ḥadīth 5506; Ṣaḥīḥ Muslim, Ḥadīth 1968)*

'Ā'ishah [(ra)] *narrated: The people said (to the Prophet* [(saws)]*), "O Messenger of God! Here are people who have recently embraced Islām,*

and they bring meat, and we do not know whether they had mentioned God's name while slaughtering the animals or not." He (the Prophet (saws)) said, "You should mention God's name and eat." (Ṣaḥīḥ Al-Bukhārī, Ḥadīth 7398)

'Ā'ishah (ra) narrated: The Messenger of God (saws) said, "When one of you eats, he should mention God's name. If he forgets to mention God's name at the beginning, he should say, 'In the name of God at the beginning of it and at the end of it.'" (Sunan Abū Dāwūd, Ḥadīth 3767; Al-Albānī graded it ṣaḥīḥ.)

Based on all of this information, it is permissible to eat meat that was slaughtered by the People of the Book (i.e., Jews and Christians), as long as it was slaughtered in the correct manner, at the throat. This means that Muslims are allowed to eat food that is kosher, as well as ḥalāl meat slaughtered by Christians. If one is uncertain as to whether the Muslim, Jew, or Christian who slaughtered the meat mentioned God's name before slaughtering, then one may simply say God's name over the meat and then eat it. This is accomplished by saying, "Bismillāh," which means, "In the name of God." This should also be said in general before eating or drinking anything. If one forgets to say this at the beginning of the meal, then, when one remembers, one should say, "Bismillāhi awwalahū wa ākhirahū," which means, "In the name of God at the beginning of it and at the end of it."

However, some Muslims are more cautious and do not eat meat unless it was slaughtered by a Muslim. This means that in countries where Muslims are a minority, certain Muslims will maintain a vegetarian or pescetarian diet, unless they have access to meat that is definitely ḥalāl.

Note also that the Islāmic method of slaughtering does not apply to seafood, and Muslims may eat any kind of seafood, no matter who caught it.

Part 2: The Messenger and Other Islāmic Figures

Chapter 4

The Prophet Muḥammad (saws)

The following biography has been constructed from several sources, namely: the Sīrah of the Prophet Muḥammad (saws) by Ibn Is'ḥāq and Ibn Hishām, translated by Alfred Guillaume; The Sealed Nectar by Safi-ur-Rahman Al-Mubarakpuri; Muḥammad: His Life Based on the Earliest Sources by Martin Lings; and The Sīrah of the Prophet by Dr. Yasir Qadhi.

Background Before the Life of the Prophet Muḥammad (saws)

Descended from Abraham (as)

Thousands of years ago, Abraham (as), a significant prophet of Allāh, had two very significant sons, both of whom became prophets as well: one son, Ishmael (as), by his wife Hagar, and one son, Isaac (as), by his wife Sarah. Both sons were blessed by God. Isaac's (as) son Jacob (as), known as Israel, was the patriarch of the Israelite nation and of all the Israelite prophets, including Moses (as) and Jesus Christ (as). Isaac (as) resided in Canaan, which was later settled by the Israelites.

Ishmael (as) and his descendants settled in Arabia and assimilated into the region. Although Abraham (as) resided in Canaan with Sarah and Isaac (as), he did visit Hagar and Ishmael (as), who had settled in a place called Bakkah (also spelled *Becca*), later to be named Makkah. Eventually, in that area, Abraham (as) and Ishmael (as) built the Ka'bah, a sacred place of worship dedicated to Allāh. A pilgrimage in honor of Allāh was established around that time and remained as a ritual among Ishmael's (as) descendants. But over the millennia, idolatry and polytheism crept into the traditions of the Ishmaelites, tainting the pure monotheism that had been taught by their ancestors. Other spiritual and societal atrocities became prevalent as well.

Arabia Before the Prophethood of Muḥammad (saws)

By the 570's C.E., idolatry and immorality were commonplace, and the Arabs had essentially forgotten the foundation of the religion of Abraham (as). The Ishmaelite Arabs did, however, retain some aspects relating to the past, such as knowledge of their genealogical roots in Abraham (as). Additionally, the Arabs maintained the annual pilgrimage (i.e., the *Ḥajj*) from the time of Abraham (as), although it too had become corrupted with idolatry and false practices. While such noble virtues as hospitality to guests and maintaining honor existed among the Arabs, the darkness of their vices overshadowed them.

Pre-Islāmic Religion

The Arabs still worshipped Allāh, but they associated false deities in worship alongside Allāh, and they depicted these false deities in the forms of stone or wood and worshipped them, as other cultures had done in the past. There were 360 idols in the Sacred Mosque, and an idol had even been placed in the Ka'bah itself. In this society, there existed widespread superstition, and people consulted soothsayers and astrologers for guidance. Moreover, the Arabs had ceased to believe in an afterlife.

Amongst the Arabs there had settled Jews and Christians, but despite having culturally assimilated into certain Arab regions, their religious influence did not take hold in the pagan societies.

Pre-Islāmic Domestic Life

While noble women in Pre-Islāmic Arabia possessed high status and freedom to a degree, other women were treated as property. A man in charge of a woman could force her into a marriage against her will or inherit her against her will. Men could marry as many women as they pleased, and people often committed adultery or fornication. Certain marriages would even commence from having intercourse with multiple men. In such an instance, if an illegitimate child resulted from the fornication, a seeress would supposedly determine who the father was. One may additionally note that illegitimate children resulting from certain out-of-wedlock sexual engagements grew up with shame.

Also not uncommon in this society, though not exactly rampant, was the occasional burying of female infants alive due to disappointment of their gender. Other times, a person in poverty would kill their child due to the fear of not having the means to provide for it. This is not to say that the killing of infants occurred often, as parents generally possess deep emotional attachment to, and love for, their children, but such instances nevertheless occurred in their society.

Pre-Islāmic Societal Life

There essentially existed no formal government among many of the Pre-Islāmic Arabs, with family relations serving as the foundation of societal life. In certain regions one tribe may have reigned over others, but there existed no formal code, and life was fairly simple, particularly outside of the cities. However, even shared ancestry did not prevent greed and competition from fueling inter-tribal wars. For this reason, tribal alliances could be weak, and war among the Arabs was not uncommon. Moreover, there generally existed no solid code of rights for the slaves or the poor, and the class system played a role in Arabian society, as it did in other cultures.

Poetry existed as the chief form of media and the chief manifestation of eloquence among Arabs, as they were a largely illiterate people. While the Arabic alphabet did exist at that time, much of what they did write was poetry, and there were no notable books from the Pre-Islāmic era. The pursuit of deep knowledge did not serve as a driving force in that time. Other recreational interests among the Arabs included the widespread activities of drinking alcohol and gambling.

Eventual Reform

There were, however, some individuals who were pure in character and intention, and through the best of them, Muḥammad (saws), all of these negative qualities of Arabia were eradicated. The fact that he achieved such a thorough, nationwide societal reformation within only 23 years is in itself a miraculous achievement. Few who claimed prophethood, or something similar, ever achieved as much. The following sections will briefly summarize the life, character, and achievements of the Prophet Muḥammad (saws).

The Lineage of Prophet Muḥammad (saws)

The following is the paternal lineage of Muḥammad (saws) back to Abraham (as), according to what was recorded by Ibn Hishām. Scholars agree on the names and number of the men up to 'Adnān, but there is doubt over the names and number of the men between 'Adnān and Ishmael (as). However, it was known in the Prophet's (saws) time that Quraysh was descended from Ishmael (as), as is evidenced in the following ḥadīth from Ṣaḥīḥ Muslim.

Muḥammad (saws) son of 'Abdullāh son of 'Abdul-Muṭṭalib (whose name was Shaybah) son of Hāshim (whose name was 'Amr) son of 'Abdu Manāf (whose name was Al-Mughīrah) son of Quṣayy (whose name was Zayd) son of Kilāb son of Murrah son of Ka'b son of Lu'ayy son of Ghālib son of Fihr (who was Quraysh) son of Mālik son of An-Naḍr son of Kinānah son of Khuzaymah son of Mudrikah (whose name was 'Āmir) son of Ilyās son of Muḍar son of Nizār son of Ma'add son of 'Adnān son of Udd (or Udad) son of Muqawwam son of Nāḥūr son of Tayraḥ son of Ya'rub son of Yashjub son of Nābit son of Ishmael (as) son of Abraham (as).

Wāthilah ibn Al-Asqa' (ra) narrated: The Messenger of God (saws) said, "Indeed, God chose Kinānah from the descendants of Ishmael, and He chose Quraysh from Kinānah, and He chose from Quraysh Banū Hāshim, and He chose me from Banū Hāshim. (Ṣaḥīḥ Muslim, Ḥadīth 2276)

A Brief Summary of the Life of the Prophet Muḥammad (saws)

Pre-Prophethood

It was into the aforementioned society that Muḥammad (saws) was born, around the year 570 C.E. in Makkah, in the region of Arabia called *Al-Ḥijāz*. He was a member of the tribe of Quraysh, belonging specifically to the tribe's clan Hāshim. Quraysh was an Ishmaelite tribe that ruled

Makkah and had the privilege of maintaining the Ka'bah. Muḥammad's (saws) father, 'Abdullāh, had passed away while he was still in the womb. Shortly after Muḥammad (saws) was born, his mother, Āminah, entrusted her son to the care of a Bedouin wetnurse, as was the custom of that time, and the wetnurse was named Ḥalīmah.

On one occasion, when Muḥammad (saws) was a toddler staying with Ḥalīmah, he was with another child when the Angel Gabriel (as) came to Muḥammad (saws) with a gold basin full of sacred water. The angel took hold of him, split open his breast, and brought out his heart, which he also split open. He took out from his heart a black clot and said, "That was the part of Satan in you." Then Gabriel (as) washed the heart in the water, joined it back together, and restored it to Muḥammad's (saws) breast. Thus, Muḥammad (saws) would be protected from evil inclinations for the rest of his life. Shortly after this event, Ḥalīmah gave Muḥammad (saws) back to his mother Āminah.

Āminah would pass away when Muḥammad (saws) was only six. Muḥammad (saws) was then taken into the care of his grandfather, 'Abdul-Muṭṭalib, who also died about two years later. At last he was taken into the care of his uncle, Abū Ṭālib, who loved and treated the boy as one of his own sons. As the years went by, Muḥammad (saws) grew into a man who sternly kept away from the vices of his society. He had stayed away from polytheism, being of those worshipped Allāh alone, and he detested idolatry. He was known as a generous person, and he avoided such idle things as drinking wine.

There was one instance in which a merchant from a Yemeni port sold some goods to a man of Quraysh, who refused to pay the due price. The Yemeni merchant brought his case to the tribe, and various representatives from clans of the Quraysh consequently made a pact in which they would stand up for those who were oppressed in Makkah until justice was done, whether the oppressed was a native or a foreigner. Thus, the Qurayshi who had wronged the merchant was forced to pay the right price. Muḥammad (saws) was among those who had taken part in this pact, and this is revealing of his just nature even before he was a prophet.

Like others around him, Muḥammad (saws) became involved in the business of merchants. He was known particularly for his honesty and reliability, so much so that he earned the nickname *Al-Amīn*, meaning "the Trustworthy." At the age of 25 he married a widowed businesswoman named Khadījah, and their marriage was a loving, harmonious one. Together they had 6 children: two sons who died around infancy, named Qāsim and 'Abdullāh, and four daughters who all lived to adulthood: Zaynab, Ruqayyah, Umm Kulthūm, and Fāṭimah. Muḥammad (saws) also adopted a son, a freed slave whose name was Zayd ibn Ḥārithah, and he took in 'Alī, the son of his uncle Abū Ṭālib.

Prophethood in the Meccan Era

Muḥammad (saws) was in the practice of taking spiritual retreats, something not unheard of in his setting, during the month of Ramaḍān to worship God. On one of the nights of Ramaḍān, when Muḥammad (saws) was 40 years old, he was engaged in worship in a cave called *Ḥirā'*, in the Mountain of Light (*Jabal An-Nūr*), when the Angel Gabriel (as) appeared to him in the form of a man. After embracing Muḥammad (saws) and commanding the illiterate man to read, the Angel Gabriel (as) spoke the following words:

1Read [O Prophet] in the name of your Lord, Who created. 2He created man from a clot. 3Read! Your Lord is the Most Bountiful 4Who taught by the pen, 5taught man what he did not know. (Qur'ān 96:1-5)

Those were the first verses of the Qur'ān to be revealed to Muḥammad (saws), who, as prophets before him, was initially startled by the experience with the spiritual world. He proceeded down the slope of the mountain, but there, filling the horizon in his angelic form, was Gabriel (as), who said, "O Muḥammad, you are the Messenger of God, and I am Gabriel." Still shaken by the experience, Muḥammad (saws) went home to his wife Khadījah, who comforted him, saying, "By Allāh, Allāh will never disgrace you. You keep good relations with your kith and kin, help the poor and the destitute, serve your guests generously and assist the deserving calamity-afflicted ones" (Ṣaḥīḥ Al-Bukhārī, Ḥadīth 3).

The revelation (Arabic: *waḥy*) from God through the Angel Gabriel (as) increased, and it came to the Prophet Muḥammad (saws) in different ways. At times, Gabriel (as) would come to the Prophet (saws) in the form of a man and communicate with him. Other times, the Prophet (saws) would hear an intense noise similar to the reverberations of a bell, and he would go into a sort of strenuous trance and communicate with Gabriel (as). The revelation sometimes caused the Prophet (saws) to break into a sweat, even on a cold day. And the revelation was also physically heavy. Once the Prophet (saws) was on a camel, and revelation came to him, forcing the camel to sit down. Another time, revelation came to the Prophet (saws) when he was touching a companion of his, and the companion feared that his own thigh would break due to the weight. On some rare occasions, the Prophet (saws) saw Gabriel (as) in his true angelic form.

Muḥammad (saws) initially preached the *dīn*, that is, the religion, to those closest to him. Among the first to accept his message were his wife Khadījah, 'Alī, Zayd, and a close friend named Abū Bakr. Soon the number of Muslims grew, and after about three years, Muḥammad (saws) began to preach openly to Quraysh. His message was a sign of its truth in and of itself, for the situation was that of a man with a reputation of complete honesty and kindness calling people away from such societal issues as idolatry, crude behavior, unjust slaughter, filth, and apathy towards the needy. The message was fresh and untampered, and this was better than that which they had at the time. Based on their knowledge and experience with him, the Quraysh had no reason to doubt him.

However, the majority of Quraysh disliked his message for primarily one reason: it required them to abandon their idols and polytheistic practices and to worship Allāh alone. Not only did this go against their traditional beliefs, which had been adhered to for generations, but it was also a threat to them economically, as the Ḥajj pilgrimage had by that time become a lucrative event to host, and they feared that Muḥammad's (saws) preaching would turn away polytheists from outside of Makkah. Early during Muḥammad's (saws) open preaching, the polytheists asked him to stop spreading his message and in exchange they would give Muhammad (saws) riches and leadership if he so wished. However, the Prophet (saws) sternly refused, as his mission was not of human origin but from God, and he did not desire materialistic wealth. The Quraysh resorted to harsher means and began persecuting Muslims. If there were Muslims who belonged to a noble family, the polytheists would ridicule them. If there were Muslims who were merchants, the polytheists would boycott them. If there were Muslims who belonged to a lower societal class, the polytheists would physically torture them in various ways, at times going so far as to even kill. Some of the leading persecutors among the polytheists were Abū Jahl and Abū Lahab, the latter being another uncle of Muhammad (saws). The Prophet (saws) himself was not spared from the persecution, and polytheists would revile him and throw trash near him or on him, but the Prophet (saws) would not retaliate. However, they would not physically torture Muḥammad (saws), as they respected the protection of his uncle, Abū Ṭālib, who was politically respected in the community. Muhammad (saws) and his followers were being persecuted in Makkah for their belief in God and their loving devotion to Him alone, but they patiently endured this. Some of the Muslims, at the suggestion of Muḥammad (saws), fled to Abyssinia, and they were led by Ja'far ibn Abū Ṭālib, a cousin of the Prophet (saws) and brother to 'Alī. There they were accepted by its Christian king, their king having the title of *negus* (Arabic: *an-najāshī*), who allowed them to practice Islām without being oppressed. That negus, whose name was Aṣḥamah, accepted Islām himself, and years later when he died, the Prophet Muḥammad (saws) prayed for him.

After the emigration to Abyssinia, the remaining Muslims in Makkah were strengthened with the conversions to Islām of two strong, influential men: Ḥamzah ibn 'Abdul-Muṭṭalib (another uncle of the Prophet (saws)) and then 'Umar ibn Al-Khaṭṭāb. Having achieved no success in hindering the progress of Islām, the polytheists of Quraysh resorted to establishing a severe boycott on the clans of Hāshim and Al-Muṭṭalib, in which no one from the rest of Quraysh could intermarry with them, buy from them, or sell to them. Nevertheless, Islām continued to flourish, persisting through the ban, and the Muslims endured patiently. After two or three years, the boycott was annulled. However, the Prophet's (saws) uncle, Abū Ṭālib, died only six months after the boycott's cancelation. In that same year, Khadījah also passed away. She had been Muḥammad's (saws) first supporter in his cause, and his only wife until her death, in the tenth year of his prophethood. Later in that year, the Prophet (saws) went with Zayd on a journey to the prominent city of Ṭā'if, in an attempt to preach the message of Islām to its people. However, the residents of Ṭā'if threw stones at the Prophet Muḥammad (saws), driving him away. That year – the year of Abū Ṭālib's death, Khadījah's death, and the incident at Ṭā'if – is known as the Year of Sorrow.

Shortly after the tragic events of that year, God showed additional favor on the Prophet (saws) through an event that would come to be known as the Night Journey and the Ascension (*Al-Isrā' wal-Mi'rāj*). On that night, the Angel Gabriel (as) woke Muḥammad (saws), and the latter was transported by a white winged horse-like creature, called Al-Burāq, larger than a donkey but smaller than a mule. It took Muḥammad (saws) to Jerusalem, and there he led previous prophets of God in prayer at Al-Masjid Al-Aqṣā. He also ascended into Heaven, where he met the Prophets Adam (as), Jesus Christ (as), John (as), Joseph (as), Idrīs (as), Aaron (as), Moses (as), and Abraham (as), before he was brought to the presence of God, and God enjoined on him and his followers the daily formal prayers. Thereafter, Muḥammad (saws) descended back and returned to Makkah on that same night. The next day, the Prophet (saws) was able to describe Al-Masjid Al-Aqṣā to the Quraysh with precision and accuracy, answering the questions asked to test him by those who had been there, and they knew he had never been there before the previous night.

The situation for the believers would significantly improve when people in a city called Yathrib began to accept Islām, and they made a covenant with Muḥammad (saws) at a place near Makkah called ‘Aqabah, in which they would shelter him and his followers. Therefore, nearly all Muslims in Makkah migrated to Yathrib. During this time, the Quraysh attempted to assassinate Muḥammad (saws). A member of each clan was going to stab him at the same time, and in this way one clan would not bear the guilt for his death alone. However, when they surrounded the house of Muḥammad (saws), it is said that he recited some verses from the Qur'ān, and God made him invisible to the would-be assassins, allowing the Prophet (saws) to escape unharmed. The Prophet Muḥammad (saws) then set out from Makkah with Abū Bakr. Although Yathrib was to the north, they went south at first in order to throw off the Quraysh and any bounty hunters in pursuit of them, as the Quraysh had offered a large reward for the capture of Muḥammad (saws). The Prophet (saws) and Abū Bakr hid in a cave in a mountain called Thawr for a few days, and at one point they were almost found, but some stories state that before the pursuers approached the cave, God had caused a spider to weave a web at its entrance, a plant to grow at the entrance, and a bird to make a nest there. The pursuers consequently decided that no one could be in the cave, so they left. Thereafter, the Prophet (saws) and Abū Bakr journeyed to Yathrib unimpeded. The migration of the Prophet Muḥammad (saws) took place in the year 622 C.E. It is known as the Hijrah, and it marks the first year of the Muslim calendar.

Prophethood in the Medinan Era

Yathrib would come to be known as Al-Madīnah, a word that literally means "the City," although it is short for Madīnatun-Nabī, the City of the Prophet, or Madīnatul-Munawwarah, the Illumined City. It was now home to many Muslims, among whom were those native to Al-Madīnah (the Helpers, or *Al-Anṣār*) and those who had emigrated to Al-Madīnah (the Emigrants, or *Al-Muhājirūn*). Two significant tribes that were native to Al-Madīnah were Aws and Khazraj. Three others were Jewish tribes: the Banū Qaynuqā‘, the Banū An-Naḍīr, and the Banū Qurayẓah. Formal alliances and treaties were formed between the Helpers and the Emigrants and between the Muslims and the Jews. It may be noted that among the Jews of Arabia were those who worshipped ‘Uzayr, often understood to be Ezra, as the son of God, differing from the majority of Jews in the world.

After a period of about six months, the mosque of the Prophet Muḥammad (saws), Masjid An-Nabawī, was built, and Muḥammad (saws) himself participated in its construction. Until then, he had stayed with a Muslim man by the name of Abū Ayyūb Al-Anṣārī, but now the Prophet’s (saws) home would be physically attached to the mosque. Approximately ten months later, God sent revelation ordering the Prophet (saws) and the Muslims to face Masjid Al-Ḥarām, the most significant part of which is the Ka‘bah, when they prayed. Until then, they had been facing Jerusalem during their prayers.

The Muslims who migrated from Makkah had left in rapidity and discretion, in order to avoid aggression and detainment by the Quraysh. In doing so, the Muslims had left land and belongings behind, which the Quraysh took. Furthermore, once the Muslims were in Al-Madīnah, the hostility of the Qurayshi polytheists in Makkah persisted: the Makkan tribe boycotted Al-Madīnah and encouraged other Arabs against the city. For these reasons, the Muslims raided some of the Quraysh’s caravans out of justice for what the tribe had done to them. In one such campaign, led by the Prophet Muḥammad (saws) himself, the Quraysh sent an army to intercept the Muslims. The two sides met in battle at a place called Badr, and God aided the outnumbered Muslims by sending angels to fight with them. The Battle of Badr ended with the Muslims being victorious. Abū Jahl was slain there, and Abū Lahab died in Makkah shortly thereafter. In subsequent years there were two other significant conflicts between the Muslims and the Quraysh, both of which were initiated by the Makkan tribe. The first was the Battle of Uḥud, in which the Muslims were not victorious, Ḥamzah was martyred, and the Prophet (saws) himself was wounded. The second was the Battle of Al-Khandaq (the Battle of the Trench; also known as the Battle of Al-Aḥzāb, the Battle of the Confederates), in which the Muslims were victorious after the Quraysh and their allies laid siege to Al-Madīnah. A man named Abū Sufyān led the Quraysh against the Muslims in both of these battles.

Once in Al-Madīnah, the Muslims were not only threatened by the Quraysh and their allies, but from within the city as well. Although the

Prophet (saw) had not provoked them, in three separate events all three of the Jewish tribes of Al-Madīnah broke their treaty with the Muslims and took up arms against them because they disliked the religious and political influence of the new Muslim community. Their revolts were unsuccessful, and on the judgment of Muḥammad (saws), the Banū Qaynuqā‘ and the Banū An-Naḍīr were exiled, without any bloodshed being had. However, the Banū Qurayẓah, who had sided with the Makkan polytheists during the Battle of the Trench, and had lost, were not judged by Muḥammad (saws). Instead, a Muslim companion by the name of Sa‘d ibn Mu‘ādh, who was the chief of one of the clans of Aws, was appointed to judge the Banū Qurayẓah, and his decision was to put the men of the tribe to death. It may be noted that this punishment was corresponding with Jewish law (Deuteronomy 20:10-14). Sa‘d ibn Mu‘ādh was highly respected by the Prophet (saws), who approved of Sa‘d's decision. The Prophet (saws) himself always attempted to avoid war and bloodshed, yet as fighting and hostility were continuously initiated against the Muslims, they had no choice but to act against those who wished for their demise.

After years of conflict with the polytheists of Quraysh, the Muslims finally formed a peace treaty with the Makkan tribe, which became known as the Treaty of Al-Ḥudaybiyah. The armistice established in this treaty was also binding upon the Banū Khuzā‘ah, a tribe allied with the Muslims, as well as upon the Banū Bakr, a tribe allied with the Quraysh. During this time of peace, Muḥammad (saws) had letters dispatched to the rulers of Roman Byzantium, Persia, and Egypt, politely inviting them to Islām. The Muslims also dealt with the hostilities they faced from Khaybar, a Jewish settlement to the north. They were of a belligerent attitude toward the Muslims, having encouraged the Quraysh and their allies regarding the Battle of the Trench. After a campaign led by Muḥammad (saws), Khaybar was surrendered to the Muslims. The Prophet (saws), however, allowed its residents to remain on the land that had been theirs.

Around this time, the Prophet (saws) sent some Muslim men to peacefully preach Islām to a tribe near the borders of Syria, but nearly all of the men were killed unjustly. Another Muslim messenger was intercepted by the tribe of Banū Ghassān, which was mainly Christian, and a chief of the tribe put him to death. In response, the Prophet Muḥammad (saws) appointed three men from among his companions to lead an army against the Banū Ghassān. The three leaders were Zayd ibn

Ḥārithah; Ja'far ibn Abū Ṭālib, and 'Abdullāh ibn Rawāḥah, a prominent companion from Al-Madīnah. The Muslim army met the army of the Banū Ghassān at a place called Mu'tah. However, several Arab Christian tribes that were allied with the Banū Ghassān came to support them, as did a small contingent of Roman forces. They greatly outnumbered the Muslim forces, and Zayd, Ja'far, and 'Abdullāh ibn Rawāḥah were all martyred in the battle. However, the Muslims did not lose too many men overall, and a Muslim by the name of Khālid ibn Al-Walīd took charge of the army and led them to safety.

It was not long before the Treaty of Al-Ḥudaybiyah was broken, when the Quraysh helped the Banū Bakr in an attack against the Banū Khuzā'ah. This violated the treaty, and the Prophet (saws) subsequently led an army of 10,000 Muslims on Makkah, but no battle was fought overall, and the polytheists peacefully ceded the city to the Muslims. Additionally, Abū Sufyān embraced Islām. The Ka'bah was rededicated to the One God alone, as it had been in the time of Abraham (as) and Ishmael (as). Additionally, Muḥammad (saws) did not exact retribution against the members of Quraysh who had subjected the Muslims to years of ridicule and torture. Instead, he forgave them. Thereafter, most of the polytheists of Quraysh decided to embrace Islām.

After the Conquest of Makkah, a tribe by the name of Hawāzin allied with the tribe of Thaqīf from Ṭā'if. These were pagan tribes that viewed the rise of Islām as a threat to their idolatrous practices, so they mobilized an army to fight the Muslims. The Prophet (saws) led a military campaign against Hawāzin and Thaqīf, and these two tribes were defeated at the Battle of Ḥunayn. The Muslims subsequently laid siege to Ṭā'if, but after almost two weeks, the Muslims abandoned the siege. Nevertheless, the Prophet (saws) did not have any animosity towards the residents of the city, and he prayed to God to guide Thaqīf.

Soon afterwards, there were rumors that the Roman Empire was mobilizing troops in the north in order to attack Al-Madīnah. Muḥammad (saws) himself led a large Muslim force towards Syria to secure the area, and the army camped at a place called Tabūk for about twenty days. During that time, it is reported that there was a well that was almost empty. The Prophet (saws) placed his hand in the water, supplicated to God, gargled the water, and spat it in the well. The well then filled with water to the top, and the entire army drank from the well for the entire stay in Tabūk. This is just one of the many reported miracles to have happened through the Prophet Muḥammad (saws), some of which will be listed later in this chapter. However, the rumors regarding the Roman mobilization were proven unfounded. Nevertheless, the Prophet (saws) made treaties of peace with nearby communities, and then he returned to Al-Madīnah.

Around that time, many delegations from different tribes came to Al-Madīnah to accept Islām or to make peace treaties with the Prophet (saws). Among them were the Banū Thaqīf from Ṭā'if, who finally made the decision to embrace Islām.

All of this time Islām had been spreading, and the number of Muslims in Arabia had increased into a nation, or an *ummah*. Muḥammad (saws) led the Muslims in the Ḥajj pilgrimage in Makkah and soon afterward passed away in Al-Madīnah at the age of 63, in the year 632 C.E. His age was determined by the Islāmic lunar calendar, which differs from the Gregorian calendar. His message had a purifying effect on people, for, within the mere 23 years of his prophethood, Arabia had been changed for the better through the moral code of Islām. Spiritually, Islām guided them to the Oneness of God; intellectually, Islām encouraged them to seek knowledge; politically, Islām encouraged them to unite under the Oneness of God; hygienically, Islām encouraged them to keep clean and to avoid impure things; and socially, Islām encouraged them to abandon prejudice, injustice, and avarice.

Muḥammad's (saws) is the example that all Muslims follow to this very day, but Muslims do not under any circumstance, or in any way, worship or deify the Prophet Muḥammad (saws). Muslims only worship God alone, without any associate. Muḥammad (saws) was only a prophet, and the Oneness of God and our duty to worship God was the fundamental aspect of Muḥammad's (saws) message, the same message of all prophets before him.

Some Narrations about the Prophet Muḥammad (saws)

Trustworthiness Before His Prophethood

Before his prophethood, Muḥammad (saws) was known for his truthfulness and good character, and it is reported that Quraysh used to refer to him as *Al-Amīn* or *the Trustworthy*. (Ibn Ishaq and Ibn Hisham. *The Prophetic Sirah [The Life of Muhammad]*. Translated by Alfred Guillaume, Oxford University Press. 1955. 2004. Pages 82, 86.)

Abū Sufyān was someone who used to be an enemy to the Prophet (saws) until he embraced Islām. While he was an enemy of the Prophet (saws), he was once questioned by the Byzantine Emperor Heraclius about Muḥammad (saws). Abū Sufyān admitted that Muḥammad (saws) did not break his covenants, prove treacherous, or lie before his prophethood. (Ṣaḥīḥ Al-Bukhārī, Ḥadīth 7)

Generosity

Ibn 'Abbās (ra) narrated: The Messenger of God (saws) was the most generous of the people; and he was the most generous during the month of Ramaḍān when Gabriel visited him every night and recited the Qur'ān to him. During this period, the generosity of the Messenger of God (saws) waxed faster than the wind that bears rain. (Ṣaḥīḥ Al-Bukhārī, Ḥadīth 6; Riyāḍ Aṣ-Ṣāliḥīn, Ḥadīth 1222)

Jābir (ra) narrated: Never was the Prophet (saws) asked for a thing to be given for which his answer was "no." (Ṣaḥīḥ Al-Bukhārī, Ḥadīth 6034)

Humble Lifestyle

'Urwah (ra) narrated from 'Ā'ishah (ra) that she used to say to 'Urwah (ra): "O son of my sister, by God, I used to see the crescent moon, then the crescent moon, then the crescent moon (i.e., three moons in two months), and a fire was not kindled in the house of the Messenger of God (saws)." I ('Urwah) said, "O my aunt, what were your means of sustenance?" She said, "Dates and water." But it (so happened) that the Messenger of God (saws) had some Anṣār neighbors who had dairy animals. They used to send the Messenger of God (saws) some milk of theirs, and he gave that to us to drink." (Ṣaḥīḥ Al-Bukhārī, Ḥadīth 2567; Riyāḍ Aṣ-Ṣāliḥīn, Ḥadīth 491)

'Amr ibn Al-Ḥārith, the brother of the wife of the Messenger of God (saws), Juwayriyah bint Al-Ḥārith (ra), narrated: When the Messenger of God (saws) died, he did not leave any dirham or dīnār (i.e., money) or a slave or a slave-woman or anything else except his white mule, his arms, and

a piece of land which he had given in charity. (Ṣaḥīḥ Al-Bukhārī, Ḥadīth 2739)

General Character

'Ā'ishah (ra) narrated: The conduct of the Prophet (saws) was entirely according to the Qur'ān. (Ṣaḥīḥ Muslim, Ḥadīth 746; Riyāḍ Aṣ-Ṣāliḥīn, Ḥadīth 1847)

'Ā'ishah (ra) narrated: The Messenger of God (saws) never hit anyone with his hand, nor any woman or servant, except when fighting in the cause of God. And if he was offended in some way, he never took revenge for his own sake, unless one of the sacred limits of God had been transgressed, then he would take steps to correct it for the sake of God. (Ṣaḥīḥ Muslim, Ḥadīth 2328; Riyāḍ Aṣ-Ṣāliḥīn, Ḥadīth 643)

Ibn Jaz (ra) narrated: I have not seen anyone who smiled more than the Messenger of God (saws). (Jāmi' At-Tirmidhī, Ḥadīth 3641; Zubayr 'Alī Za'ī graded it ḥasan.)

Anas (ra) narrated: I served the Prophet (saws) in Al-Madīnah for ten years. I was a boy. Every work that I did was not according to the desire of my master, but he never said to me, "Uff" (i.e., an expression of disgust), nor did he say to me, "Why did you do this?" or, "Why did you not do this?" (Sunan Abū Dāwūd, Ḥadīth 4774, Al-Albānī graded it ṣaḥīḥ; Riyāḍ Aṣ-Ṣāliḥīn, Ḥadīth 622)

Al-Aswad narrated that he asked 'Ā'ishah (ra): "What did the Prophet (saws) do in his house?" She replied, "He used to keep himself busy serving his family and when it was time for the prayer, he would go for it." (Ṣaḥīḥ Al-Bukhārī, Ḥadīth 676; Riyāḍ Aṣ-Ṣāliḥīn, Ḥadīth 606)

Anas (ra) narrated: I was walking with the Messenger of God (saws), who was wearing a Najrānī cloak with a very thick border, when a Bedouin happened to meet him. He took hold of the side of his cloak and drew it violently. I noticed that the violence of the jerk had bruised the neck of the Messenger of God (saws). The Bedouin said: "O Muḥammad! Give me out of God's wealth that you possess." The Messenger of God (saws) turned to him and smiled and directed that he should be given something. (Ṣaḥīḥ Al Bukhārī, Ḥadīth 6088; Riyāḍ Aṣ-Ṣāliḥīn, Ḥadīth 645)

'Abdullāh ibn 'Amr ibn Al-'Āṣ (ra) narrated: The Messenger of God (saws) neither indulged in loose talk, nor did he like to listen to it. He used to say, "The best of you is the best among you in conduct." (Ṣaḥīḥ Al Bukhārī, Ḥadīth 6035; Riyāḍ Aṣ-Ṣāliḥīn, Ḥadīth 625)

'Abdullāh ibn Mas'ūd (ra) narrated: It is as if I can see the Messenger of God (saws) tell the story of a prophet who had been beaten by his people, who was wiping the blood from his face, and who was saying, "My Lord, forgive my people, for they do not know." (Ṣaḥīḥ Al-Bukhārī, Ḥadīth 6929; Ṣaḥīḥ Muslim, Ḥadīth 1792; Riyāḍ Aṣ-Ṣāliḥīn, Ḥadīth 645)

Anas (ra) narrated: The Messenger of God (saws) was the best of all the people in behavior. (Ṣaḥīḥ Al-Bukhārī, Ḥadīth 203; Riyāḍ Aṣ-Ṣāliḥīn, Ḥadīth 621)

Respect for Non-Muslims

'Abdur-Raḥmān ibn Abū Laylā narrated: Sahl ibn Ḥunayf and Qays ibn Sa'd were sitting in the city of Al-Qādisiyyah. A funeral procession passed in front of them, and they stood up. They were told that that funeral procession was of one of the inhabitants of the land (i.e., of a disbeliever, under the protection of Muslims). They said, "A funeral procession passed in front of the Prophet (saws), and he stood up. When he was told that it was the coffin of a Jew, he said, "Is it not a human being?" (Ṣaḥīḥ Al-Bukhārī, Ḥadīth 1312)

Al-Barā' ibn 'Āzib (ra) narrated: When the Messenger of God (saws) concluded a peace treaty with the polytheists at Al-Ḥudaybiyah, 'Alī ibn Abū Ṭālib wrote the document, and he mentioned in it, "Muḥammad, the Messenger of God (saws)." The polytheists said, "Don't write 'Muḥammad, the Messenger of God,' for if you were a messenger, we would not fight with you." The Messenger of God (saws) asked 'Alī to rub it out, but 'Alī said, "I will not be the person to rub it out." The Messenger of God (saws) rubbed it out and made peace with them on the condition that the Prophet (saws) and his companions would enter Makkah (next year, to perform 'Umrah) and stay there for three days, and that they would enter with their weapons in cases. (Ṣaḥīḥ Al-Bukhārī, Ḥadīth 2698)

Bravery

Anas (ra) narrated: The Prophet (saws) was the best among the people (both in shape and character) and was the most generous of them and was the bravest of them. Once, during the night, the people of Al-Madīnah got afraid (of a sound). So the people went towards that sound, but the Prophet (saws), having gone to that sound before them, met them while he was saying, "Don't be afraid, don't be afraid." He was riding a horse belonging to Abū Ṭalḥah and it was naked without a saddle, and he was carrying a sword slung at his neck. The Prophet (saws) said, "I found it (i.e., the horse) like a sea," or, "It is the sea indeed." (Ṣaḥīḥ Al-Bukhārī, Ḥadīth 6033)

Some Miracles

The Miracle of the Qur'ān

Abū Hurayrah (ra) narrated: The Prophet (saws) said, "There was no prophet among the prophets but was given miracles because of which people had security or had belief, but what I have been given is the Divine Revelation which God has revealed to me. So I hope that my followers will be more than those of any other prophet on the Day of Resurrection." (Ṣaḥīḥ Al-Bukhārī, Ḥadīth 4981)

The Healing of 'Alī's Eyes

Sahl ibn Sa'd (ra) narrated: The Messenger of God (saws) said on the day of the Battle of Khaybar, "I will give this banner to a person at whose hands God will grant victory; a man who loves God and His Messenger (saws), and God and His Messenger love him also." The people spent the night thinking as to whom it would be given. When it was morning, the people hastened to the Messenger of God (saws). Every one of them was hoping that the banner would be given to him. He (the Prophet (saws)) asked, "Where is 'Alī ibn Abū Ṭālib?" They said, "O Messenger of God! His eyes are sore." He then sent for him and when he came, the Messenger of God (saws) applied his saliva to his eyes and supplicated. 'Alī recovered as if he had no ailment at all. He conferred upon him the banner. 'Alī said, "O Messenger of God, shall I fight against them until they are like us?" Thereupon he (the Prophet (saws)) said, "Advance cautiously until you reach their open places. Thereafter, invite them to Islām and inform them what is obligatory for them from the rights of God, for, by God, if God guides even one person through you that is better for you than possessing red camels." (Ṣaḥīḥ Al-Bukhārī, Ḥadīth 2942; Riyāḍ Aṣ-Ṣāliḥīn, Ḥadīth 175)

The Splitting of the Moon

'Abdullāh ibn Mas'ūd (ra) narrated: During the lifetime of the Prophet (saws) the moon was split into two parts and on that the Prophet (saws) said, "Bear witness (to this)." (Ṣaḥīḥ Al-Bukhārī, Ḥadīth 3636)

Narrated Anas (ra) narrated that the Makkan people requested the Messenger of God (saws) to show them a miracle, so he showed them the splitting of the moon. (Ṣaḥīḥ Al-Bukhārī, Ḥadīth 3637)

The Miracle of Water

Sālim narrated: Jābir (ra) said, "On the day of Al-Ḥudaybiyah, the people felt thirsty, and the Messenger of God (saws) had a utensil containing water. He performed ablution from it and then the people came towards him. The Messenger of God (saws) said, 'What is wrong with you?' The people said, 'O Messenger of God! We haven't got any water to perform ablution with or to drink, except what you have in your utensil.' Then the Prophet (saws) put his hand in the utensil and the water started spouting out between his fingers like springs, so we drank and performed ablution." I asked Jābir, "What was your number on that day?" He replied, "Even if we had been one hundred thousand, that water would have been sufficient for us. Regardless, we were fifteen hundred." (Ṣaḥīḥ Al-Bukhārī, Ḥadīth 4152)

Abū Hurayrah's Memory

Abū Hurayrah (ra) narrated: I said, "O Messenger of God! I hear many narrations from you, but I forget them." He said, "Spread your covering sheet." I spread my sheet, and he moved both his hands as if scooping something and emptied them in the sheet and said, "Wrap it." I wrapped it round my body, and since then I have never forgotten a single ḥadīth. (Ṣaḥīḥ Al-Bukhārī, Ḥadīth 3648)

The Miracle of Rain

Anas (ra) narrated: A man came to the Prophet (saws) on a Friday while he (the Prophet (saws)) was delivering a sermon at Al-Madīnah, and said, "There is drought, so please invoke your Lord to bless us with the rain." The Prophet (saws) looked at the sky, where no cloud could be detected. Then he invoked God for rain. Clouds started gathering together and it rained until Al-Madīnah's valleys started flowing with water. It continued raining till the next Friday. Then that man, or some other man, stood up while the Prophet (saws) was delivering the Friday sermon, and said, "We are drowned. Please invoke your Lord to withhold (the rain) from us." The Prophet (saws) smiled and said twice or thrice, "O God! (Please let it rain) round about us and not upon us." The clouds started dispersing over Al-Madīnah to the right and to the left, and it rained round about Al-Madīnah and not upon Al-Madīnah. God showed them the miracle from Him to His Prophet (saws) and His response to his invocation. (Ṣaḥīḥ Al-Bukhārī, Ḥadīth 6093)

<u>The Last Prophet</u>

Sa'd ibn Abū Waqqāṣ (ra) narrated: The Messenger of God (saws) set out for Tabūk, appointing 'Alī as his deputy (in Al-Madīnah). 'Alī said, "Do you want to leave me with the children and women?" The Prophet (saws) said, "Will you not be pleased that you will be to me like Aaron to Moses? But there will be no prophet after me." (Ṣaḥīḥ Al-Bukhārī, Ḥadīth 4416; its meaning is also in Ṣaḥīḥ Muslim, Ḥadīth 2404.)

Abū Hurayrah (ra) narrated: The Messenger of God (saws) said, "My similitude in comparison with the other prophets before me is that of a man who has built a house nicely and beautifully, except for a place of one brick in a corner. The people go about it and wonder at its beauty but say, 'Would that this brick be put in its place!' So I am that brick, and I am the last of the prophets." (Ṣaḥīḥ Al-Bukhārī, Ḥadīth 3535)

Chapter 5
Significant Islāmic Figures

The Prophets

Prophets were sent all over the world to different cultures throughout history, and we do not know the names of most of them. The Qur'ān mentions 25 prophets by name.

1. Ādam (Adam)
2. Idrīs
3. Nūḥ (Noah)
4. Ibrāhīm (Abraham)
5. Lūṭ (Lot)
6. Ismā'īl (Ishmael)
7. Is'ḥāq (Isaac)
8. Ya'qūb (Jacob)
9. Yūsuf (Joseph)
10. Hūd
11. Ṣāliḥ
12. Shu'ayb
13. Ayyūb (Job)
16. Mūsā (Moses)
17. Hārūn (Aaron)
18. Dāwūd (David)
19. Sulaymān (Solomon)
20. Ilyās (Elijah)
21. Al-Yasa' (Elisha)
22. Zakariyyah (Zachariah)
23. Yaḥyā (John)
24. 'Īsā (Jesus)
25. Muḥammad

After the Prophet Muḥammad (saws)

After the death of the Prophet Muḥammad (saws), the ruler of the Muslim community was called a *caliph* (Arabic: *khalīfah*), and the first four caliphs were his closest companions: Abū Bakr, 'Umar, 'Uthmān, and 'Alī. These four are collectively known as the *Rightly Guided Caliphs* (Arabic: *Khulafā' Ar-Rāshidūn*). The Rāshidūn Caliphate lasted from 632 to 661 C.E. During this era, wars were fought between the Muslims and other communities and nations. These wars led to the Muslim conquest of the Persian Sassanid Empire and the Middle Eastern territories of the Eastern Roman Empire as well as certain North African territories. The Rāshidūn Caliphate also oversaw the preservation of the Qur'ān. During the time of

Abū Bakr, the Qur'ān was written down into one volume, and during the time of 'Uthmān, copies of it were made and distributed. Eventually, misunderstandings among rulers, as well as the manipulations of power hungry people, led to civil war within the Muslim world, and the Rāshidūn Caliphate ended.

Thereafter, the Muslim world was ruled by the Umayyad Dynasty from 661 to 750 C.E. The generation of the *ṣaḥābah* (companions of the Prophet (saws)) was succeeded by the generation of the *tābi'ūn* (followers; Muslims who met the ṣaḥābah). The tābi'ūn were succeeded by the *tābi'ūt-tābi'*īn (followers of the followers). According to a ḥadīth of the Prophet (saws), these three generations are the best in Islām (see: Ṣaḥīḥ Al-Bukhārī, Ḥadīth 6429 and Ṣaḥīḥ Muslim, Ḥadīth 2533).

After the Umayyads, much of the Muslim world was ruled by the 'Abbāsid Dynasty, which lasted from 750 to 1258 C.E. During these two dynasties, religious schools of thought, or *madhhabs*, formed. Additionally, schools of *'aqidah*, or "creed," formed, and they differed regarding certain matters of belief. Very knowledgeable scholars also compiled ḥadīth books. These works laid the foundation for future seekers of knowledge. Although the canonical ḥadīth books were compiled around the 9th century C.E., which was approximately two centuries after the Prophet Muḥammad (saws), ḥadīths had actually been collected since the time of his companions in the 7th century C.E.

The Companions of the Prophet Muḥammad (saws)

Herein are mentioned some of the notable companions of the Prophet Muḥammad (saws).

The Arabic word for companion is *ṣaḥābī*, and the plural is *ṣaḥābah* or *aṣḥāb*. According to Ahlus-Sunnah wal-Jamā'ah, a companion is defined as anyone who met the Prophet Muḥammad (saws) while that person was a Muslim and later on died as a Muslim. Therefore, there were thousands of ṣaḥābah, but of them a few were particularly close to the Prophet (saws). After the death of Muḥammad (saws), the ruler of the Muslim community was called a *caliph* (Arabic: *khalīfah*), and the first four caliphs were his closest companions: Abū Bakr, 'Umar, 'Uthmān, and 'Alī. These four are collectively known as the *Rightly Guided Caliphs* (Arabic: *Khulafā' Ar-Rāshidūn*).

Additionally, there is a famous authentic ḥadīth (in Jāmi‘ At-Tirmidhī, Ḥadīth 3747) in which the Prophet Muḥammad (saws) listed ten companions who would be in Paradise:

1. Abū Bakr ibn Abū Quḥāfah
2. ‘Umar ibn Al-Khaṭṭāb
3. ‘Uthmān ibn ‘Affān
4. ‘Alī ibn Abū Ṭālib
5. Ṭalḥah ibn ‘Ubaydullāh
6. Az-Zubayr ibn Al-‘Awwām
7. ‘Abdur-Raḥmān ibn ‘Awf
8. Sa‘d ibn Abū Waqqāṣ
9. Sa‘īd ibn Zayd
10. Abū ‘Ubaydah ibn Al-Jarrāḥ

Note that Abū Bakr, the closest companion of the Prophet (saws), had the title of Aṣ-Ṣiddīq (the Truthful) because of his sincere conviction that what the Prophet (saws) said was true. Another ḥadīth has the Prophet (saws) describing superlative attributes of certain companions:

Anas ibn Mālik (ra) narrated: The Messenger of God (saws) said, "The most merciful of my ummah towards my ummah is Abū Bakr; the one who adheres most sternly to the religion of Allāh is ‘Umar; the most sincere of them in shyness and modesty is ‘Uthmān; the best judge is ‘Alī ibn Abū Ṭālib; the best in reciting the Book of God is Ubayy ibn Ka‘b; the most knowledgeable of what is lawful and unlawful is Mu‘ādh ibn Jabal; and the most knowledgeable of the rules of inheritance is Zayd ibn Thābit. And every nation has a trustworthy guardian, and the trustworthy guardian of this ummah is Abū ‘Ubaydah ibn Al-Jarrāḥ." (Sunan Ibn Mājah, Ḥadīth 154; Zubayr ‘Alī Za‘ī graded it ṣaḥīḥ.)

The Prophet (saws) also distinguished four companions by instructing others to learn the Qur’ān from them: ‘Abdullāh ibn Mas‘ūd, Sālim the freed slave of Abū Ḥudhayfah, Ubayy ibn Ka‘b, and Mu‘ādh ibn Jabal. (This is from Ṣaḥīḥ Al-Bukhārī, Ḥadīths 3806 and 4999.)

Other notable companions included, but were not limited to:

- ‘Abdullāh ibn Rawāḥah (a prominent companion from Al-Madīnah)

- ‘Abdullāh ibn Umm Maktūm (a blind man who was a caller to prayer)

- Abū Ayyūb Al-Anṣārī (the man with whom the Prophet (saws) stayed in Al-Madīnah before the mosque and house of the Prophet (saws) were built)
- Abū Hurayrah (the companion who narrated the most ḥadīths from the Prophet (saws))
- Al-'Abbās ibn 'Abdul-Muṭṭalib (an uncle of the Prophet (saws))
- Anas ibn Mālik (the Prophet's (saws) personal assistant)
- Bilāl ibn Rabāḥ (a freed black Abyssinian slave who became the first caller to prayer)
- Ḥamzah ibn 'Abdul-Muṭṭalib (an uncle of the Prophet (saws) who was martyred at Uḥud)
- Ja'far ibn Abū Ṭālib (the Prophet's (saws) cousin and brother to 'Alī)
- Khālid ibn Al-Walīd (a later companion who became a famous warrior)
- 'Ukkāshah ibn Miḥṣan (another companion who was promised Paradise)
- Zayd ibn Ḥārithah (the Prophet's (saws) adopted son)

The Wives of the Prophet Muḥammad (saws)

The Prophet's (saws) first wife from the age of 25 was Khadījah, and she remained his only wife until she passed away when he was in his 50's. Although Muḥammad (saws) did have several wives at once further on in his life, all of the marriages were to support widows and/or to cement political ties, with the exception of his marriage to 'Ā'ishah bint Abū Bakr, who was his only virgin wife. It is unlikely that a man of such high integrity and piety, who had been monogamous from the age of 25, and who was in his 50's, would marry multiple women out of mere lust. Additionally, the concubines of the Prophet (saws) were honored women with rights similar to those of wives.

Wives

1. Khadījah bint Khuwaylid
2. Sawdah bint Zam‘ah ibn Qays
3. ‘Ā’ishah bint Abū Bakr
4. Hafṣah bint ‘Umar
5. Zaynab bint Khuzaymah
6. Umm Salamah bint Abū Umayyah
7. Juwayriyah bint Al-Ḥārith ibn Abu Ḍirār
8. Zaynab bint Jaḥsh
9. Umm Ḥabībah bint Abu Sufyān
10. Maymūnah bint Al-Ḥārith ibn Ḥazn
11. Ṣafiyyah bint Ḥuyayy ibn Akhtab

Concubines

1. Māriyah Al-Qibṭiyyah
2. Rayḥānah
3. Jamīlah
4. The bondwoman of Zaynab bint Jaḥsh

The Children and Grandchildren of the Prophet Muḥammad (saws)

Muḥammad (saws) ibn ‘Abdullāh – Khadījah bint Khuwaylid

1. Al-Qāsim [died in childhood]
2. Zaynab – (married to) – Abu Al-‘Āṣ ibn Ar-Rabī‘
    a. Umāmah
    b. ‘Alī
3. Ruqayyah – (married to) – ‘Uthmān ibn ‘Affān
    a. ‘Abdullāh
4. Umm Kulthūm – (married to) – ‘Uthmān ibn ‘Affān
5. Fāṭimah – (married to) – ‘Alī ibn Abū Ṭālib
    a. Al-Ḥasan
    b. Al-Ḥusayn
    c. Zaynab
    d. Umm Kulthūm
6. ‘Abdullāh [died in childhood]

Muḥammad (saws) also had another son, later in Al-Madīnah, named Ibrāhīm through his concubine Māriyah, but the boy also died in childhood.

Note that all of the daughters of Muḥammad (saws) lived to be adults, but three of them (Zaynab, Ruqayyah, and Umm Kulthūm) died during his time as a prophet. Additionally, his youngest daughter, Fāṭimah, passed away shortly after he did.

Note also that the companion ‘Uthmān was first married to Muḥammad’s (saws) daughter Ruqayyah, and when she died, he married Muḥammad’s (saws) daughter Umm Kulthūm. For this reason, ‘Uthmān is known as *Dhūn-Nurayn*, “the Possessor of the Two Lights”. It may also be noted that it is forbidden to be married to two sisters at the same time, but he married one until she died, and then the other.

Muḥammad’s (saws) adopted son, Zayd ibn Ḥārithah, also had children with whom the Prophet (saws) was close.

Zayd ibn Ḥārithah – (married to) – Umm Kulthūm bint ‘Uqbah ibn Abū Mu‘ayṭ

1. Zayd
2. Ruqayyah

Zayd ibn Ḥārithah – (married to) – Umm Ayman bint Tha‘labah ibn ‘Amr

1. Usāmah
2. Zaynab

The Controversy of the Age of ‘Ā’ishah

One of the most common misunderstandings about Islām is the age at which ‘Ā’ishah was married to the Prophet (saws). The following are two authentic ḥadīths that mention her age.

Hishām’s father narrated: Khadījah died three years before the Prophet (saws) departed to Al-Madīnah. He stayed there for two years or so, and then he married ‘Ā’ishah when she was a girl of six years of age, and he consummated that marriage when she was nine years old. (Ṣaḥīḥ Al-Bukhārī, Ḥadīth 3896)

'Ā'ishah (ra) narrated: The Prophet (saws) married her when she was six years old, and he consummated his marriage when she was nine years old, and then she remained with him for nine years (i.e., till his death). (Ṣaḥīḥ Al-Bukhārī, Ḥadīth 5133; Ṣaḥīḥ Muslim 1422)

The Prophet (saws) waited to consummate his marriage with 'Ā'ishah until she had reached puberty at nine years old. This was considered normal, not just in that setting, but in cultures around the world for centuries. The concept of adolescence as we know it did not exist for many in ancient and medieval times. When a person, boy or girl, reached puberty, they were considered an adult and eligible for marriage. Further evidence that this was normal for that time and place is found in the fact that 'Ā'ishah was engaged to a man named Muṭ'im ibn 'Adī *before* she was engaged to the Prophet (saws), but her engagement to Muṭ'im was canceled. Also, a woman named Khawlah bint Ḥakīm was the one who suggested that the Prophet (saws) marry 'Ā'ishah. Lastly, the enemies of the Prophet (saws), during his lifetime and for centuries after his death, used whatever they could to slander him, but not one of his enemies used the age of 'Ā'ishah to slander him until fairly recently. This is because females were getting married at young ages in other areas too. For example, Isabelle of France married King Richard II of England when she was seven years old. This took place in 1396, long after the time of the Prophet (saws).

One cannot always judge an old situation with modern eyes, and even today the age of consent differs around the world. If in the future people around the world decided to raise the age of maturity to 30 years old, that would not retroactively make people married to individuals in their 20's in the wrong. Moreover, it is normal, medically-speaking, that a girl can reach puberty as early as eight years old, according to the United States' National Institutes of Health, the Mayo Clinic, and the United Kingdom's National Health Service.

"Early or Delayed Puberty." National Health Service. 11 Mar. 2019, https://www.nhs.uk/conditions/early-or-delayed-puberty/. Accessed 25 May 2022.

"Precocious Puberty." mayoclinic. 15 Feb. 2021, https://www.mayoclinic.org/diseases-conditions/precocious-puberty/symptoms-causes/syc-20351811. Accessed 25 May 2022.

"Puberty and Precocious Puberty." National Institutes of Health. 21 Jun. 2021, https://www.nichd.nih.gov/health/topics/puberty. Accessed 25 May 2022.

A Selection of Lineages Leading Back to Fihr (Quraysh)

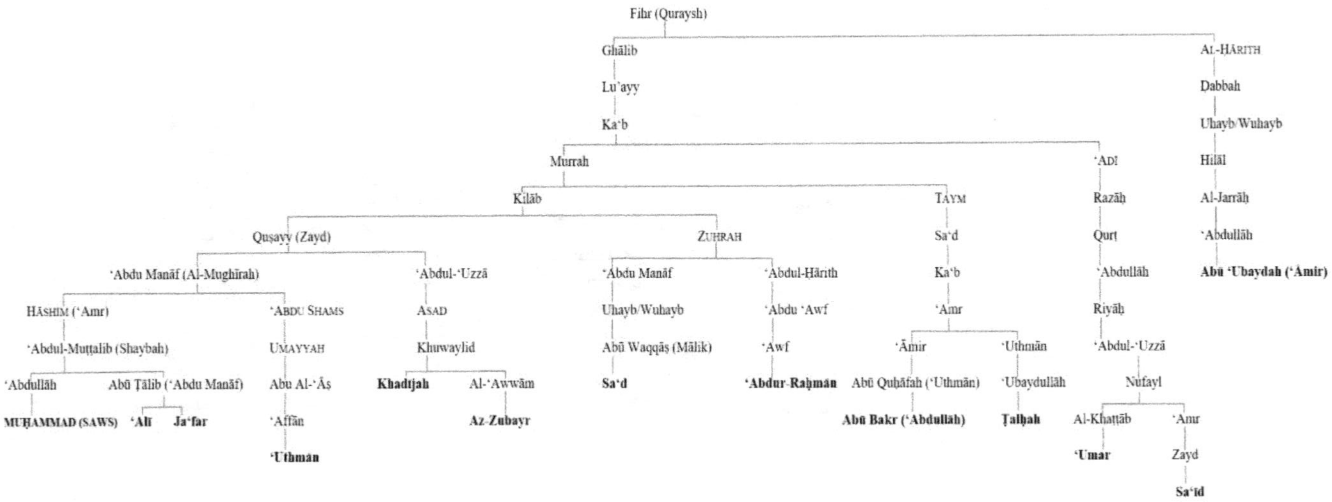

Note that names of clan founders are in small capitals.

Part 3: The Pillars of Islām

Chapter 6
Aṣ-Ṣalāh (The Prayer)

Ṣalāt (plural: *ṣalawāt*), also spelled *ṣalāh*, means "*prayer*," and the ṣalāt that is mandatory upon Muslims is the ṣalāt that is to be performed 5 times daily. In Arabic, it has an equivalent of the letter "t" at the end, but sometimes the "t" is silent, so it may also be pronounced as *ṣalāh*. Both spellings will be used herein. The five daily *ṣalawāt* are:

1. Fajr (comes in at dawn; its cutoff is at sunrise, which is called *Shurūq*)
2. Ẓuhr (comes in at the early afternoon when the sun has passed its zenith; its cutoff is at 'Aṣr)
3. 'Aṣr (comes in at the late afternoon; its cutoff is a little bit before Maghrib, when the sun turns pale yellow as it starts to set)
4. Maghrib (performed at sunset; its cutoff is when the red goes away from the sky)
5. 'Ishā' (performed in the early night; its cutoff is at midnight or Fajr, according to different scholarly opinions)

Ṣalāt is immensely beneficial for the soul. Allāh says in the Qur'ān:

114Say your prayers at both ends of the day and during parts of the night. Surely good deeds wipe out evil deeds. This is a reminder for people who pay heed. (Qur'ān 11:114)

45Recite what has been revealed to you of the Book, and pray regularly. Surely prayer restrains one from indecency and evil. And remembrance of God is greater. God has knowledge of all your actions. (Qur'ān 29:45)

And the following ḥadīth states:

Abū Hurayrah (ra) narrated: I heard the Messenger of God (saws) saying, "If there was a river at the door of anyone of you and he took a bath in it five times a day would you notice any dirt on him?" They said, "Not a trace of dirt would be left." The Prophet (saws) added, "That is the example of the five prayers with which God blots out evil deeds." (Ṣaḥīḥ Al-Bukhārī, Ḥadīth 506)

The Adhān

When one of the five *ṣalawāt* is about to be performed in congregation (Arabic: *jamā'ah*), then the *adhān*, which is the call to prayer, is generally called before the prayer starts, to let people know that it is time for *ṣalāh*. The person who says the adhān is called the *muezzin* (pronounced *mu-adh-dhin*), and many mosques have a tower from which the adhān is called, and this tower is called a *minaret* (Arabic: *manārah*). The adhān is given facing the qiblah (see the section titled *The Qiblah*), and it is said as follows:

English Translation	Arabic Transliteration
Allāh is Greater. *Allāh is Greater.* *Allāh is Greater.* *Allāh is Greater.*	*Allāhu Akbar.* *Allāhu Akbar.* *Allāhu Akbar.* *Allāhu Akbar.*
I testify that there is no god except Allāh.	*Ash hadu anlā ilāha il-lal-lāh.*
I testify that there is no god except Allāh.	*Ash hadu anlā ilāha il-lal-lāh.*
I testify that Muḥammad is the Messenger of Allāh.	*Ash hadu an-na Muḥammadar-Rasūlul-lāh.*
I testify that Muḥammad is the Messenger of Allāh.	*Ash hadu an-na Muḥammadar-Rasūlul-lāh.*

**Note:* Then the caller turns their face to the right and says:*

English Translation	Arabic Transliteration
Come to the prayer.	*Ḥaiy-ya 'alaṣ-ṣalāh.*
Come to the prayer.	*Ḥaiy-ya 'alaṣ-ṣalāh.*

**Note:* Then the caller turns their face to the left and says:*

English Translation	Arabic Transliteration
Come to success.	*Ḥaiy-ya 'alal-falāḥ.*
Come to success.	*Ḥaiy-ya 'alal-falāḥ.*

**Note:* Then the caller faces forward again and says:*

English Translation	Arabic Transliteration
Allāh is Greater.	*Allāhu Akbar.*
Allāh is Greater.	*Allāhu Akbar.*
There is no god except Allāh.	*Lā ilāha il-lal-lāh.*

Note: Only in the Fajr adhān is the following phrase said twice ***in between*** "Come to success" and "Allāh is Greater": "*The prayer is better than sleep,*" which in Arabic is, "*Aṣ-ṣalātu khayrum-minan-nawm.*"

Also, when one hears the adhān, one should repeat every phrase after it is said, except for "Come to the prayer" and "Come to success." After those two phrases, one should say, "Lā ḥawla walā quwwata illā billāh (There is no might and no strength except with God)."

Prerequisites for Ṣalāh

The prerequisites for one's ṣalāt may be counted as 9:

1. One must be a Muslim.
2. One must be sane.
3. One must have attained puberty.

4. One must be in the state of wuḍū’ (see the section *Wuḍū’ and Ghusl*).
5. One must remove any filth.
6. One must cover their ‘awrah (see the section *The ‘Awrah*).
7. It must be the correct time for the corresponding ṣalāt.
8. One must face the qiblah (see the section *The Qiblah*).
9. One must have the intention (Arabic: *niyyah*) to perform the ṣalāt.

Wuḍū’ and Ghusl

Wuḍū’ is often translated into English as “ablution,” which means “washing.” It is a state of physical and spiritual purity. In order to make wuḍū’, one must have the intention to perform it, and then one must perform the following:

- Wash the hands, starting with the right one, then the left one (1, 2, or 3 times)
- Rinse the mouth (1, 2, or 3 times)
- Rinse the nose [by sniffing in water and blowing it out] (1, 2, or 3 times)
- Wash the face (1, 2, or 3 times)
    - Run one’s fingers through the beard (if applicable)
- Wash the arms [this includes everything from the fingertips to the elbows], starting with the right one, then the left one (1, 2, or 3 times for each arm)
- Wipe the head in one motion, starting from the forehead, going back to [but not including] the nape of the neck, then back to the forehead (1 time)
- Wipe the exterior and interior of one’s ears, including behind them (1 time)
- Wash the feet [up to, and including, the ankles], starting with the right one, then the left one (1, 2, or 3 times for each foot); make sure to wash in between the toes too

The washing of the hands, face, arms, and feet three times each is *sunnah* (i.e., recommended because it is in accordance with the Prophet's (saws) example). While it is highly recommended because the Prophet (saws) did it, one time for each area will suffice.

Soap is not required for wuḍū'; only clean water is required.

If one is wearing socks that cover the ankles that were put on *while one was in wuḍū'*, then, when renewing wuḍū', one is allowed to simply wipe over the tops of their socks. This is permissible only if one has been wearing the socks within the span of one 24-hour day, or, if travelling, within the span of three days. If the socks are very thin, however, some say to take them off and wash the feet, though opinions differ on this matter.

After making wuḍū', one remains in wuḍū' unless one performs an action that nullifies it, in which case one would make another wuḍū' if one needs to pray ṣalāt or if one simply desires to make wuḍū' again. Actions that nullify wuḍū' include: deep sleep, eating camel meat, urination, defecation, flatulence, discharge of seminal fluid, and touching one's genitals.

There are three things that one has to be in wuḍū' for: praying ṣalāh, doing ṭawāf (circumambulation) around the Ka'bah, and physically touching a *muṣḥaf* (i.e., a copy of the Qur'ān written in its original Arabic).

If one has had an orgasm, sexual intercourse, or, in the case of women, just finished their period or just finished postpartum bleeding, a full bath is required. This full bath is called *ghusl*, and it consists of making the intention to do ghusl and washing the entire body once, including the roots of the hair and any crevices. This is the minimum requirement for ghusl. A more complete ghusl consists of making the intention to do ghusl, washing the hands 3 times, washing the private parts, performing the actions of wuḍū', pouring water over the head three times and rubbing the hair so that the water reaches its roots, and then washing all parts of the body starting with the right side then the left side. If one does ghusl, then they do not have to do wuḍū', unless they do something that breaks wuḍū'. It is also recommended to do ghusl on Fridays before going to Jumu'ah at the masjid.

It should also be noted that women who are on their period should not pray the five daily ṣalawāt, and they are not required to make up the missed prayers. This also applies to women who are going through postpartum bleeding, within a maximum time range of 40 days.

Tayammum

If one has no access to water to perform wuḍū' or ghusl, or if one has very limited water and needs to save it for drinking, then one should do tayammum. Tayammum involves using clean dust (dirt), sand, rocks, or pebbles to purify oneself.

First, one makes the intention to purify oneself, and then one may say, "Bismillāh (In the name of God)." Then one slaps the dust with both palms, blows the excess dust off of them, wipes one's face with their palms, and then wipes both hands (up to, and including, the wrists).

Everything that breaks wuḍū' also breaks tayammum.

Lastly, if a person has no access to water or clean dust, then one should pray ṣalāh as they are, and they do not have to redo the ṣalāh later.

Notes on Using the Toilet

Cleanliness is extremely important in Islām, and urine and feces on oneself or one's clothing will invalidate their prayer. For this reason, it is recommended that men urinate while sitting down. Both genders should also purify their private parts by pouring water on them after they have urinated or defecated. This is called istinjā', and for this reason one may find watering cans or water hoses in a Muslim's bathroom or in a mosque's restroom. When one wipes, one should also use at least three wipes, and one should use an odd number of wipes if one uses more than three. This is because God likes odd numbers because He is One, and one is an odd number. A person should also clean their private parts with their left hand, reserving the right hand for clean activities.

Removing Filth

One should be clean, wear clean clothes, and be in a clean area while praying. It is for this purpose that many Muslims choose to use a prayer rug for their prostration and sitting, as it is a clean surface. However, a prayer rug is not required for praying. It is also forbidden to pray in a bathroom, in a dump, or in a cemetery.

The 'Awrah

A person's *'awrah* is the part of their body that is not permissible to be exposed to the public and while praying. For a man, he must be covered between the knees and the navel. This means that it is better for a man to not wear shorts, particularly at the masjid. For a woman, everything must be covered except for the face and the hands. It should be noted that this is meant to preserve modesty in society and that a woman's head covering, or *ḥijāb*, helps to emphasize, and attract respect for, her character, rather than her physique. Note that "ḥijāb" literally refers to a veil or partition, and it can refer to what covers the whole body, although the term is often used to refer to a woman's headscarf. A woman may additionally wear a *niqāb*, which is a face covering, if she wishes. The wives of the Prophet Muḥammad (saws) covered their faces, and there are extra blessings in doing so. Scholars differ on whether the niqāb is mandatory, but it is not necessarily so. For both genders, clothing should not be tight-fitting, but should be loose.

Notes on Appearance

A man with long hair cannot have his hair tied back during ṣalāh, and his sleeves cannot be rolled up. This can be found in Ṣaḥīḥ Muslim, Ḥadīth 490. The reason for this is that the hair and garments are to keep hanging down out of humility, as they are part of the prostration. However, these two factors do not necessarily nullify one's ṣalāh. Additionally, one should not wear any garment with pictures of living things with faces on it, as the angels do not enter a house in which there are images, and this information is found in Ṣaḥīḥ Al-Bukhārī, Ḥadīth 3322; Sunan An-Nasa'ī, Ḥadīth 5351 (Zubayr 'Alī Za'ī graded it ṣaḥīḥ); and Sunan Abū Dāwūd, Ḥadīth 4158 (Al-Albānī graded it ṣaḥīḥ).

The Qiblah

The *qiblah* is the direction that all Muslims must face while praying. This direction is Al-Masjid Al-Ḥarām in Mecca, the most significant point of which is the Ka'bah. It must be known that Muslims do not pray *to* the qiblah, but simply *towards* the qiblah; it is a unifying point for Muslims around the world. Additionally, one should not look up or around while in ṣalāh; rather, one should keep their gaze on the place of prostration.

The Iqāmah

When a prayer in congregation behind an imām is about to start, the *iqāmah* is called, and it is said as follows:

English Translation	Arabic Transliteration
Allāh is Greater. *Allāh is Greater.*	*Allāhu Akbar.* *Allāhu Akbar.*
I testify that there is no god except Allāh.	*Ash hadu anlā ilāha il-lal-lāh.*
I testify that Muḥammad is the Messenger of Allāh.	*Ash hadu an-na Muḥammadar-Rasūlul-lāh.*
Come to the prayer.	*Ḥaiy-ya 'alaṣ-ṣalāh.*
Come to success.	*Ḥaiy-ya 'alal-falāḥ.*
The prayer is established. *The prayer is established.*	*Qad qāmatiṣ-ṣalāh.* *Qad qāmatiṣ-ṣalāh.*
Allāh is Greater. *Allāh is Greater.*	*Allāhu Akbar.* *Allāhu Akbar.*
There is no god except Allāh.	*Lā ilāha il-lal-lāh.*

Notes on Ṣalāh

The next pages detail ṣalāh from start to finish. Note that each prayer consists of a different number of units, or *rak'ahs*. Also, in congregational prayers, only the imām recites the Qur'ān out loud, as well as "Allāhu Akbar," "Sami'allāhu liman ḥamidah," and the taslīms. In the first and second rak'ahs, another part of the Qur'ān is typically recited after Al-Fātiḥah (The Opening). In the third and fourth rak'ahs, it is recommended to only recite Al-Fātiḥah with no other portions of the Qur'ān.

1. Fajr: 2 rak'ahs. The Qur'ān is recited aloud in both.
2. Ẓuhr: 4 rak'ahs. The Qur'ān is recited silently in all four.
    - The Jumu'ah prayer in congregation replaces Ẓuhr on Fridays. It is 2 rak'ahs, and the Qur'ān is recited aloud in both. If one cannot make Jumu'ah, then they should pray a normal Ẓuhr prayer. For more on Jumu'ah, see the chapter of the book titled *Al-Jumu'ah.*
3. 'Aṣr: 4 rak'ahs. The Qur'ān is recited silently in all four.
4. Maghrib: 3 rak'ahs. The Qur'ān is recited aloud in the first two and silently in the third.
5. 'Ishā': 4 rak'ahs. The Qur'ān is recited aloud in the first two and silently in the second two.

General Notes

- If you are physically unable to sit on your knees or to prostrate, then you are allowed to pray using a chair. If one is so incapacitated that they cannot even pray sitting, then they are allowed to pray lying down.
- One cannot talk, laugh, eat, drink, or move excessively in ṣalāh. Brief movement is permissible, but one must remain facing the qiblah.

- When one prays, one should try to have *khushū‘* as much as they can. Khushū‘ refers to humility and concentration.

- Before reciting the Qur'ān, in ṣalāh or at any time, one seeks refuge with God from Satan by saying: "A‘ūdhu billāhi minash-Shayṭānir-rajīm," which means, "I seek refuge in Allāh from Satan the accursed."

An Overview of Aṣ-Ṣalāh (the Prayer) from Start to Finish

Below is the English translation on the left, the Arabic transliteration on the right, and there are notes in italics.

Takbīratul-Iḥrām

**Note: This starts aṣ-ṣalāh (the prayer).*

Position

Stand upright, facing the qiblah, with the gaze on the place of prostration. Raise the hands to the shoulders, with the palms facing forward.

Words

Allāh is Greater.	Allāhu Akbar.

Qiyām (Standing)

Position

Stand with the left hand on the chest above the navel, and the right hand over the left wrist.

Words

**This opening prayer is optional to say. If one says it, it is in the beginning of the first rak'ah*:

Glorified are You, O Allāh, and praised are You, and blessed is Your name, and exalted is Your majesty, and there is no god other than You.	Subḥānakallāhumma wa biḥamdika wa tabārakasmuka wa ta'ālā jadduka wa lā ilāha ghayruka.

**Then recite:*

I seek refuge in Allāh from Satan the accursed.	A'ūdhu billāhi minash-Shayṭānir-rajīm.
In the name of Allāh, the Most Compassionate, the Most Merciful.	Bismillāhir-Raḥmānir-Raḥīm.

**Then the imām recites Al-Fātiḥah (The Opening) out loud, depending on the circumstance:*

Qiyām (Standing) – Continued

All praise is due to Allāh, the Lord of all worlds,	Al-ḥamdu lillāhi Rabbil-‘ālamīn,
the Most Compassionate, the Most Merciful,	Ar-Raḥmānir-Rahīm,
Master of the Day of Judgement.	Māliki Yawmid-dīn,
You alone we worship, and to You alone we turn for help.	Iyyāka na‘budu wa iyyāka nasta‘īn.
Guide us to the straight path,	Ihdinaṣ-Ṣirāṭal-Mustaqīm,
the path of those You have blessed,	Ṣirātalladhīna an‘amta ‘alayhim
not of those who have incurred wrath, nor of those who have gone astray.	Ghayril-maghḍūbi ‘alayhim walaḍ-ḍāllīn.
Amen.	Āmīn.

**Recite any part of the Qur'ān other than Al-Fātiḥah. If you haven't memorized any other part, then it's okay if you don't recite anything after Al-Fātiḥah. It is also not recommended to recite anything after Al-Fātiḥah in the third and fourth rak'ahs. The part of the Qur'ān presented here is sūrah 112, named Al-Ikhlāṣ (The Sincerity):*

In the name of Allāh, the Most Compassionate, the Most Merciful.	Bismillāhir-Raḥmānir-Raḥīm,
Say [O Prophet], ‘He is Allāh, the One,	Qul huwallāhu aḥad;
Allāh, the Self-Sufficient, needed by all.	Allāhuṣ-Ṣamad.
He does not have offspring, nor was He born,	Lam yalid walam yūlad.
and there is nothing like Him.	Walam yakullahū kufuwan aḥad.

**Note: When transitioning between all postures, say "Allāhu Akbar (Allāh is Greater)" except when rising from rukū' (bowing).*

Allāh is Greater.	Allāhu Akbar.

Rukū' (Bowing)

Position

Bend over at a 90 degree angle, with the legs and back straight and the hands palm-down on the knees with the fingers spread out.

Words

**Recite this 1 time, 3 times, 5 times, or any odd number of times. The standard is 3 times:*

Glorified is my Lord, the Absolute Greatest.	Subḥāna Rabbiyal-'Aẓīm.

**One may optionally add:*

Glorified are You, O Allāh, our Lord, and praised are You. O Allāh, forgive me.	Subḥānakallāhumma Rabbanā wa biḥamdika. Allāhummaghfirlī.

**Then say while rising from rukū' (bowing):*

Allāh listened to whoever praised Him.	Sami'allāhu liman ḥamidah.

2nd Qiyām (2nd Standing)

Position

This is the same position as the first. Note that many people put their arms to their sides for 2nd Qiyām, and this is acceptable.

Words

Our Lord, for You is all praise.	Rabbanā lakal-ḥamd.

**One may optionally add:*

Praises plentiful, good, and blessed,	Ḥamdan kathīran ṭayyiban mubārakan fīhi
filling the heavens and filling the earth and whatever is in between them, and filling whatever else You wish.	Mil'as-samāwāti wa mil'al-arḍi wamā bayna humā wa mil'a mā shi'ta min shay'im ba'd.

**Then say while going into sajdah/sujūd (prostration):*

Allāh is Greater.	Allāhu Akbar.

Sajdah/Sujūd (Prostrating)

Position

Lie on the ground with the forehead, hands, knees, and toes on the ground. The hands should be palm-down, the fingers should be joined together, the toes should be pointing forward, and the heels should be joined together. It is also sunnah for the nose to be touching the ground.

Words

**Recite this 1 time, 3 times, 5 times, or any odd number of times. The standard is 3 times:*

Glorified is my Lord, the Most Exalted.	Subḥāna Rabbiyal-A'lā.

**One may optionally add:*

Glorified are You, O Allāh, our Lord, and praised are You. O Allāh, forgive me.	Subḥānakallāhumma Rabbanā wa biḥamdika. Allāhummaghfirlī.

**One may then make du'ā' while prostrating if one wishes to.*

**Then say while going into jalsah/julūs (sitting):*

Allāh is Greater.	Allāhu Akbar.

Jalsah/Julūs (Sitting)

Position

Sit on your knees with your feet behind you. If you can, sit on your left foot, as demonstrated, with the right foot upright and its toes pointing forward. If this is too painful, then place your feet however you can, but you should be on your knees. The hands should be palms-down on the knees.

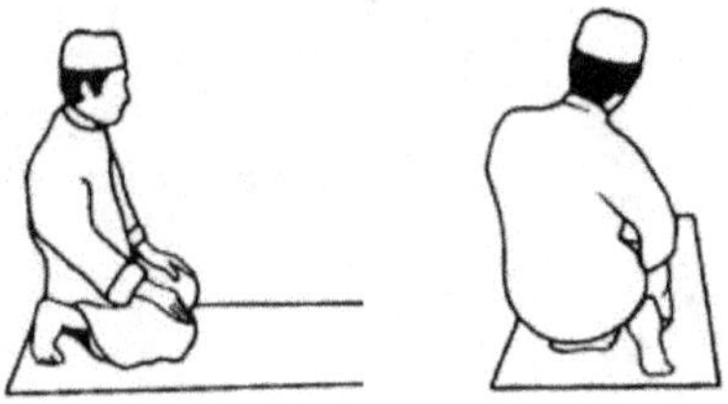

Words

My Lord, forgive me, and have mercy on me,	Rabbighfirlī, warḥamnī,

**One may optionally add:*

and strengthen me, and guide me, and raise my status, and pardon me, and provide for me.	wajbur'nī, wahdinī, warfa'nī, wa'āfinī, warzuqnī.

**Then say while going into the 2nd sajdah/sujūd (prostration):*

Allāh is Greater.	Allāhu Akbar.

2nd Sajdah/Sujūd (2nd Prostrating)

Position

This is the same position as the first prostration.

Words

**Recite this 1 time, 3 times, 5 times, or any odd number of times. The standard is 3 times:*

Glorified is my Lord, the Most Exalted.	Subḥāna Rabbiyal-A‘lā.

**One may optionally add:*

Glorified are You, O Allāh, our Lord, and praised are You. O Allāh, forgive me.	Subḥānakallāhumma Rabbanā wa biḥamdika. Allāhummaghfirlī.

**One may then make du‘ā’ while prostrating if one wishes to.*

**Then say while going into the next position:*

Allāh is Greater.	Allāhu Akbar.

**Then one gets up for the second rak‘ah and again does qiyām, rukū‘, 2nd qiyām, sujūd, julūs, and 2nd sujūd. At the end of the second rak‘ah (and at the end of the fourth rak‘ah and the third rak‘ah in Maghrib), after the 2nd sujūd, one goes into a 2nd julūs (2nd sitting).*

2nd Jalsah/Julūs (2nd Sitting)

Position

This is the same as the first sitting, except that one lightly taps the right index finger with one's gaze on the finger. The Prophet (saws) would also touch his right thumb to his right middle finger, making a circle, while tapping his right index finger.

Words

**This is known as the Tashahhud:*

All greeting, prayers, and good things belong to Allāh.	At-taḥiyyātu lillāhi waṣ-ṣalawātu waṭ-ṭayyibātu.
Peace be upon the Prophet, and (upon him be) the mercy of Allāh and His blessings.	As-Salāmu 'alan-nabiyyi wa raḥmatullāhi wa barakātuhū.
Peace be upon us and upon the righteous slaves of Allāh.	As-Salāmu 'alaynā wa 'alā 'ibādillāhiṣ-ṣāliḥīn.
I testify that there is no god except for Allāh.	Ash'hadu anlā ilāha illallāh.
And I testify that Muḥammad is His slave and His messenger.	Wa ash'hadu anna Muḥammadan 'abduhū wa rasūluhū.

2nd Jalsah/Julūs (2nd Sitting) – Continued

**Then one may recite Ṣalātul-Ibrāhīmiyyah (the Abrahamic Prayer), also known as Durūd Ibrāhīm. It is usually said at the end of the last rak'ah before one ends the prayer:*

O Allāh, send commendations on Muḥammad and on the family of Muḥammad, like how You sent commendations on Abraham and on the family of Abraham. Surely You are Praised, Glorious.	Allāhumma, ṣalli 'alā Muḥammadin wa 'alā āli Muḥammad, kamā ṣallayta 'alā Ibrāhīm wa 'alā āli Ibrāhīm. Innaka ḥamīdum-majīd.
O Allāh, send blessings on Muḥammad and on the family of Muḥammad, like how You sent blessings on Abraham and on the family of Abraham. Surely You are Praised, Glorious.	Allāhumma, bārik 'alā Muḥammadin wa 'alā āli Muḥammad, kamā bārakta 'alā Ibrāhīm wa 'alā āli Ibrāhīm. Innaka ḥamīdum-majīd.

**One may then say the following if one wishes to:*

O Allāh, indeed I seek refuge in You from the punishment of Hell and from the punishment of the grave and from the trial of life and death and from the evil of the trial of the Antichrist.	Allāhumma innī a'ūdhu bika min 'adhābi Jahannama wa min 'adhābil-qabri wa min fitnatil-maḥyā wal-mamāti wa min sharri fitnatil-Masīḥid-Dajjāl.

**One may then say any du'ā if one wishes to.*

**Then one ends the prayer by doing the* taslīm *twice. Turn to the right shoulder and say:*

Peace and mercy of Allāh be upon you.	As-Salāmu 'alaykum wa raḥmatullāh.

2nd Jalsah/Julūs (2nd Sitting) – Continued

**Then turn to the left shoulder and say:*

Peace and mercy of Allāh be upon you.	As-Salāmu 'alaykum wa raḥmatullāh.

This concludes aṣ-ṣalāh (the prayer).

[Note: When one says the taslīm towards each shoulder, one is greeting the angel on each shoulder, as well as any Muslims to their right and left.]

Forgetting Something in Ṣalāh

If someone makes a mistake in the prayer out of forgetfulness, then they must do *sujūd as-sahw*, the prostration of forgetfulness at the end of the prayer. This only takes place *after* the last tashahhud, and it consists of prostrating (doing sujūd/sajdah), sitting back up, then prostrating one more time, then sitting back up. During this, one says what one would normally say in those positions:

Subḥāna Rabbiyal-A'lā (Glorified is my Lord, the Most Exalted), during sujūd.

Rabbighfirlī, warḥamnī (My Lord, forgive me and have mercy on me), during julūs (sitting).

If someone accidentally added something extra in the prayer, then it is recommended to do sujūd as-sahw after the taslīm. If someone accidentally omitted something in the prayer, then it is recommended to do sujūd as-sahw before the taslīm.

For example, if it is 'Ishā' and one accidentally prayed 5 rak'ahs instead of 4, then, at the end of the 2nd julūs (sitting), one would give the taslīm. Then one would:

- Say "Allāhu Akbar (Allāh is Greater)"

- Prostrate on the ground and say "Subḥāna Rabbiyal-A'lā (Glorified is my Lord, the Most Exalted)"
- Say "Allāhu Akbar (Allāh is Greater)" while sitting back up
- While sitting, say, "Rabbighfirlī, warḥamnī (My Lord, forgive me and have mercy on me)"
- Say "Allāhu Akbar (Allāh is Greater)" while going back into prostration
- Prostrate on the ground and say "Subḥāna Rabbiyal-A'lā (Glorified is my Lord, the Most Exalted)"
- Say "Allāhu Akbar (Allāh is Greater)" while sitting back up
- Give the taslīms again (without doing the tashahhud again).

Or, for example, if it is 'Ishā' and one accidentally prayed 3 rak'ahs instead of 4, and they ended the prayer by giving their taslīm, then one would make up the single rak'ah, along with the second sitting and the tashahhud at the end of the rak'ah. Then *before* ending the rak'ah with the taslīm, one would:

- Say "Allāhu Akbar (Allāh is Greater)"
- Prostrate on the ground and say "Subḥāna Rabbiyal-A'lā (Glorified is my Lord, the Most Exalted)"
- Say "Allāhu Akbar (Allāh is Greater)" while sitting back up
- While sitting, say, "Rabbighfirlī, warḥamnī (My Lord, forgive me and have mercy on me)"
- Say "Allāhu Akbar (Allāh is Greater)" while going back into prostration
- Prostrate on the ground and say "Subḥāna Rabbiyal-A'lā (Glorified is my Lord, the Most Exalted)"
- Say "Allāhu Akbar (Allāh is Greater)" while sitting back up
- Give the taslīm (without doing the tashahhud again).

The Pillars and Obligatory Actions of Ṣalāh

Scholars have deduced that there are 14 pillars (arkān) of the prayer, and if one omits any of them, then the prayer is invalid and must be repeated. These pillars are:

1. Standing during obligatory prayers, if one is able to
2. Takbīratul-Iḥrām (saying "Allāhu Akbar" to begin the prayer)
3. Reciting Al-Fātiḥah during qiyām (standing)
4. Rukū' (bowing)
5. Rising from bowing
6. The second qiyām (standing)
7. Sujūd (prostrating)
8. Rising from prostrating
9. Julūs (sitting) between the two prostrations
10. Being at ease in each of these physical pillars
11. The final tashahhud
12. Sitting while reciting the final tashahhud and the taslīms
13. The two taslīms (giving the greeting of peace while facing each shoulder)
14. Doing the pillars in the correct order

If any of these is missing, then the prayer is invalid. The obligatory actions (wājibāt) of the prayer that are not pillars are:

1. Saying takbīr (Allāhu Akbar / Allāh is Greater) other than Takbīratul-Iḥrām
2. Saying Sami'allāhu liman ḥamidah" (Allāh listened to whoever praised Him.)
3. Saying "Rabbanā lakal-ḥamd" (Our Lord, for You is all praise.)

4. Saying "Subḥāna Rabbiyal-'Aẓīm" (Glorified is my Lord, the Absolute Greatest.)
5. Saying "Subḥāna Rabbiyal-A'lā" (Glorified is my Lord, the Most Exalted.)
6. Saying "Rabbighfirlī, warḥamnī" (My Lord, forgive me, and have mercy on me.)
7. Saying the first tashahhud ("All greeting, prayers," etc.…)
8. Sitting for the first tashahhud

If any of the obligatory actions of prayer are accidentally omitted, then one does not have to make them up, but one must do sujūd as-sahw at the end of their prayer.

Praying With a Sutrah

It is forbidden to walk directly in front of a praying person. Instead, one must walk around them. However, an imām leading others, or one who is praying alone, may put in front of them something called a *sutrah*. This is a barrier in front of a praying person, and it is permissible to walk in front of someone's sutrah. A sutrah does not have to be anything in particular; it can even be a stick.

Praying in Congregation Behind an Imām

The way that Muslims organize when praying in *jamā'ah* (congregation) is that the imām prays in front, and those following him form a row behind him. Those praying behind the imām stand shoulder to shoulder, with no gap in between. If the first row fills up, then a second row is formed, and so on. In order to enforce modesty in sight, touch, and thoughts, men pray in the front and women either pray in the back or in a separate area of the masjid that is designated for them.

If it is only two men praying, then they stand next to each other with the one who is the imām standing slightly ahead. If another man joins them in the middle of the prayer, then the imām walks ahead to be fully in front of the other two.

If a man and a woman are praying together, and there is no one else, then the man prays in front of the woman, even if she is his wife.

Those following the imām are silent when he recites the Qur'ān aloud. If it is a rak'ah in which the imām is reciting the Qur'ān aloud, then when he finishes Al-Fātiḥah, saying, "walaḍ-ḍāllīn," those praying behind him say out loud, "āmīn," raising their voices. It is important to note that one must wait until the imām starts to say, "āmīn," and then say it along with him.

If the imām makes a mistake while praying, then a man following him in prayer can alert him to the mistake by saying, "Subḥānallāh." A woman can alert the imām of a mistake by clapping.

When one prays behind an imām, then it is essentially the imām's prayer, although the one following him in prayer is rewarded for what the imām does. For example, if one praying behind an imām forgets to say something in a certain position, then they need not worry about it because they are following the imām. But if the imām forgets something, then he must lead the whole jamā'ah (congregation) in sujūd as-sahw at the end of the prayer.

Note also that one should *follow* the imām in his movements in the prayer, not precede him or move with him.

Joining a Prayer Once It Has Started

If someone is late to a prayer in jamā'ah (congregation), then one joins the row, silently does Takbīratul-Iḥrām, and then joins the congregation in whatever position they are in. If one joins before or during rukū', then one does not have to make up that rak'ah, but if one joins after rukū' then one makes up that rak'ah later. When the imām ends the prayer with the two taslīms, then, if one has rak'ahs to make up, one does *not* give the taslīm. Instead, one gets up and prays the remaining rak'ahs alone.

Also note that it is generally forbidden for a Muslim man to form a row by himself. However, if a man arrives at a prayer in jamā'ah that has already started, and the first row is absolutely full, and he cannot squeeze in, and there is no one else to pray next to him, then he may start the next row by himself because this is out of necessity. The next row should be started from the center.

Ṣalāh for Travelers and the Sick

If one is traveling, then one may shorten and combine certain prayers.

Fajr is still prayed on time, and it is still two rak'ahs for the traveler.

Ẓuhr and 'Aṣr are shortened to two rak'ahs each, and they are combined, meaning they are prayed one after the other. In other words, one prays two rak'ahs for Ẓuhr and then ends it with the taslīm, and then one immediately prays two rak'ahs for 'Aṣr and then ends it with the taslīm. A traveler may perform these prayers during the time for Ẓuhr or during the time for 'Aṣr.

Maghrib is still three rak'ahs, but 'Ishā' is shortened to two rak'ahs, and they are prayed one after another. A traveler may perform these prayers during the time for Maghrib or during the time for 'Ishā'.

One does not need to worry about sunnah prayers (see the section *Optional Prayers*) when traveling, but one may still pray the two sunnah rak'ahs before Fajr and the Witr prayer after 'Ishā'.

What is counted as traveling varies among different scholars. However, Shaykh Ibn Bāz said in his Majmū'ah Al-Fatāwā, Part 12, Page 267: "*Travel, according to the dominant majority of scholars, is what takes a day and night in distance. It is estimated at eighty kilometers for whoever travels by car, plane, or ship. This distance is called travel and is known to be travel according to the 'urf (custom) of Muslims. When a person travels this distance or more by camel, car, plane, ship, or on foot, he is considered a traveler.*" Note that 80 kilometers is approximately equivalent to 48 miles.

If one is sick, then one still prays Fajr on time. However, one may combine Ẓuhr and 'Aṣr without shortening them, and they are prayed during the time for Ẓuhr or during the time for 'Aṣr. A sick person may also combine Maghrib and 'Ishā' without shortening 'Ishā', and they are prayed during the time for Maghrib or during the time for 'Ishā'.

Making Up Missed Prayers

Missing one of the five *farḍ* (essential) ṣalawāt is a sin. However, if one is in a circumstance that forces them to miss a prayer, then one must make it up. In this case, one prays the missed prayer first, and then one prays the current prayer. For example, if it is time for Maghrib and someone missed ‘Aṣr, then that person would pray ‘Aṣr first and then Maghrib.

After Ṣalāh

After each obligatory ṣalāh, it is recommended to take some time individually to recite certain portions of the Qur’ān and to do dhikr (remembrance of God). It is prescribed to say immediately after the ṣalāh:

“Astaghfirullāh. Astaghfirullāh. Astaghfirullāh. Allāhumma antas-Salāmu wa minkas-salāmu tabārakta yā Dhāl-Jalāli wal-Ikrām.”

“(I seek God’s forgiveness. I seek God’s forgiveness. I seek God’s forgiveness. O God, You are the Ultimate Peace, and from You is all peace. Blessed are You, O Possessor of Majesty and Honor.)”

It is also prescribed to recite Āyatul-Kursī (the Verse of the Seat; Qur’ān 2:255) as well as the last three sūrahs of the Qur’ān (chapters 112, 113, and 114). These will be presented later in this book, in the chapter titled *Selected Portions of the Qur’ān and Their Merits*.

It is also prescribed to say:

- Subḥānallāh (“Glory be to God”) – 33 times
- Alḥamdulillāh (“All praise is for God”) – 33 times
- Allāhu Akbar (“God is Greater”) – 33 times

Then one makes it 100 by saying the following phrase once:

“Lā ilāha illallāhu waḥdahū lā sharīka lah. Lahul-mulku wa lahul-ḥamd. Wa huwa ‘alā kulli shay’in qadīr.”

“There is no god except for Allāh, alone, without associate. His is the dominion, and His is all praise. And He has power over everything.”

There are also other things that one may say after ṣalāh, but they will not all be mentioned herein.

Optional Prayers

Optional prayers that the Prophet Muḥammad (saws) performed or approved of are called *sunnah*, and there are many sunnah prayers. However, only the five prayers that have been mentioned so far are essential (*farḍ*). During optional prayers, one says exactly the same words in each rak'ah as one does during essential prayers.

Ar-Rawātib

It is recommended to pray:

- 2 rak'ahs before Fajr
- 4 rak'ahs before Ẓuhr
- 2 rak'ahs after Ẓuhr
- 2 rak'ahs after Maghrib
- 2 rak'ahs after 'Ishā'

These 12 extra rak'ahs in a day are called *rawātib*, and one may be rewarded with a house in Paradise for praying them regularly.

Umm Ḥabībah (ra) narrated: The Messenger of God (saws) said, "Whoever prays twelve rak'ahs in a day and night, a house will be built from him in Paradise: four rak'ahs before Ẓuhr, two rak'ahs after it, two rak'ahs after Maghrib, two rak'ahs after 'Ishā', and two rak'ahs before Fajr in the morning ṣalāt." (Jāmi' At-Tirmidhī, Ḥadīth 415; Zubayr 'Alī Za'ī graded it ṣaḥīḥ.)

'Ā'ishah (ra) narrated: The Messenger of God (saws) said, "Whoever is regular with twelve rak'ahs from the Sunnah, God will build a house for him in Paradise: four rak'ahs before Ẓuhr, two rak'ahs after it, two rak'ahs after Maghrib, two rak'ahs after 'Ishā', and two rak'ahs before Fajr." (Jāmi' At-Tirmidhī, Ḥadīth 414; Zubayr 'Alī Za'ī graded it ḥasan.)

Taḥiyyatul-Masjid

It is highly recommended to pray two rak'ahs whenever one enters a masjid.

Ḍuḥā

There is an optional prayer that may be prayed in the morning, after the sun has finished rising. This is prayer is called Ḍuḥā, and if it is performed early after sunrise, it is also called Ishrāq. The time for Ḍuḥā is from when the sun has risen to a certain height (the height of a spear), and its cutoff time is shortly before Ẓuhr. In terms of a clock, this equates to roughly 15 minutes after Shurūq (sunrise) until about 10 minutes before Ẓuhr. Ḍuḥā is two rak'ahs minimum, and there is no maximum number of rak'ahs set for it.

Tahajjud

One may pray additional rak'ahs at night, praying two rak'ahs, then two rak'ahs, etc., and this prayer takes place after praying 'Ishā' and before Fajr comes in. The name of this prayer is Tahajjud. It may also be called Qiyām Al-Layl (Standing at Night), but this term is general and can be applied to other actions besides ṣalāh, such as dhikr and reciting the Qur'ān.

The minimum number of rak'ahs for Tahajjud is two, and there is no maximum number. However, it was the Sunnah of the Prophet (saws) to pray eight rak'ahs, and then to follow those with three rak'ahs of Witr (see the section *Witr*). Thus, the Prophet (saws) would often pray 11 rak'ahs at night.

Tahajjud may be offered at any time between 'Ishā' and Fajr, according to the majority of scholars, with or without having slept beforehand, but a minority of scholars are of the opinion that Tahajjud should only be offered after sleeping for part of the night. Regardless, the best time for offering Tahajjud is the last third of the night, and that is also an excellent time for making du'ā'. The following ḥadīths state:

Abū Hurayrah (ra) narrated: The Messenger of God (saws) said, "Our Lord, Blessed and Exalted, descends to the lowest heaven in the last third of every night, saying, 'Who is calling upon Me that I may answer him? Who is asking from Me that I may give him? Who is seeking My forgiveness that I may forgive him?'" (Ṣaḥīḥ Al-Bukhārī, Ḥadīth 1145; Ṣaḥīḥ Muslim, Ḥadīth 758)

Abū Hurayrah (ra) narrated: The Messenger of God (saws) said, "The best prayer after what is obligatory is prayer during the night." (Ṣaḥīḥ Muslim, Ḥadīth 1163)

Abdullāh ibn 'Amr (ra) narrated: The Messenger of God (saws) said, "Verily, the most beloved fasting to God is the fasting of David, and the most beloved prayer to God is the prayer of David (as). He would sleep half of the night, stand in prayer for a third of it, and then sleep for a sixth of it. He would fast every other day." (Ṣaḥīḥ Al-Bukhārī, Ḥadīth 3420; Ṣaḥīḥ Muslim, Ḥadīth 1159)

Abdullāh ibn 'Amr ibn Al-'Āṣ (ra) narrated: The Messenger of God (saws) said, "Whoever prays Qiyām reciting ten verses will not be recorded as one of the negligent. Whoever prays Qiyām reciting one hundred verses will be recorded as one of the devout. Whoever prays Qiyām reciting one thousand verses will be recorded as one of those who receive huge rewards." (Sunan Abū Dāwūd, Ḥadīth 1398; Al-Albānī graded it ṣaḥīḥ.)

Witr

There is an optional prayer called Witr that one may perform any time after 'Ishā', and the cutoff for its time is Fajr. At its core, Witr is one rak'ah, but one should pray at least two rak'ahs before it. There are different ways to combine the two rak'ahs to the one rak'ah.

One way to pray Witr consists of praying two rak'ahs as one normally would. Then one gives the taslīm. Then the person prays one rak'ah and goes into the 2nd sitting at the end of the one rak'ah and then gives the taslīm.

Another way to pray Witr consists of praying two rak'ahs, but one does *not* go into the 2nd sitting position at the end of them. Rather, one gets up directly after the second prostration (sujūd/sajdah) of the second rak'ah, and then one prays a third rak'ah. At the end of the third rak'ah, after the second prostration, the person goes into the 2nd sitting position, and then gives the taslīm.

It is from the Sunnah of the Prophet (saws) to recite Sūratul-A'lā (chapter 87) in the first rak'ah, after reciting Al-Fātiḥah; Sūratul-Kāfirūn (chapter 109) in the second rak'ah, after reciting Al-Fātiḥah; and Sūratul-Ikhlāṣ (chapter 112) in the third rak'ah, after reciting Al-Fātiḥah. However, this is not obligatory, and one may recite whatever they wish after Al-Fātiḥah.

It is recommended by the Sunnah to make Witr the last prayer of the night. However, there is nothing wrong with praying extra prayers after Witr, but there should not be two Witrs in one night.

ʻĪd (Eid)

On the days of ʻĪd Al-Fiṭr and ʻĪd Al-Aḍḥā, a congregational prayer consisting of two rakʻahs is performed, followed by the imām giving a khuṭbah (sermon). ʻEid is *sunnah mu'akkadah*, meaning that the Prophet (saws) always did it, even though it's technically not obligatory.

Ṣalātul-Kusūf (The Eclipse Prayer)

When there is a solar eclipse or a lunar eclipse, a special prayer is offered called *Ṣalātul-Kusūf* (the Eclipse Prayer). It is prayed as follows:

- One starts their ṣalāh as they regularly would, but the recitation of the Qur'ān after Al-Fātiḥah should be long.
- Then one goes into rukūʻ for a long time.
- Then one rises from rukūʻ as they normally would, and says what they normally would, and one places the left hand on the chest above the navel, and the right hand over the left wrist, like in the 1st standing.
- Then, while standing, one recites Al-Fātiḥah again, followed by another lengthy recitation but not as long as the first.
- Then one goes into rukūʻ again for a long time.
- Then one rises again from rukūʻ, saying what one normally would.
- Then one stands for a long time.
- Then one goes into sujūd/sajdah for a long time.

- Then one sits, making it lengthy.
- Then one goes back into sujūd/sajdah for a long time.
- Then one gets up and prays the second rak'ah as they did the first, making each position lengthy but not as lengthy as in the first rak'ah.
- Then one ends the second rak'ah by going into the 2nd sitting position, saying the tashahhud and what one normally would.
- Then one gives the taslīm toward each shoulder, ending the prayer.

Thus, Ṣalātul-Kusūf is similar to regular ṣalāh, but each position is held for a long time, and there are two rukū's (bowings) and three qiyāms (standings) in each rak'ah.

Ṣalātul-Janāzah (The Funeral Prayer)

The funeral prayer is offered in congregation for a deceased Muslim or for a group of deceased Muslims. It is different from regular ṣalāh in that one stands for the entire prayer; there is no bowing or prostrating. The funeral prayer is performed as follows:

1. Raise the hands to the shoulders, with the palms facing forward, and say, "Allāhu Akbar (God is Greater)." Then place the left hand on the chest above the navel, and the right hand over the left wrist, just like in regular ṣalāh. Then say, "A'ūdhu billāhi minash-Shayṭānir-rajīm. Bismillāhir-Raḥmānir-Raḥīm. (I seek refuge in God from Satan the accursed. In the Name of God—the Most Compassionate, Most Merciful.)" Then recite Al-Fātiḥah.
2. Then raise the hands to the shoulders, with the palms facing forward, and say, "Allāhu Akbar (God is Greater)." Then place the left hand on the chest above the navel, and the right hand over the left wrist, just like in regular ṣalāh. Then say the Ṣalātul-Ibrāhīmiyyah (the Abrahamic Prayer), also known as Durūd Ibrāhīm, just as one says it at the end of regular ṣalāh.

3. Then raise the hands to the shoulders, with the palms facing forward, and say, “Allāhu Akbar (God is Greater).”).” Then place the left hand on the chest above the navel, and the right hand over the left wrist, just like in regular ṣalāh.

   Then say the following du‘ā’s:

   Allāhummaghfir lahū, warḥamhū, wa ‘āfihī, wa‘fu ‘anhū, wa akrim nuzulahū, wa wassi‘ mudkhalahū, waghsilhu bil-mā’i wath-thalji wal-barad. Wa naqqihī minal-khaṭāyā kamā naqqaytath-thawbal-abyaḍa minad-danas. Wa abdilhū dāran khayran min dārihī, wa ahlān khayran min ahlihī, wa zawjan khayran min zawjihī. Wa adkhilhul-Jannah. Wa a‘idhhū min ‘adhābil-qabri wa ‘adhābin-Nāri.

   Allāhummaghfir liḥayyinā wa mayyitinā, wa shāhidinā wa ghā’ibinā, wa ṣaghīrinā wa kabīrinā, wa dhakarinā wa unthānā. Allāhumma man aḥyaytahū minnā fa’aḥyihī ‘alāl-Islām, waman tawaffaytahū minnā fatawaffahū ‘alāl-Īmān. Allāhumma lā taḥrimnā ajrahū, walā tuḍillanā ba‘dahū.

   (O God, forgive him, and have mercy on him, and give him strength, and pardon him. Be generous to him, and cause his entrance to be wide, and wash him with water and snow and hail. Cleanse him of his transgressions as white cloth is cleansed of stains. Give him an abode better than his home, and a family better than his family, and a wife better than his wife. Take him into Paradise, and protect him from the punishment of the grave and from the punishment of the Fire.)

   (O God, forgive our living and our dead, those who are with us and those who are absent, our young and our old, our males and our females. O God, whomever you give life from among us, give him life in Islām, and whomever you take away from us, take him away in Faith. O God, do not forbid us their reward and do not send us astray after them.)

4. Then raise the hands to the shoulders, with the palms facing forward, and say, “Allāhu Akbar (God is Greater).”).” Then place the left hand on the chest above the navel, and the right hand over the left wrist, just like in regular ṣalāh.

   Then give the taslīm toward each shoulder.

This concludes the funeral prayer. Note that when one prays for the deceased, one uses the appropriate pronouns referring to them. What has been quoted above is regarding a deceased male, but for a deceased female one would simply say "she" or "her" instead of "he" or "his." And for a group, one would say "them" or "their."

When the body of the deceased is present, this prayer is known as Ṣalātul-Janāzah, but when the body is absent, this prayer is known as *Ṣalātul-Ghā'ib.*

Times in which Extra Prayers are Forbidden

There are three times of the day during which it is forbidden to pray extra prayers. These are:

1. After one prays Fajr and until the sun has risen to the height of a spear (which is about 15 minutes after Shurūq [sunrise])

2. When the sun is directly overhead at noon until it has passed its zenith (which is within about 10 minutes before Ẓuhr)

3. After one prays 'Aṣr and until Maghrib (sunset)

There are exceptions to this. If one missed the two sunnah rak'ahs before Fajr, one may make them up after Fajr and before Shurūq. And one may pray two rak'ahs of Taḥiyyatul-Masjid any time one enters the masjid, even if it is during one of the forbidden times. One may also pray the two rak'ahs of ṭawāf during the forbidden times (see the chapter *Ḥajj and 'Umrah*). And Ṣalātul-Kusūf may be prayed whenever an eclipse takes place.

Chapter 7
Al-Jumu'ah

An Introduction to Jumu'ah

As stated earlier, Al-Jumu'ah is Friday, and it is the most sacred day of the week in Islām. On Fridays, Ẓuhr is replaced with the two rak'ah Jumu'ah prayer in congregation. The Arabic word for congregation is jamā'ah – not to be confused with Jumu'ah, although the two words are related. The Jumu'ah sermon and prayer are obligatory for men but optional for women, although it is good for women to maintain a connection to the masjid, and if women do not go for Jumu'ah then they must pray Ẓuhr. It is permissible for men to miss Jumu'ah if they are sick, travelling, or under strenuous circumstances. If one cannot make Jumu'ah, then they should pray a normal Ẓuhr prayer.

It should also be noted that Jumu'ah is not a Sabbath, meaning that Muslims do not rest for the entire day of Jumu'ah. Muslims are permitted to work before and after the Jumu'ah service.

[9]Believers! When the call to prayer is made on Friday, hasten to the remembrance of God, and leave all worldly commerce. This is for your own good, if you but knew it. [10]When the prayer is ended, disperse in the land and seek to obtain [something] of God's bounty. And remember God much, so that you may prosper. (Qur'ān 62:9-10)

Abū Hurayrah (ra) narrated: The Prophet (saws) said, "The best day on which the sun has risen is Friday. On this day, Adam was created, entered the Garden, and was expelled from it, and the (Last) Hour will occur only on Friday." (Ṣaḥīḥ Muslim, Ḥadīth 854)

Aws ibn Aws Ath-Thaqafī (ra) narrated: I heard the Prophet (saws) say, "Whoever takes a bath on Friday, and bathes completely, and goes early, arriving early, and walks and does not ride (to the mosque), and sits close to the imām and listens to him, and does not engage in idle talk; for every step he takes he will have the reward of one year, the reward of a year's fasting and standing in prayer." (Sunan Ibn Mājah, Ḥadīth 1087; Zubayr 'Alī Za'ī graded it ṣaḥīḥ. Its meaning is also in Sunan Abū Dāwūd, Ḥadīth 345, and Al-Albānī graded it ṣaḥīḥ.)

Abū Al-Ja'd Aḍ-Ḍamrī (ra) narrated: The Messenger of God (saws) said, "Whoever missed three Jumu'ahs out of negligence, God will place a seal over his heart." (Sunan Abū Dāwūd, Ḥadīth 1052; Al-Albānī graded it ḥasan ṣaḥīḥ.)

The Merit of Reading Sūrah Al-Kahf on Jumu'ah

It is recommended to recite the 18th sūrah of the Qur'ān, called Al-Kahf (The Cave), on Fridays based on the following ḥadīths. Note that these ḥadīths are not in Al-Kutub As-Sittah, but they have been authenticated by scholars including Ibn Ḥajar Al-'Asqalānī and Nāṣiruddīn Al-Albānī:

Abū Sa'īd Al-Khudrī (ra) narrated: Whoever reads Sūrah Al-Kahf on the night of Jumu'ah will have a light that will stretch between him and the Ancient House (i.e., the Ka'bah). (Sunan Ad-Dārimī, Ḥadīth 3312; Al-Albānī graded it ṣaḥīḥ.)

Abū Sa'īd Al-Khudrī (ra) narrated: The Prophet (saws) said: "Whoever reads Sūrah Al-Kahf on the day of Jumu'ah will have a light that will shine from him from one Friday to the next." (The ḥadīth scholar Al-Bayhaqī recorded this ḥadīth. Ibn Ḥajar graded it ḥasan, and Al-Albānī graded it ṣaḥīḥ.)

Attending a Masjid for Jumu'ah

Many *masājid*, which is the Arabic plural for masjid, welcome non-Muslim visitors, but one should keep in mind the dress codes. It is better for men to not wear shorts in the masjid, and women are encouraged to wear a ḥijāb as well as clothing that covers their whole body and is not tight-fitting. Also, one should not wear any garment with pictures of living things with faces on it.

When one approaches a masjid, there will typically be an entrance for men and an entrance for women, as well as a place near the entrance at which one removes their shoes. Shoes are not worn in the sanctuary, which is called the *muṣallā*, and this is done in order to keep the muṣallā pure.

One should also not walk in front of, or talk to, a person who is engaged in ṣalāh. Instead, one should walk around those who are in ṣalāh.

Remember to be in wuḍū' before ṣalāh. If one is not in wuḍū', then one may find an area for wuḍū' in or near the bathroom of the masjid. If there is no area specifically for wuḍū', then using the sink is appropriate.

When one enters the muṣallā, then one should pray two rak'ahs. This is a formality that is performed to honor God, as one is in His house of worship. One should pray two rak'ahs even if one is late to Jumu'ah and the imām is giving the sermon (Arabic: *khuṭbah*). This information is learned from the following ḥadīths:

Abū Qatādah As-Salamī (ra) narrated: The Messenger of God (saws) said, "If anyone of you enters a mosque, he should pray two rak'ahs before sitting." (Ṣaḥīḥ Al-Bukhārī, Ḥadīth 444)

Jābir ibn 'Abdullāh (ra) narrated: A person entered the mosque while the Prophet (saws) was delivering the sermon on a Friday. The Prophet (saws) said to him, "Have you prayed?" The man replied in the negative. The Prophet (saws) said, "Get up and pray two rak'ahs." (Ṣaḥīḥ Al-Bukhārī, Ḥadīth 930)

After praying two rak'ahs, one sits down on the floor of the muṣallā facing the qiblah. Elderly people, people with disabilities, or anyone who is not able to sit on the floor may sit in a chair.

The Khuṭbah

The person who gives the khuṭbah is called the *khaṭīb*, and this is typically the imām, although occasionally a guest might be the khaṭīb.

When the imām enters the muṣallā and reaches the pulpit (Arabic: *minbar*), he greets the congregation by saying "As-Salāmu 'Alaykum (wa raḥmatullāhi wa barakātuhū)." The congregation then responds by saying, "Wa 'Alaykum As-Salāmu (wa raḥmatullāhi wa barakātuhū)."

From this point onward, talking and other distractions are strictly prohibited for the congregants. Even greeting another person is not allowed during the khuṭbah. If one talks, that person will lose out on the reward from listening to the khuṭbah, which is an act of worship.

Then the imām sits down and the muezzin gives the adhān. Then the imām stands up and starts to give the khuṭbah.

Although the khuṭbah is given in the native language of the congregation being addressed, the beginning of the khuṭbah is typically said in Arabic, and the imām may or may not translate it for the congregation. This Arabic opening is called *khuṭbah al-ḥājah*, which means "the sermon of necessity." While it is not required for every Muslim to memorize khuṭbah al-ḥājah, a transliteration and a translation will herein be provided so that those who are curious may know what is being said. There are also various additions to khuṭbah al-ḥājah that different imāms may make. The version presented here is from Imām Nāṣiruddīn Al-Albānī, in accordance with the authentic Sunnah.

Arabic Transliteration of Khuṭbah Al-Ḥājah

Innal-ḥamdu lillāhi. Naḥmaduhū wa nasta'īnuhū wa nastaghfiruhū, wa na'ūdhu billāhi min shurūri anfusinā wa min sayyi'āti a'mālinā. Man yahdillāhu falā muḍilla lahū, wa man yuḍlil falā hādiya lahū. Wa ash'hadu anlā ilāha illallāhu waḥdahū lā sharīka lahū. Wa ash'hadu anna Muḥammadan 'abduhū wa rasūluhū.

[102]Yā ayyuhalladhīna āmanūt-taqullāha ḥaqqa tuqātihī walā tamūtunna illā wa antum muslimūn. (Qur'ān 3:102)

[1]Yā ayyuhan-nāsut-taqū Rabbakumulladhī khalaqakum min nafsin wāḥidatin wa khalaqa minhā zawjahā wa bath-tha minhumā rijālan kathīran wa nisā'a. Wat-taqullāhalladhī tasā'alūna bihī wal-arḥām. Innallāha kāna 'alaykum raqībā. (Qur'ān 4:1)

[70]Yā ayyuhalladhīna āmanūt-taqullāha wa qūlū qawlan sadīdā. [71]Yuṣliḥ lakum a'mālakum wa yaghfir lakum dhunūbakum. Wa man yuṭi'illāha wa rasūlahū faqad fāza fawzan 'aẓīmā. (Qur'ān 33:70-71)

English Translation of Khuṭbah Al-Ḥājah

Indeed, all praise is for God. We praise Him, and we ask Him for help, and we seek His forgiveness, and we seek refuge in Him from the evils of ourselves and from the bad of our actions. Whomsoever God guides no one can lead him astray, and whomsoever He lets go astray no one can guide him. And I testify that there is no god except for Allāh, alone without associate, and I testify that Muḥammad is His slave and His messenger.

[102]Believers, fear God as is His due, and when death comes, be in a state of complete submission to Him. (Qur'ān 3:102)

[1]O humanity! Fear your Lord, who created you from a single soul. He created its mate from it and from the two of them spread countless men and women [throughout the earth]. Fear God, in Whose name you appeal to one another, and be mindful of your obligations in respect of ties of kinship. God is always watching over you. (Qur'ān 4:1)

[70]Believers, fear God, and say what is right. [71]He will bless your works for you and forgive you your sins. Whoever obeys God and His Messenger has indeed achieved a great success. (Qur'ān 33:70-71)

Then the imām will proceed with whatever his topic is in the native language of the congregation, and he will quote from the Qur'ān and the ḥadīths to support his point. After the first khuṭbah, the imām may say something along the lines of, "Aqūlu qawlī hādhā, wa astaghfirullāha lī wa lakum. Fastaghfirūhu. Innahū huwal-Ghafūr-ur-Raḥīm," which means, "I say this saying of mine, and I seek God's forgiveness for me and for you. So seek His forgiveness. Indeed, He is the Most Forgiving, the Most Merciful." However, it is not mandatory for the imām to say this. Then the imām will sit down and individuals in the congregation may make a short, silent du'ā. While nothing in particular has been prescribed to say during this short time, one may perhaps ask for God's forgiveness, among other things. Then the imām will stand up and give the second khuṭbah, which is a continuation of the first, although it is shorter than the first. Towards the end of the khuṭbah, the imām typically makes du'ā in Arabic, and the congregation may say "āmīn" during the brief pauses of the du'ā. The imām will conclude by saying "wa aqīmūṣ-ṣalāh," or a variant thereof, which means, "and establish the prayer."

After the Khuṭbah

Thereafter, the congregation will stand and line up for ṣalāh. Everyone should stand shoulder to shoulder in a straight line with no gaps in the line. The iqāmah is then given, and the imām leads the congregation in two rak'ahs of ṣalāh.

After the prayer, one may pray two or four extra rak'ahs, which are sunnah. According to a narration in Sunan Abū Dāwūd Ḥadīth 1130, which Al-Albānī graded ṣaḥīḥ, the Prophet (saws) prayed four rak'ahs if he prayed in the mosque and two rak'ahs if he prayed at home (after Jumu'ah). They are not obligatory, although it is recommended to pray them because the Prophet (saws) prayed extra rak'ahs.

This concludes the Jumu'ah service.

Chapter 8
The Importance of Ṣalāh (Prayer)

Prayer wipes out sins

114 Say your prayers at both ends of the day and during parts of the night. Surely good deeds wipe out evil deeds. This is a reminder for people who pay heed. (Qur'ān 11:114)

45 Recite what has been revealed to you of the Book, and pray regularly. Surely prayer restrains one from indecency and evil. And remembrance of God is greater. God has knowledge of all your actions. (Qur'ān 29:45)

Abū Hurayrah (ra) narrated: I heard the Messenger of God (saws) saying, "If there was a river at the door of anyone of you and he took a bath in it five times a day would you notice any dirt on him?" They said, "Not a trace of dirt would be left." The Prophet (saws) added, "That is the example of the five prayers with which God blots out evil deeds." (Ṣaḥīḥ Al-Bukhārī, Ḥadīth 506)

Abū Hurayrah (ra) narrated: the Messenger of God (saws) said, "The five daily prayers and the time between one Friday prayer and the next serve as an expiation for sins committed in between, provided that major sins are not committed." (Ṣaḥīḥ Muslim, Ḥadīth 233)

'Ubādah ibn Aṣ-Ṣāmit (ra) narrated: I bear witness that I heard the Messenger of God (saws) saying, "God, the Exalted, has made five prayers obligatory. If anyone performs ablution for them well, offers them at their time, and completely observes their bowing and concentration, it is the guarantee of God that He will forgive him. If anyone does not do so, there is no guarantee for him on the part of God; He may pardon him if He wills and punish him if He wills." (Sunan Abū Dāwūd, Ḥadīth 425; Al-Albānī graded it ṣaḥīḥ.)

Prayer is the best deed

Abū Hurayrah (ra) narrated: the Prophet (saws) said, "The prayer is the best thing prescribed, so whoever can do a great deal of it, let him do that." (Aṭ-Ṭabarānī; Al-Albānī graded it ḥasan in Ṣaḥīḥ Al-Jāmi' 3870)

Ibn Mas'ūd (ra) narrated: A man asked the Prophet (saws), "What deeds are the best?" The Prophet (saws) said: "To perform the prayers at their stated fixed times, to be good and dutiful to one's own parents, and to struggle in God's cause." (Ṣaḥīḥ Al-Bukhārī, Ḥadīth 7534)

Prayer is comfort

Anas (ra) narrated: the Messenger of God (saws) said, "In this world, women and perfume have been made dear to me, and the coolness of my eyes (i.e., my comfort) has been provided in prayer." (Sunan An-Nasā'ī, Ḥadīth 3939; Zubayr 'Alī Za'ī graded it ḥasan.)

A significance of prostration (sajdah/sujūd)

Abū Hurayrah (ra) narrated: the Messenger of God (saws) said, "A servant is closest to their Lord while in prostration, so take the opportunity to make supplications during this time." (Ṣaḥīḥ Muslim, Ḥadīth 482)

Concentration in prayer

Abū Ayyūb (ra) narrated: A man came to the Prophet (saws) and said: "O Messenger of God, teach me but make it concise." He said: "When you stand to pray, pray like a man bidding farewell. Do not say anything for which you will have to apologize. And give up hope for what other people have (i.e., do not envy)." (Sunan Ibn Mājah, Ḥadīth 4171; Al-Albānī graded it ṣaḥīḥ.)

To abandon prayer is disbelief

Jābir (ra) narrated: I heard the Prophet (saws) saying, "Indeed, the barrier between a person and polytheism and disbelief is the neglect of prayer." (Ṣaḥīḥ Muslim, Ḥadīth 82)

'Abdullāh ibn Buraydah narrated that his father (ra) said: the Messenger of God (saws) said, "The covenant that stands between us and them is the prayer. Whoever abandons it, he has committed disbelief." (Sunan An-Nasā'ī, Ḥadīth 463; Zubayr 'Alī Za'ī graded it ṣaḥīḥ.)

The first action one will be called to account for is the prayer

Abū Hurayrah (ra) narrated: the Prophet (saws) said, "The first thing about which the people will be called to account out of their actions on the Day of Judgment is the prayer. Our Lord, Sublime and Mighty, will say to the angels, though He knows better, 'Look into the prayer of My servant and see whether he has offered it perfectly or imperfectly.' If it is perfect, that will be recorded perfect. If it is defective, He will say: 'See if there are some optional prayers offered by My servant.' If there are optional prayers to his credit, He will say: 'Compensate the obligatory prayer with the optional prayer for My servant.' Then all the actions will be considered similarly." (Sunan Abū Dāwūd, Ḥadīth 864; Al-Albānī graded it ṣaḥīḥ.)

Being with the Prophet in Paradise through the prayer

Rabī'ah ibn Ka'b (ra) narrated: I was with the Messenger of God (saws) one night, and I brought him water and what he needed. He said to me, "Ask (whatever you want to)." I said, "I ask for your company in Paradise." He said, "Is there anything else?" I said, "That is all." He said, "Then help me to achieve this for you by prostrating (i.e., making sujūd) a great deal." (Ṣaḥīḥ Muslim, Ḥadīth 489)

The importance of men praying in congregation in the masjid

Abū Sa'īd Al-Khudrī (ra) narrated: the Prophet (saws) said, "The prayer in congregation is twenty five times superior to the prayer offered by a person alone." (Ṣaḥīḥ Al-Bukhārī, Ḥadīth 646)

'Abdullāh ibn 'Umar (ra) narrated: the Messenger of God (saws) said, "The prayer in congregation is twenty seven times superior to the prayer offered by a person alone." (Ṣaḥīḥ Al-Bukhārī, Ḥadīth 645; Ṣaḥīḥ Muslim, Ḥadīth 650)

Ibn 'Abbās (ra) narrated: the Prophet (saws) said, "Whoever hears the call (i.e., the adhān) and does not come, his prayer is not valid, except for those who have an excuse." (Sunan Ibn Mājah, Ḥadīth 793; Zubayr 'Alī Za'ī graded it ṣaḥīḥ.)

Abū Hurayrah (ra) narrated: the Messenger of God (saws) said, "By Him in Whose Hand my life is, I sometimes thought of giving orders for firewood to be collected, then for proclaiming the adhān for ṣalāt. Then I would appoint an imām to lead ṣalāt, and then go to the houses of those who do not come to perform ṣalāt in congregation and set fire to their houses on them." (Ṣaḥīḥ Al-Bukhārī, Ḥadīth 2420; Ṣaḥīḥ Muslim, Ḥadīth 651)

The importance of women praying at home

'Abdullah ibn Mas'ūd (ra) narrated: the Prophet (saws) said, "It is more excellent for a woman to pray in her house than in her courtyard, and more excellent for her to pray in her private room than in her house." (Sunan Abū Dāwūd, Ḥadīth 570; Al-Albānī graded it ṣaḥīḥ.)

Umm Ḥumayd (ra), the wife of Abū Ḥumayd As-Sā'idī (ra), came to the Prophet (saws) and said, "O Messenger of God, I like to pray with you." He said, "I know that you like to pray with me, but praying in your house is better for you than praying in your courtyard, and praying in your courtyard is better for you than praying in the mosque of your people, and praying in the mosque of your people is better for you than praying in my mosque." So she issued orders that a prayer-place be prepared for her in the furthest and darkest part of her house, and she used to pray there until she met God (i.e., died)." (Musnad Aḥmad, Ḥadīth 26550; Al-Albānī graded it ṣaḥīḥ.)

Ibn 'Umar (ra) narrated: the Messenger of God (saws) said, "Do not prevent your women from visiting the mosque, but their houses are better for them (for praying)." (Sunan Abū Dāwūd, Ḥadīth 567; Al-Albānī graded it ṣaḥīḥ.)

The importance of the Fajr prayer

Jundub ibn 'Abdullāh (ra) narrated: the Messenger of God (saws) said, "When anyone offers the Fajr prayer, he is in the protection of God. So let not God call him to account, withdrawing, in any respect, His protection. Because He will get ahold of him and throw him down on his face in the Hellfire." (Ṣaḥīḥ Muslim, Ḥadīth 657)

Ibn 'Umar (ra) narrated: the Messenger (saws) said: "The best prayer before God is Fajr prayer on Friday in congregation." (Shu'ab Al-Īmān by Al-Bayhaqī, Ḥadīth 2790; Al-Albānī graded it ṣaḥīḥ in Ṣaḥīḥ Al-Jāmi' 1119.)

The importance of the 'Aṣr prayer

238 Observe the ⌈five obligatory⌉ prayers—especially the middle prayer—and stand in true devotion to God. (Qur'ān 2:238)

'Abdullāh ibn Mas'ūd (ra) narrated: the Messenger of God (saws) said, "The middle prayer is the 'Aṣr prayer." (Jāmi' At-Tirmidhī, Ḥadīth 181; Zubayr 'Alī Za'ī graded it ṣaḥīḥ.)

Samurah ibn Jundab (ra) narrated: the Prophet of God (saws) said, "The middle prayer is the 'Aṣr prayer." (Jāmi' At-Tirmidhī, Ḥadīth 2983; Zubayr 'Alī Za'ī graded it ṣaḥīḥ.)

Buraydah (ra) narrated: the Prophet (saws) said, "Whoever leaves the 'Aṣr prayer, all his (good) deeds will be annulled." (Ṣaḥīḥ Al-Bukhārī, Ḥadīth 553)

Ibn 'Umar (ra) narrated: the Messenger of God (saws) said, "Whoever misses the 'Aṣr prayer (intentionally) then it is as if he lost his family and property." (Ṣaḥīḥ Al-Bukhārī, Ḥadīth 552; Ṣaḥīḥ Muslim, Ḥadīth 626)

Merits of some prayers

'Uthmān ibn 'Affān (ra) narrated: the Messenger of God (saws) said, "Whoever attends 'Ishā' in congregation, then he has (the reward as if he had) stood half of the night (in prayer). And whoever prays 'Ishā' and Fajr in congregation, then he has (the reward as if he had) spent the entire night standing (in prayer)." (Jāmi' At-Tirmidhī, Ḥadīth 221; Zubayr 'Alī Za'ī graded it ṣaḥīḥ.)

Abū Hurayrah (ra) narrated: the Messenger of God (saws) said, "If the people knew the reward for pronouncing the adhān and for standing in the first row (in congregational prayers) and found no other way to get that except by drawing lots they would draw lots. And if they knew the reward of the Ẓuhr prayer (in the early moments of its stated time) they would race for it (i.e., go early). And if they knew the reward of the 'Ishā' and Fajr prayers in congregation, they would come to offer them even if they had to crawl." (Ṣaḥīḥ Al-Bukhārī, Ḥadīth 615)

The importance of the Jumu'ah prayer

[9]Believers! When the call to prayer is made on Friday, hasten to the remembrance of God, and leave all worldly commerce. This is for your own good, if you but knew it. [10]When the prayer is ended, disperse in the land and seek to obtain [something] of God's bounty. And remember God much, so that you may prosper. (Qur'ān 62:9-10)

Abū Hurayrah (ra) narrated: The Prophet (saws) said, "The best day on which the sun has risen is Friday. On this day, Adam was created, entered the Garden, and was expelled from it, and the (Last) Hour will occur only on Friday" (Ṣaḥīḥ Muslim, Ḥadīth 854)

Aws ibn Aws Ath-Thaqafī (ra) narrated: I heard the Prophet (saws) say, "Whoever takes a bath on Friday, and bathes completely, and goes early, arriving early, and walks and does not ride (to the mosque), and sits close to the imām and listens to him, and does not engage in idle talk; for every step he takes he will have the reward of one year, the reward of a year's fasting and standing in prayer." (Sunan Ibn Mājah, Ḥadīth 1087; Zubayr 'Alī Za'ī graded it ṣaḥīḥ. Its meaning is also in Sunan Abū Dāwūd, Ḥadīth 345, and Al-Albānī graded it ṣaḥīḥ.)

'Abdullāh ibn 'Umar (ra) and Abū Hurayrah (ra) narrated that they heard the Messenger of God (saws) saying on the planks of his pulpit, "People must cease to neglect the Friday prayer or God will put a seal over their

hearts, and they will truly be among the negligent." (Ṣaḥīḥ Muslim, Ḥadīth 865)

Abū Al-Ja'd Aḍ-Ḍamrī (ra) narrated: The Messenger of God (saws) said, "Whoever missed three Jumu'ahs out of negligence, God will place a seal over his heart." (Sunan Abū Dāwūd, Ḥadīth 1052; Al-Albānī graded it ḥasan ṣaḥīḥ.)

Among the final words of the Prophet (saws)

'Alī ibn Abū Ṭālib (ra) narrated: The last words which the Messenger of God (saws) spoke were: "The prayer, the prayer. Fear God regarding those whom your right hands possess." (Sunan Abū Dāwūd, Ḥadīth 5156; Al-Albānī graded it ṣaḥīḥ.)

The reward of Ḥajj through the prayer

Abū Umāmah (ra) narrated: the Messenger of God (saws) said, "If anyone goes out from his house after performing wuḍū' for saying the prescribed prayer in congregation (in the mosque), his reward will be like that of one who goes for Ḥajj after wearing iḥrām (garments worn by the Ḥajj pilgrims). And he who goes out to say the mid-morning (Ḍuḥā) prayer, and takes the trouble for this purpose, will take the reward like that of a person who performs 'Umrah. And a prayer followed by a prayer with no worldly talk during the gap between them will be recorded in 'Illiyyūn (i.e., the record of the righteous)." (Sunan Abū Dāwūd, Ḥadīth 558; Al-Albānī graded it ḥasan).

Anas ibn Mālik (ra) narrated: the Messenger of God (saws) said, "Whoever prays Fajr in congregation, then sits remembering God until the sun has risen, then he prays two rak'ahs, then for him is the reward like that of a Ḥajj and 'Umrah." He (i.e., Anas) said: the Messenger of God (saws) said, "Complete, complete, complete." (Jāmi' At-Tirmidhī, Ḥadīth 586; Al-Albānī graded it ḥasan.)

What is the reward of Ḥajj?

'Amr ibn Al-'Āṣ (ra) narrated: When God put Islām in my heart, I came to the Prophet (saws) and said, "Hold out your right hand so that I might swear allegiance to you." So he held out his right hand, but I withdrew my hand. He said, "What is the matter, O 'Amr?" I said, "I want to stipulate a condition." He said, "What do you want to stipulate?" I said, "That I will be forgiven." He said, "Do you not know, O 'Amr, that Islām destroys whatever (sins) came before it, and that migration (i.e., hijrah) destroys whatever (sins) came before it, and that Ḥajj destroys whatever (sins) came before it?" (Ṣaḥīḥ Muslim, Ḥadīth 121)

Abū Hurayrah (ra) narrated: I heard the Prophet (saws) saying, "Whoever performs Ḥajj for the sake of God, and does not utter any obscene speech or do any evil deed, will go back (free of sin) as the day his mother bore him." (Ṣaḥīḥ Al-Bukhārī, Ḥadīth 1521; Ṣaḥīḥ Muslim, Ḥadīth 1350)

Abū Hurayrah (ra) narrated: the Messenger of God (saws) said, "An 'Umrah is an expiation for the sins committed between it and the next 'Umrah, and Ḥajj which is accepted will receive no other reward than Paradise." (Ṣaḥīḥ Al-Bukhārī, Ḥadīth 1773; Ṣaḥīḥ Muslim, Ḥadīth 1349)

'Abdullāh ibn Mas'ūd (ra) narrated: The Messenger of God (saws) said, "Alternate between Ḥajj and 'Umrah, for those two remove poverty and sins just as the bellows removes filth from iron, gold, and silver. And there is no reward for an accepted Ḥajj except for Paradise." (Jāmi' At-Tirmidhī, Ḥadīth 810; Al-Albānī graded it ṣaḥīḥ.)

Chapter 9

Az-Zakāh (The Obligatory Charity)

Zakāh is the obligatory charity that Muslims are required to give from their wealth. It is a pillar of Islām, and the Qur'ān mentions it along with ṣalāh many times. Zakāh has been translated by various people as "alms." As with the Arabic word ṣalāh, zakāh has an equivalent of the letter "t" at the end, but sometimes the "t" is silent, so it can be pronounced as "zakāh" or "zakāt."

Giving zakāh purifies one's wealth and allows for those who are poor to receive help and refrain from begging. The Qur'ān states:

103 Take alms out of their wealth to cleanse them and purify them, and pray for them; your prayer will be a comfort to them. God is All-Hearing, All-Knowing. (Qur'ān 9:103)

Zakāh is to be paid on four categories of wealth: monetary savings (including gold and silver), merchandise to be sold, harvested produce, and livestock. Zakāh is not payable on everyday items that one uses, such as their house or their car.

The Niṣāb

The *niṣāb* is the minimum amount of wealth that one must have in order to pay zakāh. If one's wealth does not reach the niṣāb after one Hijrī lunar year, then there is no zakāh due on that person.

The niṣāb for money, gold, and silver is equal to 85 grams of gold or 595 grams of silver. If one's wealth after one Hijrī lunar year is equivalent to this amount, then one must give away 2.5% of it in zakāh.

The niṣāb for merchandise to be sold is equal to 85 grams of gold or 595 grams of silver. If, after one Hijrī lunar year, the *current* value of one's merchandise is equal to this amount, then one must pay 2.5% of its value in zakāh. Note that merchandise can include retail products, real estate, animals, food, drinks, vehicles, and more.

The niṣāb for grains and produce is equal to 618 kilograms. The grains and produce must have reached their peak condition, been shelled, and cleaned of any dirt. If, after one Hijrī lunar year, one's stored grains and produce are equal to this amount, then one must pay 10% of it in zakāh if it was irrigated by rainfall or other natural means. If it was irrigated by a method that required labor and/or capital, then one must pay 5% of it in zakāh. Note that zakāh is due only on grains and produce that can be stored for one lunar year, such as dates, raisins, and nuts. Zakāh is *not* due on produce that cannot be stored for a long time, such as tomatoes, figs, melons, cucumbers, and many other fruits and vegetables.

Livestock in this context refers to sheep, goats, cows, and camels. The livestock must be free grazing and be of average quality. Low quality livestock, such as an old or sickly animal, should not be paid as zakāh. Similarly, very high quality livestock, such as a pregnant animal, should not be paid as zakāh either. The niṣāb for sheep and goats is 40 sheep and/or goats. The niṣāb for cows is 30 cows. The niṣāb for camels is 5 camels.

Sheep and Goats

- If one has 40 to 120 sheep and goats, 1 sheep is due in zakāh.
- If one has 121 to 200 sheep and goats, 2 sheep are due in zakāh.
- If one has 201 to 300 sheep and goats, 3 sheep are due in zakāh.

For every 100 extra sheep and goats, 1 extra sheep is due in zakāh.

Cows

- If one has 30 to 39 cows, 1 one-year-old cow is due in zakāh.
- If one has 40 to 59 cows, 1 two-year-old cow is due in zakāh.
- If one has 60 to 89 cows, 2 one-year-old cows are due in zakāh.

After that, for every 30 extra cows, 1 extra one-year-old cow is due. And for every 40 extra cows, 1 extra two-year-old cow is due.

Camels

- If one has 5 to 9 camels, 1 female sheep is due.
- If one has 10 to 14 camels, 2 female sheep are due.
- If one has 15 to 19 camels, 3 female sheep are due.
- If one has 20 to 24 camels, 4 female sheep are due.
- If one has 25 to 35 camels, 1 one-year-old female camel is due.
- If one has 36 to 45 camels, 1 two-year-old female camel is due.
- If one has 46 to 60 camels, 1 three-year-old female camel is due.
- If one has 61 to 75 camels, 1 four-year-old female camel is due.
- If one has 76 to 90 camels, 2 two-year-old female camels are due.
- If one has 91 to 120 camels, 2 three-year-old female camels are due.
- If one has 121 to 160 camels, 3 two-year-old female camels are due.

After that, for every extra 40 camels, 1 extra two-year-old camel is due. And for every extra 50 camels, 1 extra three-year-old camel is due.

Recipients of Zakāh

There are 8 categories of people that are eligible to receive zakāh. These are listed in the Qur'ān:

60 Alms are only for: the poor, the needy, those employed to administer alms, conciliating people's hearts, freeing slaves, those in debt, spending for God's cause, and for travelers in need. It is a legal obligation enjoined by God. God is All-Knowing and Wise. (Qur'ān 9:60)

What is the difference between the poor and the needy in this context? A poor person (*faqīr*; Arabic plural: *fuqarā'*) is one who is destitute or possesses at most half of their minimum needs. A needy person (*miskīn*; Arabic plural: *masākīn*) is one who has financial difficulty but is better off than the faqīr.

God's cause, referred to in the verse above, refers to jihād. This literally means "struggle" or "striving," and it can refer to war out of defense, justice, and security. However, there are non-combative forms of jihād too, such as seeking and spreading Islāmic knowledge.

Ony may give their zakāh directly to any of these categories, or one may give it to a trusted organization who will distribute it for them.

Zakāh may not be given to one's regular dependents (such as parents and children) or the wealthy. It may also be noted that the Prophet Muḥammad (saws) and his family were forbidden from receiving zakāh.

Chapter 10

Ṣawm (Fasting) and Ramaḍān

Ṣawm is fasting, and another word for ṣawm is *ṣiyām*. The fasting that is obligatory in Islām is during the lunar month of Ramaḍān, which is the 9th month of the Hijrī calendar. Before the first day of Ramaḍān, able-bodied Muslims make the intention to fast every day of the month from dawn (Fajr) to sunset (Maghrib). The lunar month can last either 29 or 30 days. These are the verses of the Qur'ān that mention fasting:

183 *Believers, fasting has been prescribed for you, just as it was prescribed for those before you, so that you may guard yourselves against evil.*

184 *Fast for a specified number of days, but if any one among you is ill or on a journey, let him fast the same number of days later. For those who can fast only with extreme difficulty, there is a way to compensate—the feeding of a needy person. But he who does more of his own accord shall be well rewarded. And to fast is better for you, if you only knew.*

185 *The month of Ramaḍān is the month when the Qur'ān was sent down as guidance for mankind with clear proofs of guidance and the criterion by which to distinguish right from wrong. Therefore, whoever of you is present in that month, let him fast. But he who is ill or on a journey shall fast a similar number of days later on. God desires ease for you, not hardship. He desires you to fast the whole month, so that you may glorify Him for His having guided you and so that you may be grateful to Him.*

186 *When My servants ask you about Me, say that I am near. I respond to the call of one who calls whenever he calls to Me. Let them, then, respond to Me, and believe in Me, so that they may be rightly guided.*

187 *It has been made lawful for you to be intimate with your wives on the night of the fast. They are like a garment for you, and you are like a garment for them. God is aware that you were deceiving yourselves, and He has turned in mercy towards you and pardoned you. So you may now be intimate with them and seek what God has ordained for you. Eat and drink until the white thread*

of dawn becomes distinct from the black. Then resume the fast until nightfall, and do not approach them during the nights of your devotional retreat in the mosques. These are the limits set by God, so do not approach them. Thus He makes clear His commandments to people, so that they may guard themselves [against evil].

(Qur'ān 2:183-187)

To give context and clarity to verse 187, the phrase "the night of the fast" refers to the nights of Ramaḍān. At first, Muslims during the time of the Prophet Muḥammad (saws) were not allowed to be intimate with their wives at all in Ramaḍān, even during the nights. However, a portion of them were intimate with their wives anyway; thus they were deceiving themselves. Then God revealed this verse allowing intimacy on the nights of Ramaḍān.

There are 7 things that one must refrain from when fasting because they break a person's fast:

1. Eating and drinking
2. Anything that nourishes in a similar way to eating and drinking
3. Sexual intercourse
4. Masturbation
5. Letting blood, as in through cupping or a needle
6. Vomiting intentionally
7. Menstruation and postpartum bleeding

Regarding anything that nourishes in a similar way to eating and drinking, this refers to blood transfusion, dialysis, and receiving nourishment through a needle (as in the case of having an I.V.). However, vaccinations do not break the fast.

Regarding letting blood, donating blood breaks the fast. Cupping also breaks the fast, and cupping is an old medical procedure in which a vessel such as a cup is placed on one's skin and made to stick there, usually for a few minutes. The cup is then lifted, and a small incision is made. Then the cup is put back on the site of the incision until the cup fills with blood.

Regarding masturbation, an orgasm breaks the fast. Merely touching oneself does not, but one should still repent from that. Note that wet dreams do not break one's fast because they are unintentional.

Vomiting intentionally breaks the fast, but vomiting unintentionally does not.

Those Exempt from Fasting

If one is sick or traveling during Ramaḍān, one has the option of not fasting, as long as one makes up any missed days of fasting later. What is counted as traveling varies among different scholars. However, Shaykh Ibn Bāz said in his Majmū'ah Al-Fatāwā, Part 12, Page 267: "*Travel, according to the dominant majority of scholars, is what takes a day and night in distance. It is estimated at eighty kilometers for whoever travels by car, plane, or ship. This distance is called travel and is known to be travel according to the 'urf (custom) of Muslims. When a person travels this distance or more by camel, car, plane, ship, or on foot, he is considered a traveler.*" Note that 80 kilometers is approximately equivalent to 48 miles.

Regarding sickness, if one is perpetually too ill to fast throughout the year, including medical conditions that make it dangerous to fast, then one may make up for the missed fasting by feeding at least one poor person per day. Also, a woman is not allowed to fast during her period, and, unlike with ṣalāh, she must make up the missed days of fasting after Ramaḍān. A woman is also not allowed to fast during postpartum bleeding, within a maximum time range of 40 days, and she must make up the missed days of fasting after Ramaḍān.

Before Ramaḍān

It is not recommended to fast the two days before Ramaḍān because of the ḥadīth that states:

Abū Hurayrah (ra) narrated: the Prophet (saws) said, "None of you should fast a day or two before the month of Ramaḍān unless he has the habit of fasting; then he can fast that day." (Ṣaḥīḥ Al-Bukhārī, Ḥadīth 1914)

Note that there are optional fasts that one may do throughout the year, such as the fast of David (Dāwūd) (as), which is to fast every other day, so if one is doing that then one may fast within two days before Ramaḍān.

Saḥūr and Ifṭār

During Ramaḍān, one may wake up before Fajr to have a meal. This meal is called *saḥūr* (also spelled *suḥūr*), and its cutoff is ideally a few minutes before Fajr, but the absolute cutoff for eating is at Fajr. It is from the Sunnah of the Prophet (saws) to have dates at saḥūr. When one breaks their fast at Maghrib, this meal is called *ifṭār*. It is from the Sunnah of the Prophet (saws) to break one's fast with dates. If there are no dates at all, then one should break their fast with water. In other words, a date or a sip of water should be the first thing someone consumes when they break their fast.

The evidence for saḥūr can be found in Ṣaḥīḥ Al-Bukhārī, Ḥadīth 1923 and Ṣaḥīḥ Muslim, Ḥadīth 1095. The evidence for having dates for saḥūr can be found in Sunan Abū Dāwūd, Ḥadīth 2345; Al-Albānī graded this ḥadīth ṣaḥīḥ. The evidence for breaking the fast with dates or water can be found in Jāmi' At-Tirmidhī, Ḥadīths 695-696. Al-Albānī graded these ḥadīths ṣaḥīḥ. Also note the following ḥadīths:

Abū Sa'īd Al-Khudrī (ra) narrated: The Messenger of God (saws) said, "The suḥūr is a blessed meal, so do not abandon it even if you only take a sip of water. Verily, God and His angels send commendations upon those who take the suḥūr." (Musnad Aḥmad, Ḥadīth 11086; Al-Arnā'ūṭ graded it ṣaḥīḥ.)

Abū Dharr (ra) narrated: The Messenger of God (saws) said, "My nation (i.e., all Muslims) will continue in goodness so long as they hasten to break their fast (i.e., ifṭār) and prolong the pre-fasting meal (i.e., suḥūr). (Musnad Aḥmad, Ḥadīth 21312; Al-Albānī graded it ṣaḥīḥ.)

Various Ḥadīths About Ramaḍān

Abū Hurayrah (ra) narrated: the Messenger of God (saws) said, "When the month of Ramaḍān starts, the gates of Heaven are opened, and the gates of Hell are closed, and the devils are chained." (Ṣaḥīḥ Al-Bukhārī, Ḥadīth 1899; Ṣaḥīḥ Muslim, Ḥadīth 1079)

Abū Hurayrah (ra) narrated: the Prophet (saws) said, "Whoever established prayers on the Night of Power out of sincere faith and hoping for a reward from God, then all his previous sins will be forgiven. And whoever fasts in the month of Ramaḍān out of sincere faith, and hoping for a reward from God, then all his previous sins will be forgiven." (Ṣaḥīḥ Al-Bukhārī, Ḥadīth 1901; Ṣaḥīḥ Muslim, Ḥadīth 760)

Ibn 'Abbās (ra) narrated: the Prophet (saws) was the most generous amongst the people, and he used to be more so in the month of Ramaḍān when Gabriel visited him. And Gabriel (as) used to meet him on every night of Ramaḍān till the end of the month. The Prophet (saws) used to recite the Qur'ān to him (Gabriel (as)), and when Gabriel (as) met him, he used to be more generous than a fast wind (which causes rain and welfare). (Ṣaḥīḥ Al-Bukhārī, Ḥadīth 1902; Ṣaḥīḥ Muslim, Ḥadīth 2308)

Abū Hurayrah (ra) narrated: the Messenger of God (saws) said, "Whoever does not give up lying and evil actions, God is not in need of his leaving his food and drink." (Ṣaḥīḥ Al-Bukhārī, Ḥadīth 1903)

Abū Hurayrah (ra) narrated: the Messenger of God (saws) said, "God said, 'All the deeds of the son of Adam are for him except fasting, which is for Me, and I will give the reward for it.' Fasting is a shield. If one of you is fasting, he should avoid sexual relations and quarreling. And if somebody should fight or quarrel with him, he should say, 'I am fasting.' By the One in Whose Hands is the soul of Muḥammad, the unpleasant smell coming out from the mouth of a fasting person is better in the sight of God than the smell of musk. There are two pleasures for the fasting person: one at the time of breaking his fast, and the other at the time when he will meet his Lord; then he will be pleased because of his fasting." (Ṣaḥīḥ Al-Bukhārī, Ḥadīth 1904; Ṣaḥīḥ Muslim, Ḥadīth 1151)

Abū Hurayrah (ra) narrated: the Prophet (saws) said, "If somebody eats or drinks forgetfully then he should complete his fast, for what he has eaten or drunk has been given to him by God." (Ṣaḥīḥ Al-Bukhārī, Ḥadīth 1933; Ṣaḥīḥ Muslim, Ḥadīth 1155)

Abū Hurayrah (ra) narrated: the Messenger of God (saws) said, "Whoever breaks his fast forgetfully in the month of Ramaḍān, there is no compensation or expiation for it. (Ṣaḥīḥ Ibn Ḥibbān, Ḥadīth 3521; Al-Arnā'ūṭ graded it ḥasan.)

Ibn 'Abbās (ra) narrated: The Messenger of God (saws) said, "Indeed, 'Umrah during Ramaḍān is equal to Ḥajj." (Ṣaḥīḥ Al-Bukhārī, Ḥadīth 1782; Ṣaḥīḥ Muslim, Ḥadīth 1256)

The Penalty for Sexual Intercourse during the Daytime in Ramaḍān

Abū Hurayrah (ra) narrated: A man came to the Prophet (saws), and he said, "I am ruined, O Messenger of God!" The Prophet (saws) said, "What has ruined you?" The man said, "I was intimate with my wife during Ramaḍān." The Prophet (saws) said, "Can you find a slave to set free?" He said, "No." The Prophet (saws) said, "Are you able to fast two months in a row?" He said, "No." The Prophet (saws) said, "Can you find sixty poor people to feed?" He said, "No." Then the man sat down, and someone came to the Prophet (saws) with a basket of dates. The Prophet (saws) said, "Give these dates in charity." The man said, "Is there anyone poorer than us? There is no family between the two plains of Al-Madīnah that is poorer than mine." The Prophet (saws) laughed until we could see his back teeth, and he said, "Go and feed your family." (Ṣaḥīḥ Al-Bukhārī, Ḥadīth 1936; Ṣaḥīḥ Muslim, Ḥadīth 1111)

Tarāwīḥ

During Ramaḍān, there is an optional, though highly recommended, night prayer after 'Ishā', known as Tarāwīḥ. One may pray this either alone or in congregation. The following ḥadīth states:

Abū Hurayrah (ra) narrated: the Messenger of God (saws) said, "Whoever stands in prayer during Ramadan due to faith and seeking reward, his previous sins will be forgiven." (Ṣaḥīḥ Al-Bukhārī, Ḥadīth 2009; Ṣaḥīḥ Muslim, Ḥadīth 759; Riyāḍ Aṣ-Ṣāliḥīn, Ḥadīth 1187)

The Prophet Muḥammad (saws) would pray 8 rak'ahs of Tarāwīḥ, then 3 rak'ahs for an optional prayer called Witr. After he passed away, people would pray separately in the masjid, some praying 8 rak'ahs and some praying as many as 100. During the time of Caliph 'Umar ibn Al-Khaṭṭāb, who was one of the closest companions of the Prophet (saws), 'Umar thought it would be better if the people would pray together, so he established that, and he set the number of rak'ahs at 20. And the Prophet (saws) had told people to follow his Sunnah (i.e., Example) and the Sunnah of the Rightly Guided Caliphs (see: Sunan Abū Dāwūd, Ḥadīth 4607; Al-Albānī graded it ṣaḥīḥ.). For this reason, to this day, some imāms lead Tarāwīḥ praying 8 rak'ahs while other imāms lead

Tarāwīḥ praying 20 rak'ahs. Whether 8 or 20, Tarāwīḥ is often followed by 3 rak'ahs of Witr.

Many imāms also use the opportunity of Tarāwīḥ to recite the entire Qur'ān over the course of the 29 to 30 nights of Ramaḍān. Finishing the recitation of the entire Qur'ān is known as *khaṭmul-Qur'ān*, and people often make du'ā' upon finishing the Qur'ān.

Note also that in the Hijrī calendar, the 24-hour day begins at sunset (Maghrib), so the first night of Tarāwīḥ in Ramaḍān is before the first day of Ramaḍān.

Laylatul-Qadr (The Night of Power)

The Night of Power, also translated as the Night of Glory or the Night of Decree, is the best night of the year. It is the night on which the Qur'ān was first sent down. This night is greater than 1,000 months, which equals to over 83 years; for some that is a lifetime. It is highly recommended to spend this night in worship and remembrance of God, and the Qur'ān states regarding the Night of Power:

1 We sent it [i.e., the Quran] down on the Night of Power. 2 And what will make you comprehend what the Night of Power is? 3 The Night of Power is better than a thousand months. 4 On that night, the angels and the Spirit come down by the permission of their Lord with His decrees for all matters. 5 It is all peace till the break of dawn. (Qur'ān 97)

1 Ḥā' Mīm. 2 By the Book that makes things clear, 3 surely We sent it down on a blessed night—We have always sent warnings—4 on that night every wise decree is specified 5 by Our own command. We have been sending messages, 6 as a mercy from your Lord. He hears all and knows all. 7 He is the Lord of heaven and earth and all that is between them—if only you would really believe. (Qur'ān 44:1-7)

With regard to the date of Laylatul-Qadr, we do not know for sure when it is, but we do know that it is on an odd night of one of the last ten nights of Ramaḍān (i.e., the 21st, 23rd, 25th, 27th, or 29th), and the Prophet (saws) used to increase his worship in the last ten nights:

Abū Hurayrah (ra) narrated: the Prophet (saws) said, "Whoever established prayers on the Night of Power out of sincere faith and hoping for a reward from God, then all his previous sins will be forgiven. And whoever fasts in the month of Ramaḍān out of sincere faith, and hoping for a reward from God, then all his previous sins will be forgiven." (Ṣaḥīḥ Al-Bukhārī, Ḥadīth 1901; Ṣaḥīḥ Muslim, Ḥadīth 760)

'Ā'ishah (ra) narrated: the Messenger of God (saws) said, "Search for the Night of Power in the odd nights of the last ten days of Ramaḍān." (Ṣaḥīḥ Al-Bukhārī, Ḥadīth 2017)

'Ā'ishah (ra) narrated: With the start of the last ten days of Ramaḍān, the Prophet (saws) used to tighten his waist belt (i.e., work hard), and he used to pray all the night, and he used to keep his family awake for the prayers. (Ṣaḥīḥ Al-Bukhārī, Ḥadīth 2024; Ṣaḥīḥ Muslim, Ḥadīth 1174)

'Ā'ishah (ra) narrated: I said: "O Messenger of God, what is your view if I know when the Night of Power is, then what should I say in it?" He said: "Say: 'Allāhumma innaka 'Afuwwun. Tuḥibbul-'afwa fa'fu 'annī. (O God, indeed, You are Pardoning. You love to pardon, so pardon me.)'" (Jāmi' At-Tirmidhī, Ḥadīth 3513; Zubayr 'Alī Za'ī graded it ṣaḥīḥ; Riyāḍ Aṣ-Ṣāliḥīn, Ḥadīth 1195)

There is the opinion of Ubayy ibn Ka'b, a prominent companion of the Prophet (saws) that the Night of Power was specifically on the 27th Night of Ramaḍān. Mu'āwiyah ibn Abū Sufyān, another companion, also seemed to be of this opinion.

Ubayy ibn Ka'b (ra) narrated: By God, the one whom there is no god but He, indeed it (i.e., the Night of Power) is surely in Ramaḍān. And by God, I surely know which night it is. It is the night which the Messenger of God (saws) commanded us to spend in prayer. It is the night of the twenty-seventh, and its sign is that the sun rises that day bright with no rays. (Ṣaḥīḥ Muslim, Ḥadīth 762)

Mu'āwiyah ibn Abū Sufyān (ra) narrated: the Prophet (saws) said, "The Night of Power is the twenty-seventh night." (Sunan Abū Dāwūd, Ḥadīth 1386; Al-Albānī graded it ṣaḥīḥ; Bulūgh Al-Marām, Ḥadīth 576; Ibn Ḥajar Al-'Asqalānī said the strongest opinion is that it is the saying of a companion [i.e., Mu'āwiyah].)

For these reasons, some people prioritize the twenty-seventh night in particular, but it is more correct to prioritize all the odd nights of the last ten nights of Ramaḍān.

I'tikāf (Staying)

It is from the Sunnah to observe i'tikāf in a masjid in which congregational prayers are held. However, this practice is not obligatory. If one does choose to observe i'tikāf, then this is a time specifically devoted to worshipping and remembering God. It involves residing in the masjid, and the mu'takif (i.e., one observing i'tikāf) may not visit a sick person, attend a funeral, touch or be intimate with one's spouse, or leave the masjid for any unnecessary reason.

'Ā'ishah (ra) narrated: The sunnah for one who is observing i'tikāf is not to visit a patient, or to attend a funeral, or to touch or embrace one's wife, or to go out for anything but necessary purposes. (Sunan Abū Dāwūd, Ḥadīth 2473; Al-Albānī graded it ḥasan ṣaḥīḥ.)

'Abdullāh ibn 'Umar (ra) narrated: The Messenger of God (saws) used to practice i'tikāf in the last ten days of the month of Ramaḍān. (Ṣaḥīḥ Al-Bukhārī, Ḥadīth 2025; Ṣaḥīḥ Muslim, Ḥadīth 1171)

'Ā'ishah (ra) narrated: The Prophet (saws) used to practice i'tikāf in the last ten days of Ramaḍān till he died. Then his wives used to practice i'tikāf after him. (Ṣaḥīḥ Al-Bukhārī, Ḥadīth 2026; Ṣaḥīḥ Muslim, Ḥadīth 1172)

Zakāt Al-Fiṭr

There is a special charity to be paid at the end of Ramaḍān, and it is called *zakāt al-fiṭr* or *ṣadaqat al-fiṭr*. Zakāt al-fiṭr is paid on behalf of oneself and on behalf of one's dependents. It is a *ṣā'* of food to be given to the poor among the Muslims. One ṣā' is four complete scoops as scooped up with two hands. It is approximately equal to 3 kilograms or 6.5 pounds.

Zakāt al-fiṭr is obligatory from the time of the sunset (Maghrib) that comes after the last day of Ramaḍān and brings in the first day of Shawwāl. The cutoff for zakāt al-fiṭr is when the 'Īd prayer begins. After that, anything given to the poor is considered regular ṣadaqah (charity). If one misses giving their zakāt al-fiṭr on time, they must repent. Zakāt al-fiṭr may be paid one to two days early, but no sooner than that.

Ibn 'Umar (ra) narrated: The Messenger of God (saws) enjoined the payment of one ṣā' of dates or one ṣā' of barley as zakāt al-fiṭr on every Muslim, slave or free, male or female, young or old, and he ordered that it be paid before the people went out to offer the 'Īd prayer. (Ṣaḥīḥ Al-Bukhārī, Ḥadīth 1503; Ṣaḥīḥ Muslim, Ḥadīth 984)

Ibn 'Abbās (ra) narrated: The Messenger of God (saws) prescribed the charity relating to the breaking of the fast as a purification of the fasting person from empty and obscene talk and as food for the poor. If anyone pays it before the prayer (of 'Īd), it will be accepted as zakāt. If anyone pays it after the prayer, that will be a ṣadaqah (charity) like other charities. (Sunan Abū Dāwūd, Ḥadīth 1609; Al-Albānī graded it ḥasan.)

'Īd Al-Fiṭr

'Īd Al-Fiṭr (often spelled "Eid Al-Fiṭr") is a holiday that takes place directly after Ramaḍān, on the first day of the month of Shawwāl. It is forbidden to fast on this day. There is a common misconception that 'Īd Al-Fiṭr lasts for three days, but this is just a custom that people later developed, and the religion only establishes one day for 'Īd Al-Fiṭr.

Abū Sa'īd (ra) narrated: The Prophet (saws) forbade fasting on the day of Al-Fiṭr and the day of An-Naḥr (i.e., 'Īd Al-Aḍḥā, the other Muslim holiday). (Ṣaḥīḥ Al-Bukhārī, Ḥadīth 1991, 1992)

There is a special khuṭbah (sermon) delivered on the morning of 'Īd, followed by a two-rak'ah congregational prayer. Some authentic practices from the Sunnah regarding 'Īd Al-Fiṭr include eating an odd number of dates before one goes out for the prayer, men adorning themselves with their best clothes, Muslims greeting and congratulating one another, and reciting takbīr from the night before until the time that the imām enters the muṣallā (sanctuary) to lead the 'Īd prayer. The takbīr for 'Īd has more words than usual. It is chanted, and a basic way of saying it is:

"Allāhu Akbar. Allāhu Akbar. Allāhu Akbar. Lā ilāha illallāh. Allāhu Akbar. Allāhu Akbar. Wa lillāhil-ḥamd."

"God is Greater. God is Greater. God is Greater. There is no god except for Allāh. God is Greater. God is Greater. And for God is all praise."

Extra Fasts

According to the Sunnah of the Prophet (saws), it is recommended to fast on other days of the year outside of Ramaḍān. Other recommended times of fasting include:

- Any time during the month of Sha'bān (the lunar month before Ramaḍān) except for the last two days. This is the month during which one's deeds are taken up to God. (See: Ṣaḥīḥ Al-Bukhārī, Ḥadīth 1969; Ṣaḥīḥ Muslim, Ḥadīth 1156| Sunan An-Nasā'ī, Ḥadīth 2357; Al-Albānī graded it ḥasan.)

- Any six days during the month of Shawwāl (the lunar month after Ramaḍān) other than the first day (which is 'Īd Al-Fiṭr). The reward of good deeds is generally tenfold, so if Ramaḍān is 30 days, then fasting it is like fasting for 300 days. Adding 6 days of fasting during Shawwāl to it will be like adding 60 days. The lunar year is approximately 360 days, so fasting during Ramaḍān and 6 days of Shawwāl can be like fasting for a whole year. (See: Ṣaḥīḥ Muslim, Ḥadīth 1164| Ṣaḥīḥ Al-Bukhārī, Ḥadīth 6491; Ṣaḥīḥ Muslim, Ḥadīth 131)

- The Day of 'Arafah (Yawm 'Arafah). It is the 9th day of the month of Dhūl-Ḥijjah (the 12th month of the Hijrī calendar), and it is the best day of the year. The Day of 'Arafah is the day on which the religion was completed, and fasting on it is an expiation for the minor sins of the previous year and the minor sins of the coming year. (See: Ṣaḥīḥ Muslim, Ḥadīth 1162| Ṣaḥīḥ Al-Bukhārī, Ḥadīth 4606; Ṣaḥīḥ Muslim, Ḥadīth 3017)

- The 10th of the month of Muḥarram (the 1st month of the Hijrī calendar). It is recommended to also fast either the 9th or the 11th of Muḥarram, along with the 10th. The 10th of Muḥarram is called Yawm 'Āshūrā'. It is the day on which God saved Moses (as) and the Israelites and drowned Pharaoh, and fasting on it is an expiation for the minor sins of the previous year. (See: Ṣaḥīḥ Muslim, Ḥadīth 1162| Ṣaḥīḥ Al-Bukhārī, Ḥadīth 3397; Ṣaḥīḥ Muslim, Ḥadīth 1130)

- Any three days of each Hijrī month, but in particular the 13th, 14th, and 15th of each Hijrī month. These three days are called Ayyām Al-Bīḍ (the White Days) because of the fullness of the moon during this time. Because deeds are generally rewarded tenfold, fasting for 3 days is like fasting for 30 days. (See: Ṣaḥīḥ Al-Bukhārī, Ḥadīth 1178| Ṣaḥīḥ Muslim, Ḥadīth 1162| Jāmi' At-Tirmidhī, Ḥadīth 761; Zubayr 'Alī Za'ī graded it ḥasan; Ibn Ḥibbān graded it ṣaḥīḥ)

- Mondays and Thursdays. Deeds are shown to God on these days of the week. Furthermore, the Prophet Muḥammad (saws) was born on a Monday, and the revelation of the Qur'ān first came to him on a Monday. (See: Ṣaḥīḥ Muslim, Ḥadīth 1162| Jāmi' At-Tirmidhī, Ḥadīth 747; Zubayr 'Alī Za'ī graded it ḥasan.)

- Every other day throughout the year (except when such fasting is not allowed). This is called the fast of David (Dāwūd) (as), and it is the most beloved form of fasting to God that is not obligatory. (See: Ṣaḥīḥ Al-Bukhārī, Ḥadīth 3420; Ṣaḥīḥ Muslim, Ḥadīth 1159| Ṣaḥīḥ Muslim, Ḥadīth 1162)

It should also be noted that singling out Fridays and Saturdays as days of fasting should not be done. (See: Ṣaḥīḥ Muslim, Ḥadīth 1144| Sunan Abū Dāwūd, Ḥadīth 2421; Al-Albānī graded it ṣaḥīḥ.) The reason behind this may be to preserve one's strength for Jumu'ah and to avoid imitating the Jews because they venerate Saturday as the Sabbath. However, one may fast on a Friday and/or a Saturday if it falls in the pattern of a permissible fast that one is doing, or if it falls on a specific day on which fasting is recommended.

Chapter 11
Ḥajj and ‘Umrah

Ḥajj is a pillar of Islām, and it is an obligation for every Muslim, man and woman, to perform it at least once in their lifetime if they are a sane adult and physically and financially able to. Children who have not yet reached puberty do not have to perform Ḥajj, but if they do, they must perform it again as an adult, and one is considered an adult in Islām when one reaches puberty. There are extra acts of worship in the religion that may give one the reward of Ḥajj, such as going from one's house to the masjid for an obligatory prayer while in the state of wuḍū' or performing ‘Umrah during Ramaḍān. However, these extra acts of worship do not take away the obligation of performing the actual Ḥajj.

26 We assigned to Abraham the site of the House, saying, 'Do not associate with Me anything and purify My House for those who circumambulate [the Ka'bah] and those who stand upright, and those who bow and prostrate themselves. 27 Call humanity to the Pilgrimage. They will come to you, on foot, and on every kind of lean camel, by every distant track 28 so that they may witness its benefit for them and, on the appointed days may utter the name of God over the cattle He has provided for them. Then eat their flesh, and feed the distressed and the needy. 29 Then let the pilgrims purify themselves and fulfil their vows and perform the circumambulation of the Ancient House.' (Qur'ān 22:26-29)

96 The first House [of worship] to be built for humanity was the one at Bakkah [i.e., Makkah]. It is a blessed place; a source of guidance for the whole world. 97 There are clear signs in it; it is the place where Abraham stood. Anyone who enters it will be secure. Pilgrimage to the House is a duty to God for anyone who is able to undertake it. Anyone who disbelieves should remember that God is independent of all creatures. (Qur'ān 3:96-97)

Ibn 'Abbās (ra) narrated: The Messenger of God (saws) said, "He who intends to perform Ḥajj should hasten to do so." (Sunan Abū Dāwūd, Ḥadīth 1732; Al-Albānī graded it ḥasan.)

Abū Hurayrah (ra) narrated: The Messenger of God (saws) said, "The guests of God, Mighty and Sublime, are three: the warrior (fighting in a just cause), the pilgrim performing Ḥajj, and the pilgrim performing 'Umrah." (Sunan An-Nasā'ī, Ḥadīth 3121; Zubayr 'Alī Za'ī graded it ṣaḥīḥ.)

'Ā'ishah (ra) narrated: I said, "O Messenger of God! Is jihād obligatory for women?" He said, "Yes. Upon them is a jihād in which there is no fighting: the Ḥajj and the 'Umrah." (Sunan Ibn Mājah, Ḥadīth 2901; Bulūgh Al-Marām, Ḥadīth 580; Ibn Ḥajar Al-'Asqalānī said its chain of narrators is ṣaḥīḥ, and Zubayr 'Alī Za'ī graded it ṣaḥīḥ.)

Conditions for an Accepted Ḥajj (Al-Ḥajj Al-Mabrūr)

In order for Ḥajj to be accepted, it must be paid for with money earned in a ḥalāl (permissible) way. One should also avoid evil, sin, and unjust arguments during Ḥajj. One should properly perform all the rituals of Ḥajj according to the Sunnah of the Prophet Muḥammad (saws), and one should not show off in it. Ḥajj should only be done for the pleasure of God, and one should avoid sins following their Ḥajj. A woman performing Ḥajj must also be traveling with a mahram because it is forbidden for a woman to travel without one. A mahram is a sane man who protects a woman, and it can be her husband or one whom she is forbidden to marry due to blood ties or other reasons (such as her father, brother, uncle, nephew, etc.).

The Reward for an Accepted Ḥajj (Al-Ḥajj Al-Mabrūr)

The reward of Ḥajj is that the ḥajjī (one who performs Ḥajj) will be purified of sins to the point where they are as they were on the day that their mother gave birth to them. In other words, they will be starting again with a clean slate, free of sins. And one who performs Ḥajj will have earned the reward of Al-Jannah (Paradise). This is all depending on whether one's Ḥajj was accepted by God, and only God has knowledge of that.

‘Amr ibn Al-‘Āṣ (ra) narrated: When God put Islām in my heart, I came to the Prophet (saws) and said, “Hold out your right hand so that I might swear allegiance to you.” So he held out his right hand, but I withdrew my hand. He said, “What is the matter, O ‘Amr?” I said, “I want to stipulate a condition.” He said, "What do you want to stipulate?” I said, “That I will be forgiven.” He said, “Do you not know, O ‘Amr, that Islām destroys whatever (sins) came before it, and that migration (i.e., hijrah) destroys whatever (sins) came before it, and that Ḥajj destroys whatever (sins) came before it?” (Ṣaḥīḥ Muslim, Ḥadīth 121)

Abū Hurayrah (ra) narrated: I heard the Prophet (saws) saying, “Whoever performs Ḥajj for the sake of God, and does not utter any obscene speech or do any evil deed, will go back (free of sin) as the day his mother bore him.” (Ṣaḥīḥ Al-Bukhārī, Ḥadīth 1521; Ṣaḥīḥ Muslim, Ḥadīth 1350)

Abū Hurayrah (ra) narrated: the Messenger of God (saws) said, “An ‘Umrah is an expiation for the sins committed between it and the next ‘Umrah, and Ḥajj which is accepted will receive no other reward than Paradise.” (Ṣaḥīḥ Al-Bukhārī, Ḥadīth 1773; Ṣaḥīḥ Muslim, Ḥadīth 1349)

‘Abdullāh ibn Mas‘ūd (ra) narrated: The Messenger of God (saws) said, “Alternate between Ḥajj and ‘Umrah, for those two remove poverty and sins just as the bellows removes filth from iron, gold, and silver. And there is no reward for an accepted Ḥajj except for Paradise.” (Jāmi‘ At-Tirmidhī, Ḥadīth 810; Al-Albānī graded it ṣaḥīḥ.)

The Types of Ḥajj and the Time for It

There are three types of Ḥajj: Tamattu‘, Qirān, and Ifrād. The best type of Ḥajj is Tamattu‘.

Ḥajj Tamattu‘ involves assuming iḥrām (see the section *Iḥrām*) for ‘Umrah, performing ‘Umrah, then exiting iḥrām. Then one assumes iḥrām for Ḥajj and performs it. Thus, Ḥajj Tamattu‘ consists of ‘Umrah then Ḥajj, with a gap in the middle.

Ḥajj Qirān involves assuming iḥrām for ‘Umrah and Ḥajj together, then performing ‘Umrah, then performing Ḥajj. Thus, Ḥajj Qirān consists of ‘Umrah then Ḥajj, with no gap in the middle.

Ḥajj Ifrād involves assuming iḥrām for Ḥajj by itself then performing it, with no 'Umrah at all.

The months of the Hijrī calendar after Ramaḍān are considered the months of Ḥajj. These are the months of Shawwāl (the 10th month), Dhūl-Qa'dah (the 11th month), and Dhūl-Ḥijjah (the 12th month). The reason these are known as the months of Ḥajj is because one can only assume iḥrām for Ḥajj during them.

However, Ḥajj itself only takes place during certain days, and these are the 8th to the 12th of the month of Dhūl-Ḥijjah, and it can also be extended to the 13th of Dhūl-Ḥijjah.

Iḥrām

Iḥrām is a spiritual state of being in which one intends to perform 'Umrah and/or Ḥajj, and in which certain things become forbidden to an individual. Iḥrām is the first pillar of 'Umrah, and it is the first pillar of Ḥajj. Without iḥrām, there is no 'Umrah or Ḥajj. Before entering iḥrām, it is recommended for one to perform ghusl (i.e., take a full bath). Then men may apply whatever perfume they wish to wear, but women should not apply any perfume.

Afterwards, a man puts on two white pieces of unstitched cloth. Unstitched does not mean that it is not sewn at all, but it means that it is not stitched to another piece of cloth. Essentially, a man in iḥrām wears two large white sheets/towels. One (called an *izār*) is tied at the waist, and the other (called a *ridā'*) is draped around the shoulders. As far as footwear, one is only allowed to wear sandals in iḥrām, or any type of simple footwear that exposes the ankle, heel, and top of the foot. Shoes that cover the whole foot are forbidden in iḥrām. A man in iḥrām cannot wear any other clothes besides the two white iḥrām garments and sandals (or sandal-like shoes). The head must also not be covered. However, wearing items that are not clothes, such as a waist pack, a drawstring bag, a ring, or a watch are permissible. One may also use safety pins if they are having trouble keeping their ridā' in place.

A woman does not have special iḥrām garments to wear. Instead, she wears her normal, modest clothing. The only things a women may not wear in iḥrām are the niqāb (i.e., face veil) and gloves. She must also wear sandals or sandal-like footwear.

Then one makes the intention to perform ‘Umrah, Ḥajj, or both, depending on what type of pilgrimage they are undertaking. The intention is made in the heart. One also says when they enter iḥrām for ‘Umrah or Tamattu‘: “Labbayk Allāhumma ‘Umratan.” This phrase translates to: “Here I am, O God, making ‘Umrah.”

If one is doing Qirān, then one says, “Labbayk Allāhumma Ḥajjan wa ‘Umrah,” which means, “Here I am, O God, making Ḥajj and ‘Umrah.”

If one is doing Ifrād, one says, “Labbayk Allāhumma Ḥajjan,” which means, “Here I am, O God, for Ḥajj.

Thus, iḥrām consists of wearing the special garments (for men) and the intention (for both men and women). Once one makes their intention that places them in iḥrām, several things become forbidden to them as long as they remain in iḥrām.

Things forbidden for a muḥrim (i.e., someone in iḥrām) include:

- Sex
- Touching the opposite sex with desire
- Sinning
- Arguing
- Wearing stitched clothes (such as shirts, pants, robes, and thobes) and wearing regular shoes. Note that this prohibition only applies to men.
- Putting on perfume
- Arranging a marriage
- Proposing a marriage
- Getting married
- Trimming one’s nails
- Intentionally removing any hair
- Hunting land animals
- Slaughtering land animals
- Helping one hunt or slaughter a land animal

Note that while hunting land animals is forbidden in iḥrām, fishing is permissible. Also, putting on perfume includes putting on scented moisturizers, soaps, shampoos, deodorants, and toothpastes. However, unscented moisturizers, soaps, shampoos, deodorants, and toothpastes are permissible. If one does any of these things out of ignorance, forgetfulness, or having been forced to do it, then they are excused, but they must stop committing the forbidden action when it comes to their attention, if they are able to. However, if one does certain forbidden actions deliberately and with no excuse, then a *fidyah* (ransom) is required.

There is no fidyah for entering into a marriage contract.

For those who intentionally remove any hair or nails, put on perfume, touch the opposite sex with desire (but without having intercourse), or if a woman wears a niqāb or gloves, or if a man wears stitched clothing, then these individuals have a choice as to the type of fidyah they may offer:

1. They may fast for three days, consecutively or non-consecutively
2. They may feed six poor people, giving each poor person half a ṣā‘ of food. Half a ṣā‘ is two complete scoops as scooped up with two hands, and it is approximately 1.5 kilograms or 3.3 pounds.
3. They may sacrifice a sheep and distribute its meat among the poor, not eating any of it them self.

If someone has sex with their spouse while in iḥrām, then their ‘Umrah and/or Ḥajj is rendered invalid.

If someone has hunted game while in iḥrām, then they must sacrifice an animal that is equivalent to it and distribute the meat to the poor, if there is an equivalent to the game that was killed. Or they can find out its value and give food of an equal value to the poor, giving each poor person half a ṣā‘. Or they can fast one day for each poor person they should feed.

There are five places in Arabia, on the way to Makkah, at which one must assume iḥrām before passing if they are performing ‘Umrah or Ḥajj. Each of these five places is called a mīqāt (Arabic plural: mawāqīt). The 5 mawāqīt are:

- **Dhūl-Ḥulayfah**. It is the mīqāt for the pilgrims coming from Al-Madīnah.

- **Al-Juḥfah**. It is the mīqāt for the pilgrims coming from Egypt, Ash-Shām (Syria, Palestine, Jordan, and Lebanon), and the West in general. Pilgrims from Al-Madīnah can also come this route.

- **Qarn Al-Manāzil**. It is the mīqāt for the pilgrims coming from the Najd (a region of the Arabian peninsula), and that includes the cities of Ṭā’if and Riyāḍ. Pilgrims from the Gulf countries, the Indian subcontinent, Australia, Malaysia, Indonesia, and Singapore may also pass through this mīqāt.

- **Yalamlam**. It is the mīqāt for pilgrims coming from Yemen. Pilgrims coming from southern parts of Africa can also pass through this mīqāt.

- **Dhātu ‘Irq**. It is the mīqāt for pilgrims coming from ‘Irāq. Pilgrims from Iran, China, and Russia may also use this mīqāt.

For those who reside in the *Ḥaram* (i.e., the sacred boundary of Makkah), or for those who have completed ‘Umrah and have not yet left the Ḥaram, a popular spot for assuming, or reassuming, iḥrām is Masjid ‘Ā’ishah, also known as Masjid At-Tan‘īm. Note that one can put on iḥrām garments before reaching a mīqāt, and the intention must be made either before one reaches the mīqāt or at the mīqāt.

The Talbiyah

After the pilgrim assumes iḥrām, they are supposed to recite the *talbiyah* until they reach Masjid Al-Ḥarām and perform ṭawāf around the Ka‘bah. The talbiyah is as follows:

“Labbayk Allāhumma labbayk. Labbayka lā sharīka laka labbayk. Innal-ḥamda wan-ni‘mata laka wal-mulk lā sharīka lak.”

“Here I am, O God, here I am. Here I am, You have no partner; here I am. Indeed, all praise and all blessings are Yours, and all dominion. You have no partner.”

An Overview of 'Umrah

When one approaches Masjid Al-Ḥarām, it is good to be in wuḍū' already. It is sunnah to enter with one's right foot first and to say the du'ā' for entering a masjid, which is:

"A'ūdhu billāhil-'Aẓīm, wa biwajhihil-karīm, wa sulṭānihil-qadīm, minash-shayṭānir-rajīm. Bismillāhi, waṣ-ṣalātu was-salāmu 'alā Rasūlillāhi. Allāhummaf-taḥlī abwāba raḥmatika."

"I seek refuge in God, the Absolute Greatest, and in His noble Face, and in His primordial power, from Satan the accursed. In the name of God, and commendations and peace be upon the Messenger of God. O God, open for me the doors of Your mercy."

[Tip: When one removes their sandals or shoes before entering Masjid Al-Ḥarām, one may put them in a drawstring bag and hold on to them. If one leaves them at the entrance, those shoes will very likely become lost. One should also keep their important possessions near them, perhaps in a waist pack. This includes items such as money, cards, passports, and other forms of I.D. One should also be on guard against pickpockets – even in Masjid Al-Ḥarām!]

Around this point, one can stop saying the talbiyah.

Ṭawāf

One then approaches the *maṭāf*, which is the flat, wide area around the Ka'bah, where pilgrims circle the Ka'bah. The act of circling the Ka'bah is called *ṭawāf*. Another English word for ṭawāf is circumambulation. One must be in wuḍū' in order to perform ṭawāf, and ṭawāf is a pillar of 'Umrah, so without it 'Umrah is incomplete.

[Note: Thousands of years ago, a stone was sent from Paradise, and it was built into the Ka'bah. The stone had descended from Paradise whiter than milk, but the sins of the sons of Adam (as) made it black. (See Jāmi' At-Tirmidhī, Ḥadīth 877; Zubayr 'Alī Za'ī graded it ḥasan.) This stone is known as *Al-Ḥajar Al-Aswad*, or the Black Stone. It is built into the south-eastern corner of the Ka'bah.]

In recent times, green lights have been installed in a wall of Masjid Al-Ḥarām to signify the point where ṭawāf starts, and one starts ṭawāf at Al-

Ḥajar Al-Aswad (the Black Stone). At the start, one says, “Bismillāh, Allāhu Akbar (In the name of God, God is Greater).” If one is able to, one may kiss the stone. This is from the Sunnah of the Prophet (saws). If one cannot kiss it, one may touch it, and if one cannot touch it, then one should point to it and say, “Allāhu Akbar.”

[Tip: Do not overexert yourself trying to touch the Black Stone. It is sunnah, not obligatory. The crowd around it is usually very thick, and reaching it can be a challenge, especially for those who are weak.]

[Tip: When doing ṭawāf with a partner, try to walk one in front of another, not side by side, otherwise people may walk in between the two of you and separate you.]

One then proceeds to circle the Ka‘bah in a counterclockwise direction. There is no specific du‘ā’ or dhikr to make when doing ṭawāf. One may say whatever du‘ā’ or dhikr one wishes to say, or one may recite whatever portion of the Qur’ān they want to. When one reaches the Yemeni Corner of the Ka‘bah, it is sunnah to touch it. However, if one cannot touch it, then one should neither point to it nor say “Allāhu Akbar.”

Between the Yemeni Corner and the Black Stone, it is sunnah to say:

“Rabbanā ātinā fid-dunyā ḥasanatan wa fil-ākhirati ḥasanatan wa qinā ‘adhāban-nār.”

“Our Lord, give us good in this world, and give us good in the Hereafter, and protect us from the punishment of the Fire.”

From the Black Stone, around the Ka‘bah, and back to the Black Stone is one circuit. One must do seven circuits around the Ka‘bah. Each time one passes the Black Stone, one should point to it and say, “Allāhu Akbar,” if one does not touch it or kiss it. For the first three circuits, it is sunnah for men to lightly jog, or at least to move their legs as if they are jogging. This light jogging is called *raml*. One walks the next four circuits in a normal manner. However, jogging is not obligatory, and if one is not able to, one may walk all seven circuits. It is also sunnah for men to uncover their right shoulder during the first three circuits of ṭawāf. This is done by placing the middle of the upper garment under the right armpit and the ends of it over the left shoulder. The uncovering of the right shoulder is called *al-iḍṭibā‘*.

Maqām Ibrāhīm and Zamzam

When one has completed their seven circuits around the Ka'bah, then one covers their right shoulder and proceeds to *Maqām Ibrāhīm*, the Station of Abraham. It is a stone where Abraham (as) stood while building the Ka'bah. Then one recites the verse from the Qur'ān:

"Wat-takhidhū mim-maqāmi Ibrāhīma muṣallā."

125 Make the place where Abraham stood a place of worship. (Qur'ān 2:125)

One then prays two rak'ahs of ṣalāh behind Maqām Ibrāhīm, reciting Sūratul-Kāfirūn (chapter 109) after Al-Fātiḥah in the first rak'ah and Sūratul-Ikhlāṣ (chapter 112) after Al-Fātiḥah in the second rak'ah. If one cannot find space to pray behind Maqām Ibrāhīm, then one can pray anywhere in the Ḥaram (Sanctuary) near the Ka'bah (but of course not where people are making ṭawāf). After this point, it is common for people to make a lot of du'ā' and to drink *Zamzam* water, but neither of these are required parts of 'Umrah.

[Note: Thousands of years ago, Prophet Abraham (as) was guided to leave his wife Hagar (in Arabic: Hājar) and their infant son Ishmael (as) in Bakkah, the old name for Makkah, which was a barren, waterless valley at the time. Hagar feared for Ishmael's (as) life, and she walked and ran in between the two hills of *Ṣafā* and *Marwah* seven times looking for water, until God sent the Angel Gabriel (as) to cause a spring of water to miraculously form nearby. (See Ṣaḥīḥ Al-Bukhārī, Ḥadīth 3364.) This spring became known as the well of Zamzam, and, as it had a miraculous origin, it is regarded as sacred, and there is blessing in drinking its water.

Ibn 'Abbās (ra) narrated: The Messenger of God (saws) said, "The best water on the face of the earth is Zamzam water. In it is food for nourishment and healing for illness." (Al-Mu'jam Al-Kabīr by Aṭ-Ṭabarānī, Ḥadīth 11011; Al-Albānī graded it ḥasan.)

Jābir ibn 'Abdullāh (ra) narrated: The Messenger of God (saws) said, "The water of Zamzam is for whatever it is drunk for." (Sunan Ibn Mājah, Ḥadīth 3062; Zubayr 'Alī Za'ī graded it ḥasan.)

The second ḥadīth means that whatever one intends or makes du'ā' for when drinking Zamzam may be fulfilled, if God wills.]

Sa‘ī

Thereafter, one starts the next pillar of ‘Umrah, which is called *sa‘ī*, and it consists of walking between the two hills of Ṣafā and Marwah in imitation of what Hagar did thousands of years ago. Sa‘ī is done at the *mas‘ā*, the path at the ends of which are the two hills. Approaching the hill of Ṣafā, the hill where one begins sa‘ī, one should recite the following verse of the Qur’ān:

Innaṣ-Ṣafā wal-Marwata min sha‘ā’irillāh. Faman ḥajjal-bayta awi‘tamara falā junāḥa ‘alayhi an yaṭṭawwafa bihimā. Wa man taṭawwa‘a khayran fa innallāha shākirun ‘alīm.

158 *Indeed, Ṣafā and Marwah are among the symbols set up by God. If anyone goes on a pilgrimage to the House, or performs a minor pilgrimage, let them walk between them. And whoever does good of his own accord, God is Appreciative, and All-Knowing. (Qur’ān 2:158)*

One should also recite:

“Abda’u bimā bada’ Allāhu bihī.” or “Nabda’u bimā bada’ Allāhu bihī.”

“I begin with what God began with.” or “We begin with what God began with.”

This line signifies that God mentioned Ṣafā first, so the pilgrims start sa‘ī at Ṣafā. Also, the above Qur’ān verse and statement should only be recited at the beginning of sa‘ī, not every time one approaches Ṣafā and Marwah.

When one is on Ṣafā, one faces the Ka‘bah and raises one’s hands with the palms facing upwards in supplication. One then says the following dhikr:

“Allāhu Akbar. Allāhu Akbar. Allāhu Akbar. Lā ilāha illallāhu waḥdahū lā sharīka lah. Lahul-mulku wa lahul-ḥamd. Wa huwa ‘alā kulli shay’in qadīr. Lā ilāha illallāhu waḥdah. Anjaza wa‘dah, wa naṣara ‘abdah, wa hazamal-aḥzāba waḥdah.”

“God is Greater. God is Greater. God is Greater. There is no god except for Allāh, alone, without associate. His is the dominion, and His is all praise. And He has power over everything. There is no god except for Allāh, alone.

He fulfilled His promise, and He granted victory to His slave, and He defeated the confederates alone."

[Note: The confederates, or *al-aḥzāb*, were those disbelievers who had banded together seeking to destroy the Muslims.]

Then one makes du'ā' for whatever one wishes. One may repeat this dhikr and make du'ā' two more times, making it three times in all, but once is sufficient.

Then one proceeds down the mas'ā to the hill of Marwah. In between Ṣafā and Marwah, there are green markers, and men are supposed to run in between these. However, if one cannot run, walking is sufficient. One can also make whatever dhikr or du'ā' they wish, or they can recite whatever they want to of the Qur'ān. At Marwah, when one is facing the qiblah, one says the same dhikr as they said on Ṣafā and makes du'ā'. Three times is preferable, but once is sufficient. From Ṣafā to Marwah is one round, then from Marwah to Ṣafā is the second round, and so on. One makes seven rounds in all between Ṣafā and Marwah, ending at Marwah.

Shaving the Head or Cutting the Hair

Then a man shaves his head or at least cuts his hair, but shaving the head is better. Women must cut the length of a fingertip from their hair, but they cannot shave their heads.

Abū Hurayrah (ra) narrated: The Messenger of God (saws) said, "O God, forgive those who get their heads shaved." The people said, "And those who get their hair cut." The Prophet (saws) said, "O God, forgive those who get their heads shaved." The people said, "And those who get their hair cut." The Prophet (saws) said his supplication a third time and added to it, "and those who get their hair cut short." (Ṣaḥīḥ Al-Bukhārī, Ḥadīth 1728; Ṣaḥīḥ Muslim, Ḥadīth 1302)

Thus, the Prophet (saws) prayed for forgiveness for those who get their heads shaved three times, and he only prayed for forgiveness for those who cut their hair once. People can cut their hair or shave their head themselves, or they can pay a barber to do it for them.

Cutting the hair or shaving the head is a pillar of ‘Umrah, and it ends ‘Umrah, and one exits from iḥrām after this. Then the things that were forbidden to one in iḥrām become permissible to them again, and a man can wear regular clothes again.

[Note: If one is doing Ḥajj Qirān, then one does *not* exit iḥrām, and they do not cut their hair or shave their head.]

This concludes the overview of ‘Umrah.

Between ‘Umrah and Ḥajj

If one is performing Ḥajj Tamattu‘, then, after finishing ‘Umrah, one may reside in Makkah until the first day of Ḥajj starts. During this time, one may perform many acts of worship.

An Overview of Ḥajj

The 8th Day of Dhūl-Ḥijjah

The first day of Ḥajj is the 8th of Dhūl-Ḥijjah, and this day is called *Yawm At-Tarwiyah.* After Fajr, one assumes iḥrām from wherever one has been staying since their ‘Umrah, whether it is in Makkah or in a city outside of Makkah. In this instance, it does not have to be from a mīqāt. One says: “Labbayk Allāhumma Ḥajjan,” which means, “Here I am, O God, for Ḥajj.”

Then one recites the talbiyah and proceeds to a place near Makkah called *Minā*, where there is a tent city, and the people pray Ẓuhr, ‘Aṣr, Maghrib, ‘Ishā’, and Fajr there. The prayers that are 4 rak‘ahs (Ẓuhr, ‘Aṣr, and ‘Ishā’) are shortened to two rak‘ahs each, but the prayers are not combined.

[Note: Technically, staying at Minā on the 8th of Dhūl-Ḥijjah is only sunnah. It is not obligatory, so if one cannot go there for whatever reason, then one can proceed to ‘Arafāt on the 9th, and their Ḥajj will still be valid. The starting time for reaching ‘Arafāt is Fajr on the 9th of Dhūl-Ḥijjah, and the cutoff for reaching ‘Arafāt is Fajr on the 10th of Dhūl-Ḥijjah.]

[Note: If one is performing Ḥajj Ifrād, then it is sunnah, but not obligatory, to do *ṭawāf al-qudūm* (the ṭawāf of arrival) and sa'ī.]

The 9th Day of Dhūl-Ḥijjah

The second day of Ḥajj is the 9th of Dhūl-Ḥijjah, and this day is called *Yawmu 'Arafah*. Standing at *Arafāt* is a pillar of Ḥajj, and without it, Ḥajj is invalid.

'Abdur-Raḥmān ibn Ya'mar (ra) narrated: The Messenger of God (saws) said, "The Ḥajj is Arafāt. The Ḥajj is Arafāt. The Ḥajj is Arafāt." (Jāmi' At-Tirmidhī, Ḥadīth 2975; Zubayr 'Alī Za'ī graded it ṣaḥīḥ.)

[Note: While it is highly recommended to fast on the Day of 'Arafah for non-pilgrims, pilgrims at 'Arafāt should not fast.]

After Fajr is prayed in Minā on the 9th of Dhūl-Ḥijjah, the pilgrim starts heading towards 'Arafāt, which is a large plain with a hill to the southeast of Makkah, and it is recommended to recite the talbiyah while going there. On the way to Arafāt, it is recommended to stop at a place called *Namirah* until noon. When the sun passes its zenith, the pilgrim moves to a place called *'Uranah*, which is next to 'Arafāt and in front of Masjid Namirah. There the imām gives a khuṭbah (sermon), and he then leads the people in praying Ẓuhr and 'Aṣr. Ẓuhr and 'Aṣr are shortened to two rak'ahs each, and they are combined (i.e., prayed one directly after another) during the time of Ẓuhr. One adhān is given, and two iqāmahs are given, and no extra prayer is prayed between Ẓuhr and 'Aṣr. Whoever is unable to pray with the imām should pray in the same way on their own, or with others in a similar situation.

Then the pilgrim proceeds to 'Arafāt, and if they are able to, they should stand on the hill, which is called *Jabal Ar-Raḥmah (the Mount of Mercy)*. If one is not able to stand on the hill, then all of Arafāt is a place for standing. One should face the qiblah and busy themselves with worship, reciting the Qur'ān or raising their hands with their palms upward in supplication. One can make du'ā' or recite the talbiyah, and it is highly recommended to say the following dhikr:

"Lā ilāha illallāhu waḥdahū lā sharīka lah. Lahul-mulku wa lahul-ḥamd. Wa huwa 'alā kulli shay'in qadīr."

“There is no god except for Allāh, alone, without associate. His is the dominion, and His is all praise. And He has power over everything.”

And the pilgrim can occasionally add in the talbiyah:

“Innamal-khayru khayrul-ākhirati.”

“Indeed, all good is the good of the Hereafter.”

And the following ḥadīth states:

‘Ā’ishah (ra) narrated: The Messenger of God (saws) said, “There is no day when God ransoms more slaves from the Fire than the day of ‘Arafah. He draws near, then He boasts about them before the angels and says, ‘What do these people want?’” (Ṣaḥīḥ Muslim, Ḥadīth 1348)

When the sun sets, the pilgrim calmly leaves ‘Arafāt for a place called *Muzdalifah.* In Muzdalifah, one adhān is given, and then Maghrib and ‘Ishā’ are prayed by combining them (i.e., praying one directly after another), with two iqāmahs. Also, ‘Ishā’ is shortened to two rak‘ahs. No extra prayer is prayed between Maghrib and ‘Ishā’, and no extra prayer is prayed after ‘Ishā’. Then one may rest until Fajr. However, the weak and the women may proceed after half of the night has passed in order to avoid the heaviness of the crowd the next day. One may also collect pebbles, the size of date seeds, in Muzdalifah to use for a later ritual called *ramī* (stoning). At least 49 pebbles will be needed, but one may collect more. Also, the pebbles do not have to be from Muzdalifah.

The 10th Day of Dhūl-Ḥijjah

The third day of Ḥajj is the 10th of Dhūl-Ḥijjah, and this day is called *Yawm An-Naḥr*, the Day of Sacrifice. This is also the holiday of ‘Īd Al-Aḍḥā, although pilgrims do not partake in the celebrations of this day that non-pilgrims partake in.

In Muzdalifah, one prays Fajr in the early part of its time, and then goes to *Mash‘ar Al-Ḥarām*, which is a small mountain in Muzdalifah. The pilgrim faces the qiblah and does dhikr, saying, “Lā ilāha illallāh (There is no god except for Allāh)” and, “Allāhu Akbar (God is Greater).” One may also make du‘ā’. If one cannot reach Mash‘ar Al-Ḥarām, then one may do dhikr and make du‘ā’ anywhere in Muzdalifah. This continues until the sun becomes very bright. Before the sun has finished rising, one calmly leaves for Minā while reciting the talbiyah. When one reaches the river valley called *Wādī Muḥassar*, one should hurry through it, if possible. This is because this valley is where God destroyed the army of an Abyssinian ruler named Abraha when he attempted to destroy the Ka'bah. The army was destroyed by a flock of birds that pelted them with stones. This occurred the year that the Prophet (saws) was born, and he did not like to spend too much time in a place where people had met God's wrath.

In Minā, *after sunrise*, one performs ramī, or stoning, in which one stones a certain pillar. If one has no pebbles, one picks up pebbles in Minā. *Jamarāt* is the Arabic plural of *jamrah*, which means "pillar."

[Note: The story behind stoning the jamarāt is that thousands of years ago, God commanded Prophet Abraham (as) to sacrifice his son. Muslims believe that the son to be sacrificed was Ishmael (as), and Ishmael (as) consented to this. Then Satan came to Abraham (as) to tempt him into not sacrificing Ishmael (as). However, Abraham (as) resisted Satan's temptation and threw pebbles at Satan to drive him away. For this reason, the pilgrims throw stones at the jamarāt, and this is a symbolic act that represents driving away Satan. Like all acts of worship, this is meant to venerate God, and one should avoid getting angry or exaggerating when throwing the pebbles because Satan is not literally in the jamarāt.]

One proceeds to *jamratul-'aqabah*, which is the last of the jamarāt and the closest one to the direction of Makkah. Then the pilgrim faces jamratul-'aqabah, and it is sunnah to have Makkah to their left and Minā to the right. Then the pilgrim throws at the pillar seven pebbles, one after another. When throwing each pebble, the pilgrim says, "Allāhu Akbar." The pebbles must either hit the pillar or land in the pit around the pillar. After the stoning is finished, the time for reciting the talbiyah is finished. If one is not able to perform ramī in the morning after sunrise, then they may perform it in the afternoon, or even up until the night.

[Note: If one is too old, weak, or sick, one may appoint someone to throw the pebbles for them.]

After performing ramī, this is considered the first stage of exiting iḥrām for Ḥajj. What was forbidden to one in iḥrām becomes permissible *except* for any form of intimacy with one's spouse. That is still forbidden. But a man may put on regular clothes and use perfume. However, if one wants to remain in this state of having partially exited iḥrām, then one must perform *ṭawāf al-ifāḍah* on that same day, after sacrificing an animal and shaving the head or cutting the hair. If one does not do this by Maghrib, then one returns to the complete state of iḥrām.

After performing ramī, one slaughters a sacrificial animal, or *hadī*, anywhere in Minā or Makkah. One may also appoint someone else to do the actual slaughtering on their behalf. If the pilgrim is doing Tamattu‘ and cannot afford an animal, then they must fast for three days during Ḥajj and seven days when they return from Ḥajj. One may sacrifice a sheep or share in a seventh of a cow or a camel that is being sacrificed.

[Note: The slaughtering of a sacrificial animal, in addition to benefiting the poor who receive its meat, may be a reminder of when God allowed Abraham [(as)] to sacrifice a ram instead of his son Ishmael [(as)].]

[Note: Slaughtering a sacrificial animal is not obligatory for those doing Ḥajj Ifrād, but it is *mustaḥabb* (favored), and there is blessing in doing it.]

The method of slaughtering is to have the animal face the qiblah, lying on its left side and putting one's right foot on the animal's right side. In the case of a camel, one slaughters it while it is standing and facing the qiblah with its left leg tied. At the time of slaughtering, one says:

"Bismillāhi, wallāhu akbar. Allāhumma minka wa laka. Allāhumma taqabbal minnī."

"In the name of God, and God is greater. O God, (this is) from You and for You. O God, accept it from me."

Then one slaughters the animal by slicing it at the throat. If one does not perform their sacrifice on Yawm An-Naḥr, then one may do it on *Ayyām At-Tashrīq (the Days of Drying Meat)*, which are the 11th, 12th, and 13th of Dhūl-Ḥijjah. Regardless, the pilgrim eats from the hadī and feeds the poor with it.

[Note: It is highly recommended that all Muslims around the world sacrifice an animal – a goat, sheep, cow, or camel – on Yawm An-Naḥr, which is ‘Īd Al-Aḍḥā, or on Ayyām At-Tashrīq. The sacrifice is called *uḍḥiyah* or *qurbāni,* and the meat is given to the poor or divided into three shares: one share for oneself, one share for one's family and friends, and one share for the poor and the needy. This sacrifice is not obligatory, but it is *sunnah mu'akkadah*, which means that the Prophet (saws) always did it.]

After sacrificing an animal, one shaves their head or cuts their hair, if they are a man. A woman only cuts her hair the length of a fingertip.

It is also sunnah for the imām to give a khuṭbah on Yawm An-Naḥr in Minā, during the forenoon.

Then one returns to Masjid Al-Ḥarām in Makkah and performs ṭawāf around the Ka'bah, and this ṭawāf is called ṭawāf al-ifāḍah, and it is also called *ṭawāf az-ziyārah*. Ṭawāf al-ifāḍah is a pillar of Ḥajj, and without it one's Ḥajj is invalid. It is performed in the exact manner as the ṭawāf of 'Umrah except that the male pilgrim does not uncover his right shoulder or jog. After ṭawāf, it is sunnah to pray two rak'ahs behind Maqām Ibrāhīm. Then the pilgrim does sa'ī, going between Ṣafā and Marwah seven times, as it is done in 'Umrah. The sa'ī of Ḥajj is also a pillar of Ḥajj, and without it one's Ḥajj is invalid.

After this, the pilgrim exits iḥrām completely, and everything that was forbidden in iḥrām becomes permissible, even sexual intercourse with one's spouse. Then the pilgrim prays Ẓuhr in Makkah, and one may drink from the well of Zamzam. Thereafter, one returns to Minā for Ayyām At-Tashrīq and their nights.

The 11th Day of Dhūl-Ḥijjah

On the 11th of Dhūl-Ḥijjah, the pilgrim again performs ramī, also called *ramī al-jamarāt*, or the stoning of the pillars, of which there are three, and this time the pilgrim stones all three jamarāt. This stoning takes place *after* noon (Ẓuhr) comes in, and the time for its permissibility lasts until night.

The pilgrim begins with the first jamrah, which is the closest to Masjid Al-Khayf. One throws seven pebbles, one after another, and when throwing each pebble the pilgrim says, "Allāhu Akbar." The pebbles must either hit the pillar or land in the pit around the pillar. Then one goes onward a little, faces the qiblah, raises their hands with the palms upward, and makes du'ā'.

Then the pilgrim goes to the second jamrah, which is in the middle. One throws seven pebbles, one after another, and when throwing each pebble the pilgrim says, “Allāhu Akbar.” The pebbles must either hit the pillar or land in the pit around the pillar. Then one moves to the left, faces the qiblah, raises their hands with the palms upward, and makes du‘ā’.

Then the pilgrim goes to the third jamrah, jamratul-‘aqabah, which is the last of the jamarāt and the closest one to the direction of Makkah. Then the pilgrim faces jamratul-‘aqabah, with Makkah to their left and Minā to the right, and throws seven pebbles, one after another. As before, when throwing each pebble the pilgrim says, “Allāhu Akbar.” The pebbles must either hit the pillar or land in the pit around the pillar. Then the pilgrim does not make du‘ā’ and leaves the jamarāt, returning to their tent in Minā.

The 12th and 13th Days of Dhūl-Ḥijjah

On the 12th of Dhūl-Ḥijjah, the pilgrim again performs ramī al-jamarāt, in exactly the same manner as the day before. As before, this stoning takes place *after* noon (Ẓuhr) comes in, and the time for its permissibility lasts until night.

After stoning the jamarāt on the 12th of Dhūl-Ḥijjah, if the pilgrim wants to hasten to leave Minā, that is permissible. However, if one is still in Minā by Maghrib, then one must stay there for the 13th of Dhūl-Ḥijjah. Regardless, staying in Minā for the 13th of Dhūl-Ḥijjah is sunnah, so it is better to do that.

If one is in Minā on the 13th of Dhūl-Ḥijjah, the pilgrim again performs ramī al-jamarāt, in exactly the same manner as they did on the 11th and 12th days. As before, this stoning takes place *after* noon (Ẓuhr) comes in, and the time for its permissibility lasts until night.

After completing ramī al-jamarāt on the 12th or 13th of Dhūl-Ḥijjah, then one returns to Makkah and stays there as long they want to. When one decides to end their Ḥajj and leave Makkah, then one must perform the *farewell ṭawāf (ṭawāf al-wadā‘)*, and it must be the last thing one does in Makkah. One performs ṭawāf as they normally would, except that for men there is no jogging or uncovering the right shoulder.

Then one may pray two rak‘ahs behind Maqām Ibrāhīm and drink Zamzam water. One may also take some Zamzam water with them.

Afterwards, one exits Masjid Al-Ḥarām with their left foot first, and one may say the du'ā' for leaving the masjid, which is:

"Bismillāhi, waṣ-ṣalātu was-salāmu 'alā Rasūlillāhi. Allāhumma innī as'aluka min faḍlika. Allāhumma 'ṣimnī minash-shayṭānir-rajīm."

"In the name of God, and commendations and peace be upon the Messenger of God. O God, indeed, I ask You for Your favor. O God, protect me from Satan the accursed."

Then one's Ḥajj is complete.

This concludes the overview of Ḥajj.

Menstruation during 'Umrah and Ḥajj

As wuḍū' is a prerequisite for ṭawāf and ṣalāh, female pilgrims who are menstruating are not allowed to perform ṭawāf or pray ṣalāh.

If a woman is doing 'Umrah by itself, without performing Ḥajj, then she must wait until her period is over, do ghusl, and then perform 'Umrah.

If a woman is doing Ḥajj Tamattu', and she is on her period when it is time to perform 'Umrah, then her Ḥajj automatically becomes a type of Ḥajj Qirān. This is because later, if her period is finished by the time she does ṭawāf al-ifāḍah, she must make the intention that the one ṭawāf counts for both the ṭawāf of 'Umrah and ṭawāf al-ifāḍah. Thus, she gets rewarded for two ṭawāfs by doing one ṭawāf. The same applies for when she does sa'ī after ṭawāf al-ifāḍah: she makes the intention that the one sa'ī counts for both the sa'ī of 'Umrah and the sa'ī of Ḥajj.

The female pilgrim who is menstruating during ṭawāf al-ifāḍah should not perform it when everyone else does, nor should she pray the two rak'ahs behind Maqām Ibrāhīm. It is permissible to delay ṭawāf al-ifāḍah until one has stopped menstruating. When the female pilgrim who had been menstruating performs ṭawāf al-wadā', she may also intend that she is performing ṭawāf al-ifāḍah. Thus, she is rewarded for two ṭawāfs by performing one ṭawāf because she has the intention for it to count for both.

Also, the only people exempt from ṭawāf al-wadā‘ are menstruating women, and they do not have to make it up, as long as they did ṭawāf al-ifāḍah because ṭawāf al-ifāḍah is a pillar of Ḥajj. However, if they did not do ṭawāf al-ifāḍah due to menstruation, then they must do ṭawāf al-wadā‘ with the intention for it to count for both ṭawāfs. If one is still menstruating by the end of Ḥajj, then one must wait for their menstruation to end and *then* perform ṭawāf al-wadā‘ with the intention for it to count for both ṭawāfs.

The Pillars and Obligatory Acts of Ḥajj

Scholars have deduced that the pillars (arkān) of Ḥajj are four, to be performed in the following order, and without them Ḥajj is invalid:

1. Iḥrām
2. Staying at ‘Arafāt
3. Ṭawāf al-ifāḍah
4. Sa‘ī

The obligatory (wājibāt) acts of Ḥajj are necessary parts of Ḥajj, but if one misses an obligatory act, then one must sacrifice a sheep as compensation, and its meat goes to the poor, and then one's Ḥajj will be valid. The obligatory acts of Ḥajj are:

1. Assuming iḥrām from the mīqāt
2. Extending one's stay at ‘Arafāt from the afternoon until a part of the night
3. Staying overnight in Muzdalifah until halfway through the night, except for those whose job it is to bring water or tend to livestock
4. Staying overnight in Minā during Ayyām At-Tashrīq, except for those whose job it is to bring water or tend to livestock
5. Stoning the jamarāt in the correct order
6. Shaving the head or cutting the hair
7. Ṭawāf al-wadā‘, except for menstruating women who have performed ṭawāf al-ifāḍah

Visiting the Mosque of the Prophet (saws) in Al-Madīnah

Visiting Masjid An-Nabawī in Al-Madīnah is not a part of Ḥajj or 'Umrah, although many people visit Masjid An-Nabawī before or after undertaking a pilgrimage to Makkah. This is permissible because of the blessings to be gained in visiting Masjid An-Nabawī. And the following ḥadīths state:

Abū Hurayrah (ra) narrated: The Prophet (saws) said, "Do not set out on a (religious) journey except to three mosques: Al-Masjid Al-Ḥarām, the Masjid of the Messenger of God (saws), and Masjid Al-Aqṣā." (Ṣaḥīḥ Al-Bukhārī, Ḥadīth 1189; Ṣaḥīḥ Muslim, Ḥadīth 1397)

'Abdullāh ibn Az-Zubayr (ra) narrated: The Messenger of God (saws) said, "Prayer in this masjid of mine is better than a thousand prayers in any other masjid, except Al-Masjid Al-Ḥarām. Prayer in Al-Masjid Al-Ḥarām is one hundred times better than prayer in this mosque of mine." (Musnad Aḥmad, Ḥadīth 15685; Ibn Ḥibbān and Al-Albānī graded it ṣaḥīḥ.)

Abū Ad-Dardā' (ra) narrated: The Prophet (saws) said, "The virtue of prayer in Al-Masjid Al-Ḥarām is one hundred thousand times better than prayer elsewhere, prayer in this masjid of mine is one thousand times better than prayer elsewhere, and prayer in Bayt Al-Maqdis (i.e., Masjid Al-Aqṣā) is better than five hundred prayers elsewhere." (Shu'ab Al-Īmān by Al-Bayhaqī, Ḥadīth 3845; Al-Bazzār graded it ḥasan.)

The Rawḍah and the Grave of the Prophet (saws)

Abū Hurayrah (ra) narrated: The Prophet (saws) said, "Between my house and my pulpit there is a garden of the gardens of Paradise, and my pulpit is on my fountain tank (i.e., Al-Kawthar – a blessed fountain in the Hereafter)." (Ṣaḥīḥ Al-Bukhārī, Ḥadīth 1196; Ṣaḥīḥ Muslim, Ḥadīth 1391)

Note that the Arabic word for pulpit is *minbar*, and the word for garden used in the ḥadīth is *rawḍah*, the plural of which is *riyāḍ*, and the word for fountain tank is *ḥawḍ*. One is likely to encounter these words when visiting that location of Masjid An-Nabawī, which is called the *Rawḍah*. It is a very special place, filled with peace, where many people try to pray.

Directly next to the Rawḍah is the grave (Arabic: *qabr*) of the Prophet Muḥammad (saws). His closest companion, Abū Bakr, is buried next to him; and his second closest companion, ‘Umar, is buried next to them. Note that the Prophet (saws) warned people against taking the graves of prophets as places of worship (see Ṣaḥīḥ Al-Bukhārī, Ḥadīth 1390 and Ṣaḥīḥ Muslim, Ḥadīth 532), but his house was already connected to the masjid. Moreover, he taught that prophets should be buried in the place where they die, so when he when died in ‘Ā’ishah’s room, he was buried there. Over the years, the masjid grew in size and encompassed what used to be the house of the Prophet (saws). However, Muslims are *not* under any circumstance supposed to pray *to* the grave of the Prophet (saws), nor are they supposed to seek blessings from it. Doing these things would be acts of shirk (associating partners with God). Nevertheless, one is allowed to greet the Prophet Muḥammad (saws), Abū Bakr, and ‘Umar at this site, and this does not count as shirk, as one does not *pray to* any of them, one just greets them. One may greet them as follows:

As-Salāmu ‘alayka yā Rasūlallāh. (Peace be upon you, O Messenger of God.)

As-Salāmu ‘alayka yā Abā Bakr. (Peace be upon you, O Abū Bakr.)

As-Salāmu ‘alayka yā ‘Umar. (Peace be upon you, O ‘Umar.)

Masjid Qubā’

While one is in Al-Madīnah, it is also permissible to visit Masjid Qubā’ and to pray there. When the Prophet Muḥammad (saws) made his Hijrah and arrived at the outskirts of Al-Madīnah, he laid the foundations for the first masjid to be built since God renewed Islām through him. In other words, no masjid had been built in Makkah or Al-Madīnah since the Prophet (saws) received his first revelation until Masjid Qubā’, and it even chronologically preceded Masjid An-Nabawī. The following ḥadīth states:

Sahl ibn Ḥunayf (ra) narrated: The Messenger of God (saws) said, “Whoever purifies himself in his house, then comes to the mosque of Qubā’ and prays in it, he will have a reward like ‘Umrah.” (Sunan Ibn Mājah, Ḥadīth 1412; Al-Albānī graded it ṣaḥīḥ.)

Part 4: Miscellaneous Topics

Chapter 12

The Islāmic View of Different Scriptures

Belief in All of the Scriptures

Islām teaches that Abraham (as) was given scriptures called the Ṣuḥuf (literally meaning "Pages" or "Scrolls"), Moses (as) was given the Tawrāh (Torah), David (as) was given the Zabūr (often said to be the Psalms), Jesus (as) was given the Injīl (Gospel), and Muḥammad (saws) was given the Qur'ān. Another name for the Qur'ān is the Furqān (the Criterion). Muslims are required to believe in all of these scriptures.

136 Believers, believe in God and His Messenger and in the Book He sent down to His Messenger, as well as what He sent down before. He who denies God, His angels, His books, His messengers and the Last Day has surely gone far astray. (Qur'ān 4:136)

But what does belief in these scriptures mean? Belief in the previous scriptures simply means believing that they were sent down in the past. Belief in the previous scriptures does *not* mean *following* them all in the present day. There is a clear distinction between believing in something and following it. The Qur'ān replaces the previous scriptures that established authority, namely the Torah and the Gospel. Therefore, Muslims believe in the Torah and the Gospel, but they only follow the Qur'ān.

Additionally, belief in previous scriptures means believing in what was sent down *originally*, not in what people claim are scriptures today. This distinction is made because Muslims believe that the Torah and the Gospel were changed by people over time. So when God says to believe in what He sent down, it means to believe in what *He* sent down, not in what people *claim* He sent down. If Person A leaves Person B a note, and someone changes the note, and then Person A tells Person B,

"Believe in what I wrote," Person A is referring to what was *originally* written, even if Person B thinks the note says something different.

The Alteration of the Torah and the Gospel

So why do Muslims believe that the Torah and the Gospel were changed? Critics of Islām sometimes claim that nowhere in the Qur'ān does it state that the Torah and the Gospel have been changed. While details of the alteration of the Torah and the Gospel have not been provided in the Qur'ān and the Sunnah, the notion that they have been changed is attested to. The Qur'ān states:

75 Do you then hope that they will believe in you when some of them have already heard the word of God and then, after having understood it, they knowingly distort it? (Qur'ān 2:75)

13 Since they broke their solemn pledge, We laid on them Our curse and hardened their hearts. They distorted the meaning of the revealed words, taking them out of their context, and forgot much of what they were enjoined. You will constantly discover treachery on their part, except for a few of them. But pardon them, and bear with them. Truly, God loves the doers of good. 14 We also made a covenant with those who say, 'We are Christians.' But they too have forgotten much of what they were enjoined. So, We have put enmity and hatred between them till the Day of Judgement. And soon God will declare to them what they have been doing. 15 People of the Book! Our Messenger has come to make clear to you much of what you have hidden of the Scriptures and disregarding much. A light has now come to you from God and a clear Book, 16 whereby God guides to the ways of peace all who seek His good pleasure, bringing them from darkness to the light, by His will, and guiding them to a straight path. (Qur'ān 5:13-16)

Critics of Islām state that the verses quoted above are merely stating that people in the time of the Prophet Muḥammad (saws) were intentionally misquoting scriptures or taking them out of context, not that those scriptures had been permanently changed in the past. However, it appeared to be the opinion of the Prophet Muḥammad (saws) himself, as well as the opinion of his young companion, Ibn 'Abbās, that the Muslims should not trust everything that is said in what people now claim to be the Torah and the Gospel.

Abū Hurayrah [(ra)] *narrated: The People of the Book used to read the Torah in Hebrew and then explain it in Arabic to the Muslims. The Messenger of God* [(saws)] *said (to the Muslims), "Do not believe the People of the Book, nor disbelieve them, but say, 'We believe in God and whatever is revealed to us, and whatever is revealed to you.'" (Ṣaḥīḥ Al-Bukhārī, Ḥadīth 7362)*

Ibn 'Abbās [(ra)] *narrated: O Muslims! How do you ask the People of the Book, though your book (i.e., the Qur'ān) which was revealed to His Prophet* [(saws)] *is the most recent information from God, and you recite it, the book that has not been distorted? God has revealed to you that the People of the Book have changed with their own hands what was revealed to them, and they have said, "This is from God," in order to get some worldly benefit thereby. Is not the knowledge revealed to you sufficient to prevent you from asking them? By God, I have never seen any one of them asking (Muslims) about what has been revealed to you. (Ṣaḥīḥ Al-Bukhārī, Ḥadīth 2685)*

So why would the Prophet Muḥammad [(saws)] and his companions warn people about trusting the scriptures of the People of the Book if those scriptures had not been altered? And Ibn 'Abbās even said that the People of the Book changed what had been revealed to them whereas the Qur'ān was not distorted. Furthermore, suppose that one believes that the Qur'ān is the literal, dictated word of God, and one reads the Torah and the Gospel, which were also the words of God. However, when one reads the Torah and the Gospel, they find things in them that contradict the Qur'ān. It then follows that the Torah and the Gospel must have been changed, at least in part, because they do not match up with the Qur'ān. And this does not contradict the Qur'ān or the Sunnah because of the verses and the ḥadīths that have been quoted above. Of course, this rationale depends upon one's acceptance of the Qur'ān as the word of God.

The Permissibility of Reading the Torah and the Gospel

Despite the alteration of the Torah and the Gospel, the Qur'ān and the Sunnah do affirm the permissibility of consulting them to show that they confirm that the Qur'ān is also from God.

[94]If you [O Prophet] are in any doubt concerning what We have sent down to you, then question those who have read the Book before you. The truth has come to you from your Lord, so do not be one of the doubters. (Qur'ān 10:94)

Ibn 'Umar (ra) narrated: A group of Jews came and invited the Messenger of God (saws) to Quff. So he visited them in their school. They said, "O Abū Al-Qāsim (i.e., a nickname for the Prophet Muḥammad (saws), meaning "Father of Al-Qāsim"), one of our men has committed fornication with a woman, so pronounce judgment upon them." They placed a cushion for the Messenger of Allah (saws), who sat on it and said, "Bring the Torah." It was then brought. He then withdrew the cushion from beneath him and placed the Torah on it, saying, "I believe in you and in Him Who revealed you." (Sunan Abū Dāwūd, Ḥadīth 4449; Al-Albānī graded it ṣaḥīḥ.)

Regarding the Qur'ān verse cited above, it refers to observing that the Torah and the Gospel have similar stories and commands to what is in the Qur'ān, so this shows that they all came from the same source, which is God. And regarding the Prophet Muḥammad (saws) consulting a copy of the Torah in order to give a legal verdict, he judged Jews by the Torah, not by the Qur'ān. This may demonstrate the Prophet's (saws) fair nature in that he did not impose all the commands of the Qur'ān and the Sunnah upon people who did not accept them. Rather, he allowed them to abide by their previously established laws in what they claimed was the Torah. Furthermore, his saying to the copy of the Torah, "I believe in you," meant that he believed in the original Torah and this applied to the parts of that Torah copy that were unaltered.

There is no contradiction between being skeptical of details in the modern-day Torah and Gospel and using them in a general sense to confirm that the Qur'ān is from God. This is because not *everything* in the Torah and the Gospel has been changed, and one may clearly see this by observing the parts of them that align with the Qur'ān and the Sunnah.

Changing the Words of God

There are also those who say that the notion of people changing parts of the Torah and the Gospel contradict the parts of the Qur'ān which state that none can change the words of God.

[27]Proclaim what has been revealed to you from your Lord's Book. None can change His words. You shall find no refuge besides Him. (Qur'ān 18:27)

The Qur'ān also states that none can change the words of God in 6:34, 6:115, and 10:64. However, this refers to the *decrees* of God, and it may also refer to the Heavenly transcription of His words. This does not refer to when people write down His words in this world. Obviously, anyone can come along and change what is written on a piece of paper, so in that way people changed the Torah and the Gospel, but they could not change the decrees of God. This leads people to ask, "Why did God not prevent people from changing the Torah and the Gospel?" The answer is that God does what He wills, and He does not reveal all of His wisdom. We can only speculate on the wisdom of allowing the Torah and the Gospel to be altered. Perhaps it was because God wanted to test the People of the Book by allowing them to change their scriptures and by Him giving more importance to the Qur'ān.

However, the Qur'ān in a way preserves the Torah and the Gospel because it contains the essence of their message, which is the Oneness of God and the necessity to believe in Him and to serve Him through good deeds. The Qur'ān itself states this:

[48]We have sent down the Book to you with the truth, fulfilling [the predictions] revealed in the previous scriptures and determining what is true therein, and as a guardian over it. Judge, therefore, between them by what God has revealed, and do not follow their vain desires turning away from the truth that has come to you. To every one of you We have ordained a law and a way, and had God so willed, He would have made you all a single community, but He did not so will, in order that He might try you by what He has given you. Compete, then, with one another in doing good works. To God you shall all return. Then He will make clear to you about what you have been disputing. (Qur'ān 5:48)

The Torah and the Gospel point to the Qur'ān

Some may also wonder why the Qur'ān states the following:

[68]Say [O Prophet], 'People of the Book, you have no ground to stand on until you observe the Torah and the Gospel and what is revealed to you from your Lord.' What is revealed to you from your Lord will surely increase many of

them in rebellion and in their denial of the truth. But do not grieve for those who deny the truth. (Qur'ān 5:68)

In telling people to observe the Torah and the Gospel, the Qur'ān is saying to follow those scriptures by following the Qur'ān. Note that the verse says, "and what has been revealed to you from your Lord," and this refers to the Qur'ān. The Qur'ān states that the Prophet Muḥammad (saws) was prophesized in the Torah and the Gospel in places such as the following:

157 *Also for those who follow the Messenger—the unlettered prophet they find described in the Torah that is with them, and in the Gospel—who commands them to do right and forbids them to do wrong, who makes good things lawful to them and bad things unlawful, who will relieve them of their burdens and of the shackles that weigh upon them. Those that believe in him and honor him, those that aid him and follow the light sent down with him, shall surely triumph. (Qur'ān 7:157)*

The Qur'ān gives similar statements in 3:81-82 and 61:6. As to where one may find mention of the Prophet Muḥammad (saws) in what Jews and Christians claim are the Torah and Gospel, some point to passages in the Hebrew and Christian Bibles that include Deuteronomy 18:15-22 and John 14:16. However, Jewish rabbis and Christian priests and pastors interpret these verses differently.

When and how could the Torah and the Gospel have been changed?

As to when and how the Torah and the Gospel were changed, Islām does not give us details. However, one may look to history to see how there is reason to doubt their complete preservation. Regarding the Torah, the majority of the Israelites rejected it for hundreds of years after Moses (as) and up until the time of Ezra. Some did keep it, but they were in the minority, and the prophets were entrusted to preserve it, but the people rejected the prophets. Most of the Israelites adopted the practices of their neighboring pagan nations, taking to idolatry and polytheism, and, as the Qur'ān and the Hebrew Bible both state, they threw the Torah behind their backs (see: the Qur'ān 2:101 and 3:187 and Nehemiah 9:26). This persisted for hundreds of years in a time long before books could be printed and widely distributed. Thus, there was plenty of opportunity for lapses in the preservation of the Torah to occur during this time.

Regarding the Gospel, Christians believe that certain apostles and disciples of Jesus (as), as well as people who knew Jesus's (as) apostles, authored the New Testament. However, there existed other early groups of Christians, and they had beliefs about Jesus (as) that differed from what was written in what would later become the standard New Testament. Among these groups were the Ebionites, who are mentioned by the bishop Irenaeus, the early church historian Eusebius, and other Christian writers. The Ebionites believed that although Jesus (as) was the Messiah, he was fully human, and they had their own writings and their own alleged ties to Jesus's (as) apostles. So there was not one agreed upon narrative about the nature of Jesus (as) after his time, and this leaves room for the Gospel to have been altered.

Note that this is the speculation of the author, and there is no standard Islāmic narrative regarding who changed what in the Torah and the Gospel and when.

The Preservation of the Qur'ān

Muslims believe that the Qur'ān has been, and will be, preserved and that it is the final revelation from God.

9It is We who have sent down the Reminder and We will, most surely, safeguard it. (Qur'ān 15:9)

Regarding the history of preservation of the Qur'ān in its written form, companions of the Prophet Muḥammad (saws) wrote it down during his lifetime on whatever they could, using materials such as palm stalks or stones. The preservation of the Qur'ān after the Prophet's (saws) life is mentioned in long ḥadīths in Ṣaḥīḥ Al-Bukhārī, Ḥadīths 4986 and 4987. The summary of these ḥadīths is that when Abū Bakr was the caliph, he ordered Zayd ibn Thābit to collect the portions of the Qur'ān that had previously been written and use them to write a single, standardized codex of the Qur'ān. Zayd did this, and the codex was kept with Abū Bakr. After the death of Abū Bakr the codex passed to Caliph 'Umar, and after 'Umar's death the codex passed to his daughter Ḥafṣah, a widow of the Prophet (saws). During the reign of Caliph 'Uthmān, he obtained the codex from Ḥafṣah, and he appointed a committee, which included Zayd ibn Thābit, to make copies of the written Qur'ān. They wrote it in the dialect of the Quraysh because the Qur'ān had been revealed in that dialect. The copies were then distributed to different Muslim provinces, and 'Uthmān had the old Qur'ān fragments and copies, that were not official codices, burnt. 'Uthmān ordered the Qur'ān fragments to be burnt because some people may have spelled words according to their own Arabic dialects. This affected the pronunciation of certain words but not their meaning. Nevertheless, with many non-Arabs embracing Islām, there needed to be a standardized version of the Qur'ān and any manuscripts with spellings that indicated different pronunciations could not be circulated because that might have confused people. Therefore, 'Uthmān had all the extra Qur'ān copies and fragments burnt, except for those that had been standardized. None of the companions of the Prophet (saws) objected to this, as is stated in the narration that reads:

Muṣ'ab ibn Sa'd narrated: I saw a large number of people present when 'Uthman burnt the manuscripts. They liked it. And not one of them opposed it. (Kitāb Al-Maṣāḥif by Ibn Abū Dāwūd; Ibn Kathīr graded it ṣaḥīḥ.)

Furthermore, Muslim historians never shied away from recording controversial things, and there was no group of companions of the Prophet (saws) with a different version of the Qur'ān complaining that the real Qur'ān was being destroyed or changed. And there was never a time when the majority of Muslims abandoned the Qur'ān in favor of idolatry, as happened with the ancient Israelites and the Torah. The only thing that some non-Muslim critics point to is the objections of the companion 'Abdullāh ibn Mas'ūd during the caliphate of 'Uthmān. However, Ibn Mas'ūd's objections were to the young age of Zayd ibn Thābit and to giving up his personal Qur'ān copy. Regarding 'Uthmān's actions in general, Ibn Mas'ūd came to view them favorably, as the scholar Ibn Kathīr explained in his history book Al-Bidāyah wa An-Nihāyah.

It should also be noted that the Qur'ān was preserved not only in written form but orally too. Many companions of the Prophet Muḥammad (saws) memorized the entire Qur'ān by heart. Among them would have been the four caliphs: Abū Bakr, 'Umar, 'Uthmān, and 'Alī. This is because they were the leaders of the Muslims not just politically but spiritually, and the Prophet (saws) stipulated that those who know the most Qur'ān should lead the ṣalāh (prayer) (see Ṣaḥīḥ Muslim, Ḥadīth 673). 'Abdullāh ibn Mas'ūd, Sālim the freed slave of Abū Ḥudhayfah, Ubayy ibn Ka'b, and Mu'ādh ibn Jabal would likely also have had the entire Qur'ān memorized because the Prophet (saws) said that people should learn the Qur'ān from them (see Ṣaḥīḥ Al-Bukhārī, Ḥadīths 3806 and 4999). From these and other companions, many learned and memorized the entire Qur'ān, and in each generation up until the present day there have been, and are, many who memorize the entire Qur'ān. One who has the entire Qur'ān memorized is called a *ḥāfiẓ* (preserver) of the Qur'ān.

Chapter 13

Accurate Prophecies in the Qur'ān

A Prophecy about the Romans

During the lifetime of the Prophet Muḥammad (saws), the Romans (i.e., the Byzantines) and the Persians (i.e., the Sasanians), the two great empires of that setting, were at war with one another. Around the time when Muḥammad (saws) and the Muslims were being persecuted by the disbelievers in the tribe of Quraysh in Makkah, the Romans suffered heavy losses from the Persians, who captured from the Romans Damascus, in 613, and Jerusalem, in 614.

Around that time, God revealed the following to Muḥammad (saws):

2The Romans have been defeated 3in a nearby land. They will reverse their defeat with a victory 4within three to nine years, [for] with God rests all power of decision, first and last. On that day the believers too will have cause to rejoice 5with the help of God. He helps whom He pleases. He is the Almighty, and the Most Merciful. 6[This is] God's promise. Never does God fail to fulfil His promise—but most people do not know this. (Qur'ān 30:2-6)

In the year 622 the Romans, led by Emperor Heraclius, won a crushing victory over the Persians in Cappadocia. The Hijrah from Makkah to Al-Madīnah also took place in 622. It may therefore be concluded that this twofold prophecy, of the Byzantines gaining a victory within three to nine years as well as the Muslims' rejoicing at that time, was fulfilled.

A Prophecy about the Muslim Victory at Badr

On the day of the Battle of Badr, before the fighting started, the Prophet (saws) recited the following from the Qur'ān:

45The hosts shall soon be routed and they shall be put to flight. (Qur'ān 54:45)

This prophecy was fulfilled in that the polytheists of Quraysh were soundly defeated by the Muslims at the Battle of Badr. Not only were the Quraysh routed, and not only did they retreat, but those who were slain died as disbelievers who had heard, rejected, and persecuted the Prophet (saws) and his followers. With all of this considered, one can conclude that this prophecy came true. The specificity of the time in which this verse was recited is narrated in the following ḥadīth:

Ibn 'Abbās (ra) narrated: On the day of the Battle of Badr, the Prophet (saws) said, "O God! I appeal to You (to fulfill) Your Covenant and Promise. O God! If Your Will is that none should worship You, (then give victory to the pagans)." Then Abū Bakr took hold of him by the hand and said, "This is sufficient for you." The Prophet (saws) came out saying, "'Soon' their united front will be defeated and 'forced to' flee. (Qur'ān 54:45)" (Ṣaḥīḥ Al-Bukhārī, Ḥadīth 3953.)

A Prophecy about God protecting Muḥammad (saws)

God says the following in the Qur'ān:

67O Messenger, deliver whatever has been sent down to you by your Lord. If you do not do so, you will not have conveyed His message. God will defend you from people. For God does not guide those who deny the truth. (Qur'ān 5:67)

This prophecy was fulfilled in that Muḥammad (saws) was never fatally harmed by any human, and he died a natural death, despite being threatened by disbelievers for the 23-year duration of his mission. This was also fulfilled in that the Prophet's (saws) Sunnah was preserved throughout the centuries.

A Prophecy about Muslims in the World

God says in the Qur'ān:

55God has promised to those among you who believe and do good works that He will surely grant them power in the land as He granted to those who were before them; and that He will surely establish for them their religion which He has chosen for them. He will cause their state of fear to be replaced by a sense of security. Let them worship Me and associate no other with Me. Whoever still chooses to deny the truth is truly rebellious. (Qur'ān 24:55)

The above prophecy was fulfilled in that Islām was well established in the earth and remains so to this day, and it is the second-largest world religion. The Muslims went from being a persecuted minority in Makkah to being rulers of Arabia. Moreover, several Muslim-majority empires have dominated throughout history, including the Rāshidūn Caliphate, the Umayyad Empire, the 'Abbāsid Empire, the Ottoman Empire, and the Mughal Empire. Not every Islāmic kingdom or country may have had a pure government, but in many of them, nonetheless, Muslims could openly practice their faith, and many pious Muslims have served as influential leaders. Islām has thrived through many empires and is still thriving through many nations, yet this prophecy was revealed during the time of the Prophet (saws), when Islām was consolidated mostly in Arabia.

Chapter 14
Signs of the Last Day

There are many signs that signal that we are in the last days and that the Last Day, the Final Hour, is approaching. Scholars have divided these into minor signs and major signs. The minor signs include many things, such as an increase in earthquakes and landslides, the Euphrates River uncovering a mountain of gold which people will fight over, people who were once destitute competing in constructing tall buildings, a general uprise in bad behavior, widespread indulgence in forbidden actions, and people viewing as lawful that which is unlawful. In the last days, those practicing genuine Islām will be few. For brevity, more examples of the many minor signs will not be given herein.

The major signs have been numbered as ten, based on the following ḥadīth:

Ḥudhayfah ibn Asīd Al-Ghifārī (ra) narrated: The Prophet (saws) came to us while we were talking. He (the Prophet (saws)) said, "What are you talking about?" They said, "We are talking about the (Last) Hour." He said, "It will never come until you see ten signs." He mentioned: the Smoke; the Antichrist; the Beast; the rising of the sun from its place of setting; the descent of Jesus (saws) son of Mary; Gog and Magog; and three landslides – one in the east, one in the west, and one in the Arabian peninsula. And the last of that will be a fire which will emerge from Yemen and drive the people to their place of gathering. (Ṣaḥīḥ Muslim, Ḥadīth 2901)

There is no ḥadīth that clearly indicates the chronological order of these signs, but the order of some of them is known. The following information is all taken from ṣaḥīḥ (authentic) ḥadīths, or ḥadīths that are at least ḥasan (good).

A man known as the Mahdī will appear. He will be a righteous and just Muslim leader through whom God will grant prosperity. He will be a descendant of the Prophet Muḥammad (saws) through Fāṭimah, and he will have the same name as the Prophet (saws), which is Muḥammad ibn ʻAbdullāh. The Mahdī will have a high forehead and a long, thin, curved nose, and he will rule for about seven years.

Around the time of the Mahdī, the Antichrist will appear. The actual term used to refer to the Antichrist is *Al-Masīḥ Ad-Dajjāl*, the Imposter Messiah, or just "Ad-Dajjāl" for short. The Antichrist will be a short, well-built man with thick, curly hair and a ruddy complexion. He will be blind in his right eye, which will bulge out like a grape, and his left eye will also be defective. He will be pigeon-toed, and he will have the Arabic word *kāfir* (disbeliever) written between his eyes. The Antichrist also will not have children. He will come from Khorasan (i.e., the Iranian Plateau) in the east, and he will be from among the Jews of Isfahan, and there will be 70,000 Jews with him.

The Antichrist will have a paradise and a fire with him. This paradise and this fire will each take the form of a river that people may drink from. However, his paradise will actually be a fire, and his fire will actually be a paradise. Thus, he will deceive people.

The Antichrist will travel throughout the earth for forty days – one day like a year, one day like a month, one day like a week, and the rest like normal days. He will travel the earth like clouds driven by the wind, and he will command the sky to rain and the earth to bring forth vegetation, and he will enhance people's livestock. This will be for those who accept him. As for those who reject him, he will strike them with famine and poverty. The Antichrist will also bring forth treasure from ruins. A certain young man will disbelieve in the Antichrist, so the Antichrist will kill the young man by cutting him in two. Then the Antichrist will bring him back to life in order to persuade his followers. The young man, however, will still disbelieve in the Antichrist.

The Antichrist will also ask a Bedouin if the latter will accept him as his lord if he resurrects the Bedouin's father and mother. The Bedouin will respond in the affirmative, after which two devils will appear to him in the image of his father and mother, attempting to persuade him to accept the Antichrist as his lord.

The Antichrist will enter every town on earth except for Makkah and Al-Madīnah because there are angels guarding those cities. The Antichrist will also not be able to enter Al-Masjid Al-Ḥarām, Al-Masjid An-Nabawī, Al-Masjid Al-Aqṣā, and the Masjid of Sinai. However, he will come close to Al-Madīnah, and many of those who go out to him will be women. Muslims are advised to keep far away from the Antichrist. Furthermore, whoever memorizes the first ten verses of Sūratul-Kahf and the last ten verses of Sūratul-Kahf will be protected from the Antichrist, and Sūratul-Kahf is chapter 18 of the Qur'ān.

During the time of the Mahdī and the Antichrist, Jesus (as) will descend to earth from Heaven, and the place of his descension will be a white minaret on the eastern side of Damascus. Jesus (as) will be wearing two lightly dyed yellow garments, and his hands will be on the wings of two angels. Jesus (as) will be of medium height with a reddish fair complexion. When he lowers his head, drops of water will fall from it, and when he raises his head, drops like pearls will scatter from it. Every disbeliever within the range of the sight of Jesus (as) will die. The Mahdī will try to get Jesus (as) to lead him and the Muslims with him in ṣalāh, but Jesus (as) will insist that the Mahdī leads the prayer, and Jesus (as) will pray behind the Mahdī. This symbolizes that Jesus (as) is a Muslim and will follow what was sent to the Prophet Muḥammad (saws), and Jesus (as) will not come with a new revelation.

Jesus (as) will then search for the Antichrist, catch hold of him at the gate of Ludd (a village near Jerusalem), and Jesus (as) will kill the Antichrist. Then the Muslims will come to Jesus (as), and he will wipe their faces and inform them of their ranks in Paradise. Then two peoples known as Ya'jūj and Ma'jūj (i.e., Gog and Magog) will appear, and they will be so numerous that other people will not be able to fight them. They will swarm down from every slope and will drink all the water in Lake Tiberias in Palestine. Jesus (as) and his Muslim companions at that time will take refuge on a mountain, and they will be in dire straits. But they will make du'ā' to God, and God will send insects that will attack the necks of Gog and Magog until they are dead, and their corpses and stench will fill the earth. Jesus (as) and his companions will come down from the mountain and will again make du'ā', and God will send birds to dispose of the corpses of Gog and Magog, and He will send down rain to wash the earth. Then the earth will bring forth plentiful produce and livestock will give abundant milk.

During the time of Jesus (as), there will be a period of peace for seven years, and he will judge humanity justly. At some point, Jesus (as) will do away with pigs, break the cross, and abolish the tax that non-Muslims must pay in Muslim lands (i.e., the jizyah), and there will come a time during his days when money will be so abundant that no one will accept it. Jesus (as) will also perform Ḥajj or 'Umrah, and all religions besides Islām will perish during his time. Jesus (as) will be on the earth for a total of 40 years, and then he will die, and the Muslims will pray the funeral prayer over him.

After that time, God will send a pleasant wind that will soothe people, even under their armpits, and the wind will take the lives of every believer and every Muslim until only the wicked will survive, who will commit adultery in public. They will not appreciate good or condemn evil. Shortly after that, the trumpet signaling the Last Day will be sounded, and the world will end.

There are other major signs of the Last Day, and we do not know the order in which they will occur. One of these signs is the Smoke. It will be visible and will cover the people and bring painful torment. The sun will also rise from the west, and at that time people will believe but believing will not avail one at that time if they had not believed before, and repentance will not be accepted after that time. A Beast of the earth will also emerge that will mark people on their noses. There will also be three great landslides, and a great fire from Yemen. All of the signs of the Last Day will follow each other quickly, and the following ḥadīth states:

Abū Hurayrah (ra) narrated: The Prophet (saws) said, "The signs of the Hour will emerge in quick succession, one after another, just like the beads of a string." (Al-Mu'jam Al-Awsaṭ by Aṭ-Ṭabarānī, Ḥadīth 4271; Al-Albānī graded it ṣaḥīḥ.)

Chapter 15
Will God Answer My Supplications?

A person's du'ā' (supplication) is generally answered in some way by God. However, there are etiquettes to making du'ā' that the Muslim should observe. One should avoid that which is unlawful (ḥarām); supplicate with certainty, focus, humility, and persistence; not grow impatient; and not supplicate for something unlawful. If one supplicates in this manner, then God will respond in one of three ways:

1. Fulfilling the supplication
2. Storing it for the supplicant in the Hereafter
3. Diverting an evil from the supplicant

186 *When My servants ask you about Me, say that I am near. I respond to the call of one who calls whenever he calls to Me. Let them, then, respond to Me, and believe in Me, so that they may be rightly guided. (Qur'ān 2:186)*

55 *Call on your Lord with humility and in secret. He does not like the transgressors. (Qur'ān 7:55)*

Abū Hurayrah (ra) narrated: The Messenger of God (saws) said, "O people, God is good and does not accept anything but that which is good. God has enjoined upon the believers that which He has enjoined upon the Messengers. He says, 'Messengers, eat what is wholesome and do good deeds. I am well aware of what you do (Qur'ān 23:51).' And He says, 'Believers, eat the wholesome things which We have provided for you and give thanks to God, if it is Him you worship (Qur'ān 2:172).'" Then he mentioned a man who has undertaken a lengthy journey and is disheveled and dusty, raising his hands towards heaven and saying, "O Lord, O Lord!" But his food is unlawful, his drink is unlawful, his clothing is unlawful, and he is nourished with what is unlawful, so how can he receive a response? (Ṣaḥīḥ Muslim, Ḥadīth 1015)

Abū Hurayrah (ra) narrated: The Prophet (saws) said, "A person will still be answered so long as his supplication does not involve sin or severing ties of kinship, and so long as he does not become impatient." It was said, "O Messenger of God, what does being impatient mean?" He said, "Saying, 'I supplicated, and I supplicated, and I did not receive any response,' then he becomes disappointed and stops supplicating." (Ṣaḥīḥ Muslim, Ḥadīth 2735)

Abū Hurayrah (ra) narrated: The Messenger of God (saws) said, "Call upon God with certainty that He will answer you. Know that God will not answer the supplication of an unmindful and distracted heart." (Jāmi' At-Tirmidhī, Ḥadīth 3479; Al-Albānī graded it ḥasan.)

'Ubādah ibn Aṣ-Ṣāmit (ra) narrated: The Messenger of God (saws) said, "There is no Muslim on earth who calls upon God in supplication but that God will grant it to him or divert some evil away from him, so long as he does not ask for something sinful or to cut off family ties." A man said, "In that case we will ask for more." He (the Prophet (saws)) said, "God has even more." (Jāmi' At-Tirmidhī, Ḥadīth 3573; Zubayr 'Alī Za'ī graded it ḥasan.)

Abū Sa'īd Al-Khudrī (ra) narrated: The Prophet (saws) said, "There is no Muslim who calls upon God, without sin or cutting family ties, but that God will give him one of three answers: He will quickly fulfill his supplication, He will store it for him in the Hereafter, or He will divert an evil from him similar to it." They said, "In that case we will ask for more." He (the Prophet (saws)) said, "God has even more." (Musnad Aḥmad, Ḥadīth 11133; Al-Albānī graded it ṣaḥīḥ.)

Chapter 16

Why Do Bad Things Happen?

Acclaimed astrophysicist Dr. Neil deGrasse Tyson, PhD appeared on an episode of the television program CBS Sunday Morning, and correspondent Martha Teichner asked the astrophysicist if he believed in God. The video clip of the question and Tyson's response was uploaded to the YouTube channel CBS Sunday Morning on April 30th, 2017, and in it Tyson states:

"If your concept of a creator is someone who's all-powerful and all-good, that's not an uncommon pairing of powers that you might ascribe to a creator – all-powerful and all-good. And I look at disasters that afflict Earth and life on Earth – volcanoes, hurricanes, tornadoes, earthquakes, disease, pestilence, congenital birth defects. You look at this list of ways that life is made miserable on Earth by natural causes, and I just ask: how do you deal with that? So philosophers rose up and said, 'If there is a God, God is either not all-powerful or not all-good.'"

This is a succinctly worded explanation that is common among atheists and agnostics. If God is all-good and all-powerful, why would He allow bad things to happen?

The Islāmic answer is that life is a test, and the purpose of a test is to make one grow. One passes the test of life and grows by serving God and holding on to Him through all the ups and downs of life. God states in the Qur'ān:

1 Blessed is He in whose hand is the Kingdom. He has power over all things. 2 He created death and life so that He might test which of you is best in conduct. He is the Almighty, the Most Forgiving. 3 He created seven heavens one above the other in layers. You will not find any flaw in the creation of the Most Compassionate. Then look once again; can you see any flaw? (Qur'ān 67:1-3)

The commentary that the translator Dr. Mustafa Khattab wrote in *The Clear Qur'an* for verse 3 reads as follows: "*Some may point to birth defects, genetic mutations, etc. and say these are flaws. This verse means that, in the grand scheme of creation, everything created has its place, form, and purpose, and that it does exactly what Allah ordained for it.*" In other words, it may be understood that this verse is stating that everything is as it should be. Notice that God's name, Ar-Raḥmān (the Most Compassionate / the Most Gracious / the Infinitely Good), is mentioned in this verse, and it may be understood that this implies that everything was created with a compassionate intention even if it appears negative.

Moreover, one calamity can mean different things for different people, and what may be a punishment for one person may be a mercy for another person because bearing it with patience can lead to an immense reward with God. The religious evidence for this is that God says in the Qur'ān:

155 We shall certainly test you with fear and hunger, and loss of property, lives and crops. Give good news to those who endure with fortitude. 156 Those who say, when afflicted with a calamity, 'We belong to God and to Him we shall return,' 157 are the ones who will have blessings and mercy from their Lord. It is they who are on the right path! (Qur'ān 2:155-157)

And the following ḥadīths state:

Abū Sa'īd and Abū Hurayrah (ra) narrated: The Prophet (saws) said, "Never is the Muslim stricken with a discomfort, an illness, an anxiety, a grief or mental worry or even the pricking of a thorn except that God will expiate his sins." (Ṣaḥīḥ Al-Bukhārī, Ḥadīth 5641; Ṣaḥīḥ Muslim, Ḥadīth 2573; Riyāḍ Aṣ-Ṣāliḥīn, Ḥadīth 37)

Abū Yaḥyā Ṣuhayb ibn Sinān (ra) narrated: The Messenger of God (saws) said, "How wonderful is the case of a believer. There is good for him in everything, and this applies only to a believer. If prosperity comes to him, he expresses gratitude to God, and that is good for him. And if adversity befalls him, he endures it patiently, and that is good for him." (Ṣaḥīḥ Muslim, Ḥadīth 2999; Riyāḍ Aṣ-Ṣāliḥīn, Ḥadīth 27)

There are other hadiths to this effect, including Ṣaḥīḥ Al-Bukhārī, Ḥadīth 5648 / Ṣaḥīḥ Muslim, Ḥadīth 2571 / Riyāḍ Aṣ-Ṣāliḥīn, Ḥadīth 38 and Ṣaḥīḥ Al-Bukhārī, Ḥadīth 3474 / Riyāḍ Aṣ-Ṣāliḥīn, Ḥadīth 33. These hadiths will not be quoted herein for the sake of brevity. Nevertheless, calamities can be means of becoming closer to God and becoming a better person, depending on how one reacts to them. And one calamity or natural disaster may be a means of averting another calamity or natural disaster that is worse. For example, a child that is born with a congenital birth defect or who dies young may be prevented from committing major sins or causing others to sin. Or it could be that the child may face so many difficulties that dying or being handicapped are mercies for the child. These examples are not the definite answers for each case, but it could be that there is something worse being averted through congenital birth defects and infant mortality that we do not have the wisdom to see. In other words, a handicap could cause someone to be a better person than they would have been without the handicap. Regardless, bearing a congenital handicap with patience through love of God and worshipping Him will lead to great reward.

The religious evidence for wisdom behind calamities is in the Qur'ān, chapter (sūrah) 18, verses 60-82. This part of the Qur'ān narrates the story of Moses (as) and Al-Khiḍr (as). There were three instances in which Al-Khiḍr (as) did something that looked like a calamity to Moses (as), but there was a purpose behind each deed that Al-Khiḍr (as) did which Moses (as) did not know.

We must also remember that calamities happened to the Prophet Muḥammad (saws) himself. His father died while he was in the womb, his mother died when he was six years old, and his grandfather died two years later. What was the wisdom in making him an orphan from a young age? We ultimately do not know, but it may have led to him being kinder, more understanding, and more hospitable to the disadvantaged, among other benefits that we cannot see. Later in his life, all of the Prophet's (saws) children died during his lifetime except for his youngest daughter, Fāṭimah. But that meant that the Prophet Muḥammad (saws) had to bury six of his children during his lifetime. Moreover, all three of his sons, Al-Qāsim, 'Abdullāh, and Ibrāhīm, were very young children when they died. What was the wisdom in causing such young children to die? We cannot know what God intended through their deaths, but we do know that their deaths never made the Prophet (saws) question his relationship with God.

There also occurred what is known as the Year of Sorrow, when the Prophet's (saws) wife and his first supporter, Khadījah, passed away. That same year, his beloved uncle Abū Ṭālib, who as a chieftain gave the Prophet (saws) protection from the physical hostility of the disbelievers of Quraysh, also passed away. And later in that same year, the Prophet (saws) was rejected and stoned out of the city of Aṭ-Ṭā'if after preaching there. And through all of this, the Prophet (saws) never questioned his relationship with God. He always relied on God, and God thereafter rewarded the Prophet (saws) with the Night Journey and the Ascension (Al-Isrā' Wal- Mi'rāj). Living through the deaths of these loved ones – of his children, his wife, and his uncle – caused the Prophet (saws) to turn to God, trusting in God's mercy and wisdom, and trusting that everything was as it should be.

God says in the Qur'ān:

5So, surely with every hardship there is ease. (Qur'ān 94:5)

God does not say "after" every hardship comes ease. He uses the Arabic word *ma'a*, literally meaning "with." So with every hardship there is some form of ease. One just has to know where to look for it, and even if outer ease does not come immediately, inner ease can be attained through knowing that God remembers those who remember Him. God says in the Qur'ān:

152So remember Me; I will remember you. Be thankful to Me, and do not be ungrateful. 153You who believe, seek help through patience and prayer. Surely, God is with the patient. (Qur'ān 2:152-153)

28those who believe and whose hearts find comfort in the remembrance of God. Surely in the remembrance of God hearts can find comfort. (Qur'ān 13:28)

And the following ḥadīths state:

Abū Hurayrah (ra) narrated: The Prophet (saws) said, "Indeed, God, Mighty and Sublime, says, 'I am with My slave when he remembers Me and his lips move with My mention.'" (Sunan Ibn Mājah, Ḥadīth 3792; Bulūgh Al-Marām, Ḥadīth 1332; Ibn Ḥibbān and Al-Albānī graded the ḥadīth ṣaḥīḥ.)

Ibn 'Umar (ra) narrated: The Messenger of God (saws) said, "Do not speak too much without mentioning God. Verily, talking too much without remembering God hardens the heart. The furthest of people from God is one with a hard heart." (Jāmi' At-Tirmidhī, Ḥadīth 2411; Ibn Ḥajar Al-'Asqalānī graded the ḥadīth ḥasan.)

Abū Dharr (ra) narrated: The Messenger of God (saws) said, "Wealth is in the heart and poverty is in the heart. Whoever is wealthy in his heart will not be harmed no matter what happens in the world. Whoever is impoverished in his heart will not be satisfied no matter how much he has in the world. Verily, he will only be harmed by the greed of his own soul." (Al-Mu'jam Al-Kabīr by Aṭ-Ṭabarānī, 2/154; Al-Albānī graded the ḥadīth ṣaḥīḥ.)

Ma'qil ibn Yasār (ra) narrated: The Messenger of God (saws) said, "Your Lord Almighty said, 'Son of Adam, be free for My worship. I will fill your heart with richness and fill your hands with provision. Son of Adam, do not distance yourself from Me, or else I will fill your heart with poverty and fill your hands with worthless distractions.'" (Al-Mu'jam Al-Kabīr by Aṭ-Ṭabarānī, Ḥadīth 500; Al-Albānī graded the ḥadīth ṣaḥīḥ.)

Taking all of this into account, one may understand that true happiness is in the heart, and the heart is enriched and softened by the loving and humble remembrance of God and being content with what one has. Trusting in God's wisdom leads to contentment, and contentment leads to patience, and God is with the patient. Reliance, or putting one's trust in someone, is called *tawakkul* in Arabic, and a believer should have tawakkul (reliance) on God. And the Qur'ān states:

159Surely God loves those who place their trust in Him. (Qur'ān 3:159)

Here is a quote to part of the answer to the question of why God decrees disasters for children, as it was stated on the website islamqa.info. On the website, it is question 13610, and it was published on April 11th, 2009:

"If we accept the words of human specialists when they are dealing with their specialties, and we do not argue with them – such as doctors, engineers, etc. – because our educational level does not enable us to understand everything that they know, then it is even more appropriate that we should accept that however the All-Knowing, from Whose knowledge nothing is hidden, deals with the affairs of His creation is undoubtedly correct and wise.

We humans sometimes think that it is wise to do some things that we dislike, because there is some benefit in that for us, and if we did not do them we would be accused of being lacking in wisdom and reason. For example, if a person is sick and there is the fear that he may die, but it is known that he may be cured – by Allah's leave – if he takes a certain medicine, then the wise thing for him to do is to take that medicine even if it is bitter; if he fails to take it, that is regarded as a shortcoming and lack of reason on his part. There are many things that we do in life that we dislike, because of the benefits that they bring to us."

And God says in the Qur'ān:

58 The blind and the sighted are not equal, just as those who believe and do good works and those who do evil are not equal. How seldom you reflect! (Qur'ān 40:58)

It seems logical that the evildoers are not equal to the doers of good, and that the impatient are not equal to the patient. The doers of good and the patient are of a higher status, and it seems logical that God will accommodate them accordingly after death if God is just.

Some may ask: "Why is there so much suffering and evil in the world?"

The answer is that, although God is One, there is duality in His creation, and a concept can be more deeply understood by experiencing its opposite. Therefore, evil allows us to understand and appreciate good, and suffering causes us to grow spiritually, mentally, and physically. If there existed a world without tension of any sort, then we would not grow, or at least we would not grow as fast as we do with tension. Compare this to physical exercise. Working out tears muscle fibers, and when those fibers repair, our muscles grow stronger. Similarly, certain puzzles, mathematical equations, and the memorization of facts cause our minds to grow, even if those things may seem challenging at first. Related to these examples is the growth, or enhancing, of the soul through worship and experiencing tests – both tests of ease and tests of hardship. This does not mean that one should seek out suffering in order to grow. One should avoid suffering as much as one can, and there is spiritual growth in avoiding suffering, as that requires effort, and effort results in growth. There is also spiritual growth in helping others to avoid suffering. However, sometimes calamities are unavoidable, but we must view calamities as opportunities to grow ourselves spiritually. Life is ultimately not about whether calamities will happen to people. Instead, it's about how people react to those calamities.

Some may also ask: "Why does life have to be a test? If God is the Infinitely Good, why did He not just create us all in Paradise to live there forever?"

The answer is that God wanted to create a being with free will that He would test because He wanted that being to earn its virtue, and that being is the human. If God just gave us our virtue freely and had us live in Paradise with no evil inclinations to avoid, then we would have been like angels because angels are inherently righteous and cannot disobey God. But God wanted to create something different from angels, and God can do whatever He wants, so He created a being that is supposed to go through trials. That is what God wanted to do, but God is also the Most Loving, and He would not have created His creation if He did not love it. So our benefit and reward, in this life and the next, comes to us through loving God and worshipping Him no matter the circumstance.

13 It is He who begins and repeats [His creation]. 14 And He is the Most Forgiving and the Most Loving, 15 the Lord of the glorious Throne, 16 Doer of whatever He wills. (Qur'ān 85:13-16)

And God knows best.

Chapter 17

Have I Sinned Too Much For God To Forgive Me?

God's Names and Attributes of Forgiveness, Mercy, and Love

Throughout the Qur'ān, God refers to Himself with names of greatness and positivity, including:

- Ar-Raḥmān (the Most Compassionate / the Most Gracious / the Infinitely Good)
- Ar-Raḥīm (the Most Merciful)
- Al-Ghafūr (the Most Forgiving)
- Al-Ghaffār (the Constantly Forgiving)
- Al-Wadūd (the Most Loving)
- As-Salām (the Ultimate Peace)
- At-Tawwāb (the Accepter of Repentance)
- Al-Mu'min (the Giver of Security)

Knowing and trusting that these are God's names should bring an individual peace. Moreover, God says in the Qur'ān:

53Say [O Prophet, that God says], 'O My servants, who have committed excesses against their own souls, do not despair of God's mercy, for God surely forgives all sins. He is truly the Most Forgiving, the Most Merciful. (Qur'ān 39:53)

64God is the best Guardian, and He is the Most Merciful of the merciful. (Qur'ān 12:64)

32Your Lord is infinite in His forgiveness. (Qur'ān 53:32)

222God loves those who turn to Him in repentance, and He loves those who keep themselves clean. (Qur'ān 2:222)

And the following ḥadīths state:

Anas (ra) narrated: The Messenger of God (saws) said, "God, the Exalted, has said: 'O son of Adam, I forgive you as long as you pray to Me and hope for My forgiveness, whatever sins you have committed. O son of Adam, I do not care if your sins reach the height of the sky, then you ask for My forgiveness, I would forgive you. O son of Adam, if you come to Me with a load of sins nearly as great as the earth, and meet Me associating nothing with Me, I would match it with forgiveness.'" (Jāmi' At-Tirmidhī, Ḥadīth 3540; Riyāḍ Aṣ-Ṣāliḥīn, Ḥadīth 442, 1878; Al-Albānī graded it ḥasan.)

Abū Hurayrah (ra) narrated: The Prophet (saws) said, "If your sins were to reach the sky and then you repented, God would still accept your repentance." (Sunan Ibn Mājah, Ḥadīth 4248; Al-Albānī graded it ḥasan.)

Abū Hurayrah (ra) narrated: The Messenger of God (saws) said, "God divided mercy into one hundred parts. He kept ninety-nine parts with Him and sent down one part to the earth. And because of that, its one single part, His creations are merciful to each other, so that even the mare lifts up its hoofs away from its baby animal, lest it should trample on it." (Ṣaḥīḥ Al-Bukhārī, Ḥadīth 6000; Ṣaḥīḥ Muslim, Ḥadīth 2752; Riyāḍ Aṣ-Ṣāliḥīn, Ḥadīth 420)

'Umar ibn Al-Khaṭṭāb (ra) narrated: Some prisoners were brought to the Messenger of God (saws). Among them was a woman who was running (searching for her child). When she saw a child among the captives, she took hold of it, pressed it against her chest and nursed it. The Messenger of God (saws) said, "Do you think this woman would ever throw her child in the fire?" We said, "By God, no." Thereupon the Messenger of God (saws) said, "God is more kind to His slave than this woman is to her child." (Ṣaḥīḥ Al-Bukhārī, Ḥadīth 5999; Ṣaḥīḥ Muslim, Ḥadīth 2754; Riyāḍ Aṣ-Ṣāliḥīn, Ḥadīth 418)

Abū Hurayrah (ra) narrated: The Messenger of God (saws) said, "When God created creation, He wrote in a book which is with Him over His Throne: 'Indeed, My mercy overcomes over My wrath.'" (Ṣaḥīḥ Al-Bukhārī, Ḥadīth 7404; Ṣaḥīḥ Muslim, Ḥadīth 2751; Riyāḍ Aṣ-Ṣāliḥīn, Ḥadīth 419)

And Martin Lings (Abū Bakr Sirājud-Dīn) wrote in his biography of the Prophet (saws), *Muhammad: His Life Based on the Earliest Sources* (published in 2006 by Inner Traditions, pages 47-48):

"Amongst the most striking features of the Revelation were the two Divine Names *ar-Raḥmān* and *ar-Raḥīm*. The word *raḥīm*, an intensive form of *rāḥim*, merciful, was current in the sense of very merciful or boundlessly merciful. The still more intensive *raḥmān*, for lack of any concept to fit it, had fallen into disuse. The Revelation revived it in accordance with the new religion's basic need to dwell on the heights of Transcendence. Being stronger even than *ar-Raḥīm* (the All-Merciful), the Name *ar-Raḥmān* refers to the very essence or root of Mercy, that is, to the Infinite Beneficence or Goodness of God, and the Koran expressly makes it an equivalent of *Allāh*."

God's mercy is infinite. He is more merciful than anyone can imagine. His mercy is greater than a loving mother's mercy for her child. There is no sin that God cannot forgive. And as long as we keep sincerely repenting, God will keep forgiving us, and He will love us because He loves at-tawwābīn, those who repent, as is quoted in the verse of the Qur'ān above (2:222). Notice that God does not just say He has mercy on those who repent. He *loves* those who repent. So if an individual keeps sincerely repenting to God, then that person can have the hope that God loves them.

The Conditions for Valid Repentance

Just because God can forgive all sins does not mean that we can do whatever we want and then say that we're sorry. According to Islām, Hellfire is real, and the validity of a believer's īmān (faith) depends in part upon acceptance of the reality of Hellfire and the reality of Paradise. There is a balance in Islām of fearing God's wrath and trusting in His mercy. One should neither believe with certainty that they are safe from God's wrath, nor should one ever despair of God's mercy. However, if we repent, then God shows us His love and His mercy, and His mercy surpasses His wrath. So how does one perform a valid repentance?

Imām An-Nawawī, one of the most significant scholars in the history of Islām, wrote in his book Riyāḍ Aṣ-Ṣāliḥīn, in the chapter about repentance (Bāb At-Tawbah):

"Scholars said: It is necessary to repent from every sin. If the offense involves the right of God, not a human, then there are three conditions to be met in order that repentance be accepted by God:

1. *To desist from committing it.*
2. *To feel sorry for committing it.*
3. *To decide not to recommit it.*

Any repentance failing to meet any of these three conditions would not be sound.

But if the sin involves a human's right, it requires a fourth condition (i.e., to absolve oneself from that right). If it is property, he should return it to its rightful owner. If it is slandering or backbiting, one should ask the pardon of the offended."

One may find the evidence for these conditions in the following Qur'ān verse and ḥadīth, among other places:

135 And who, when they have committed an indecency or have wronged their souls, remember God and pray that their sins be forgiven—for who but God can forgive sins?—and do not knowingly persist in their misdeeds. (Qur'ān 3:135)

'Abdullāh ibn Mas'ūd (ra) narrated: The Messenger of God (saws) said, "Regret is repentance." (Sunan Ibn Mājah, Ḥadīth 4252; Al-Albānī graded it ṣaḥīḥ.)

From all of this, it is to be understood that in order for repentance to be accepted, one must stop committing the sin and regret it. One can, and should, say something along the lines of, "Astaghfirullāha wa atūbu ilayhi (I seek God's forgiveness, and I turn to Him in repentance)." However, true repentance is more than mere words, and it should come from the heart.

Furthermore, there are two deadlines by which repentance must be made, and repentance will not be accepted after those two deadlines. One deadline applies on an individual basis, and it is when a person dies. The other deadline applies on a collective basis, and it is when the sun will rise from the west, which is a major sign of the Last Day. The evidence for these two deadlines is in the following Qur'ān verses and ḥadīths:

17 But God undertakes to accept repentance only from those who do evil out of ignorance and those who repent soon after. God turns towards such people with mercy. He is All-Knowing and All-Wise. 18 Repentance is not for those who continue to do evil deeds until, when death comes upon one of them, he says: 'Now I repent!' nor from those who die as deniers of the truth. We have prepared a painful punishment for them. (Qur'ān 4:17-18)

Ibn 'Umar (ra) narrated: The Prophet (saws) said, "Indeed, God accepts the repentance of His slave as long as the death rattle has not reached his throat." (Jāmi' At-Tirmidhī, Ḥadīth 3537; Riyāḍ Aṣ-Ṣāliḥīn, Ḥadīth 18; Al-Albānī graded it ḥasan.)

'Abdur-Raḥmān ibn Al-Baylamānī (ra) narrated: The Prophet said, "Whoever repents before he utters the death rattle, God will accept it from him." (Musnad Aḥmad, Ḥadīth 23068; Al-Albānī graded it ṣaḥīḥ.)

Abū Mūsā Al-Ash'arī (ra) narrated: The Prophet (saws) said, "God, the Exalted, will continue to stretch out His Hand in the night so that the sinners of the day may repent, and He will continue to stretch His Hand in the daytime so that the sinners of the night may repent, until the sun rises from the west." (Ṣaḥīḥ Muslim, Ḥadīth 2759; Riyāḍ Aṣ-Ṣāliḥīn, Ḥadīth 16)

Abū Hurayrah (ra) narrated: The Messenger of God (saws) said, "He who repents before the sun rises from the west, God will forgive him." (Ṣaḥīḥ Muslim, Ḥadīth 2703; Riyāḍ Aṣ-Ṣāliḥīn, Ḥadīth 17)

One should not delay their repentance from a sin until death because one never knows when they will die.

Does God forgive shirk (associating partners with Him)?

The word *shirk* is an Arabic word, and it refers to associating partners with God. God is alone in His supremacy, and there is nothing and no one like Him. Based on the Qur'ān and the Sunnah, shirk is the worst of the major sins, and God says in the Qur'ān:

48 God will not forgive anyone for associating something with Him, but He will forgive whoever He wishes for anything besides that. Whoever ascribes partners to God is guilty of a monstrous sin. (Qur'ān 4:48)

Does this mean that whoever commits shirk will go to Hell, even if they repent? No, this does not mean that. The verse above refers only to those who *die* while committing shirk. In other words, they die while believing that God has an equal. Those who were brought up in, or converted to, a religion that sets up partners with God will be forgiven of all their misdeeds if they embrace Islām. And even Muslims who commit shirk but then turn to God in repentance, and return to Islām, may be forgiven by God. The evidence for this is in the Qur'ān:

68[They are] those who never invoke any other deity besides God; nor take a life which God has made sacred, except with the right to do so; nor commit adultery. Anyone who does that shall face punishment: 69he shall have his suffering doubled on the Day of Resurrection, and he will abide forever in disgrace, 70except for those who repent and believe and do good deeds. God will change the evil deeds of such people into good ones. He is Most Forgiving and Most Merciful. 71He who repents and does good deeds has truly turned to God. (Qur'ān 25:68-71)

85If anyone seeks a religion other than Islām, it will not be accepted from him. He will be among the losers in the Hereafter. 86How would God bestow His guidance upon people who have opted for unbelief after having embraced the faith and having borne witness that this Messenger is true and [after] all evidence of the truth has come to them? For God does not guide such wrongdoers. 87Such people will be recompensed with rejection by God, by the angels, by all humanity. 88In this state they shall abide forever; their punishment shall not be lightened nor shall they be granted respite. 89Except for those who afterwards repent and reform. God is Forgiving and Merciful. (Qur'ān 3:85-89)

72Indeed, they are deniers of the truth who say, 'God is the Christ, the son of Mary.' For the Christ himself said, 'Children of Israel, serve God, my Lord and your Lord.' If anyone associates anything with God, God will forbid him the Garden, and the Fire will be his home. The wrongdoers shall have no helpers. 73They are deniers of the truth who say, 'God is one of three.' There is only One God. If they do not desist from saying this, a painful punishment is bound to befall such of them as are bent on denying the truth. 74Why do they not turn to God in repentance and ask for His forgiveness? God is Forgiving and Merciful. (Qur'ān 5:72-74)

And the following ḥadīths state:

'Abdullāh ibn Mas'ūd (ra) narrated: The Messenger of God (saws) said, "The one who repents from sin is like one who did not sin." (Sunan Ibn Mājah, Ḥadīth 4250; Al-Albānī graded it ḥasan.)

Abū Sa'īd Al-Anṣārī (ra) narrated: The Messenger of God (saws) said, "Regret is part of repentance, and one who truly repents is like one without sin." (Al-Mu'jam Al-Kabīr by Aṭ-Ṭabarānī 22/306; Al-Albānī graded it ḥasan.)

A Muslim is forgiven for being forced into sin or forgetting

'Umar ibn Al-Khaṭṭāb (ra) narrated: The Messenger of God (saws) said, "The reward of deeds depends upon the intentions." (Ṣaḥīḥ Al-Bukhārī, Ḥadīth 1; Ṣaḥīḥ Muslim, Ḥadīth 1907; Riyāḍ Aṣ-Ṣāliḥīn, Ḥadīth 1)

Ibn 'Abbās (ra) narrated: The Messenger of God (saws) said, "Indeed, God has forgiven my nation (i.e., all Muslims) for mistakes and forgetfulness, and what they are forced to do." (Sunan Ibn Mājah, Ḥadīth 2045; Al-Albānī graded it ṣaḥīḥ.)

Seeking Forgiveness (Istighfār) and Repentance (Tawbah)

Seeking forgiveness (istighfār) is essentially supplication (du'ā'). It is the literal process of asking God for forgiveness. Repentance (tawbah) involves regretting the sin. It is possible to commit a sin, ask for forgiveness, and not regret it. There is great benefit in istighfār and tawbah, but tawbah is deeper. Another understanding is that istighfār is seeking protection from the evil of one's bad deeds that occurred in the past, whereas tawbah is seeking protection from the evil of one's possible bad deeds in the future. This is because tawbah involves resolving not to commit a sin again.

A Benefit of Abandoning Sin

Abū Qatādah (ra) narrated: The Prophet (saws) said, "Verily, you will never leave anything for the sake of God, Mighty and Sublime, but that God will replace it with something better for you." (Musnad Aḥmad, Ḥadīth 23074; Al-Arnā'ūṭ graded it ṣaḥīḥ.)

Some Benefits of Istighfār

There are many benefits in seeking forgiveness from God out of sincerity, with humility and concentration. Seeking forgiveness brings one closer to God, and it can bring one provision in this life as well.

[52]My people, seek forgiveness of your Lord and turn to Him in repentance. He will send from the sky abundant rain upon you. He will add strength to your strength. Do not turn away from Him as doers of evil.' (Qur'ān 11:52)

[8]Then I called them openly, [9]and spoke to them in public and in private.' [10]Then I said, 'Ask forgiveness of your Lord. Surely He is the Most Forgiving. [11]He will send down abundant rain from the sky for you, [12]provide you with wealth and children, and grant you gardens and waterways. (Qur'ān 71:8-12)

From these verses of the Qur'ān, we learn that istighfār can bring us strength, abundant rain, wealth, and children, for those who want these things. And the following ḥadīths state:

'Abdullāh ibn Busr [(ra)] narrated: The Prophet [(saws)] said, "Glad tidings to those who find a lot of seeking forgiveness in the record of their deeds." (Sunan Ibn Mājah, Ḥadīth 3818; Al-Albānī graded it ṣaḥīḥ.)

Az-Zubayr [(ra)] narrated: The Messenger of God [(saws)] said, "Whoever would love to be pleased with his record, let him increase seeking forgiveness on it." (Shu'ab Al-Īmān by Al-Bayhaqī, Ḥadīth 648; Al-Albānī graded it ṣaḥīḥ.)

'Ubādah ibn Aṣ-Ṣāmit [(ra)] narrated: The Messenger of God [(saws)] said, "Whoever seeks forgiveness for the believing men and women, God will record a good deed for him by each man and woman." (Musnad Ash-Shāmiyīn by Aṭ-Ṭabarānī, Ḥadīth 2118; Al-Albānī graded it ḥasan.)

Some Du'ā's regarding Istighfār and Tawbah

Shaddād ibn Aws [(ra)] narrated: The Prophet [(saws)] said, "The best way to seek forgiveness (sayyidul-istighfār) is that you say:

Allāhumma, anta Rabbī, lā ilāha illā anta, khalaqtanī wa anā ‘abduka, wa anā ‘alā ‘ahdika wa wa‘dika mastaṭa‘tu. A‘ūdhu bika min sharri mā ṣana‘tu. Abū’u laka bini‘matika ‘alayya wa abū’u laka bidhanbī. Faghfirlī, fa’innahū lā yaghfirudh-dhunūba illā anta.

(O God, you are my Lord. There is no god except for You. You created me, and I am your servant, and I hold to Your covenant and Your promise as much as I can. I seek refuge in You from the evil of what I have done. I acknowledge before You Your favors upon me, and I confess to You my sins, so forgive me, for indeed no one can forgive sins except for You.) *”*

He (the Prophet (saws)) said, “Whoever says this in the day with conviction and dies before evening, he will be among the people of Paradise. Whoever says this in the night with conviction and dies before morning, he will be among the people of Paradise.” (Ṣaḥīḥ Al-Bukhārī, Ḥadīth 6306; Riyāḍ Aṣ-Ṣāliḥīn, Ḥadīth 1875)

Zayd (ra), a freed slave of the Prophet (saws), narrated: The Messenger of God (saws) said, “Whoever says:

Astaghfirullāhal-‘Aẓīm alladhī lā ilāha illā huwal-Ḥayyul-Qayyūmu wa atūbu ilayhi.

(I seek the forgiveness of God, the Absolute Greatest, whom there is no god except for Him, the Ever-Living, the All-Sustaining, and I turn to Him in repentance.)

then God will forgive him, even if he fled from battle.” (Sunan Abū Dāwūd, Ḥadīth 1517; Jāmi‘ At-Tirmidhī, Ḥadīth 3577; Riyāḍ Aṣ-Ṣāliḥīn, Ḥadīth 1874; Al-Albānī graded it ṣaḥīḥ, and Zubayr ‘Alī Za’ī graded it ḥasan.)

Abū Bakr Aṣ-Ṣiddīq (ra) narrated that he asked the Messenger of God (saws), “Teach me a supplication which I can say during my prayer.” He (the Messenger of God (saws)) said, “Say:

Allāhumma innī ẓalamtu nafsī ẓulman kathīran walā yaghfirudh-dhunūba illā anta, faghfirlī maghfiratam-min ‘indika warḥamnī. Innaka antal-Ghafūr-ur-Raḥīm.

***(O God, I have wronged myself greatly and no one forgives sins except for You, so grant me forgiveness from Yourself, and have mercy on me, for You are the Most Forgiving, the Most Merciful.)*"** *(Ṣaḥīḥ Al-Bukhārī, Ḥadīth 834; Ṣaḥīḥ Muslim, Ḥadīth 2705; Riyāḍ Aṣ-Ṣāliḥīn, Ḥadīth 1475)*

Chapter 18

Will Non-Muslims Be In Hell?

The notion of whether one will be in Hellfire applies on an individual basis, and that judgment is for God alone. None of the creations of the Creator may sentence an individual to Hellfire. God knows what is in a person's heart, so He is the best judge. Someone may outwardly appear to be misguided, but God may love them. We must remember the ḥadīth that states:

Sahl ibn Sa'd As-Sā'idī (ra) narrated: The Messenger of God (saws) said, "Verily, a man may appear to people as doing the deeds of the people of Paradise, yet he is among the people of Hellfire. Verily, a man may appear to people as doing the deeds of the people of Hellfire, yet he is among the people of Paradise." (Ṣaḥīḥ Al-Bukhārī, Ḥadīth 2898; Ṣaḥīḥ Muslim, Ḥadīth 112)

However, it is permissible to talk about the fate of certain groups of people in a general sense, instead of an individual sense, using evidence from the Qur'ān and the Sunnah. So, generally-speaking, will non-Muslims be in Hell? Note the following Qur'ān verses and ḥadīth:

62 The believers, the Jews, the Christians, and the Sabians—all those who believe in God and the Last Day and do good deeds—will be rewarded by their Lord. They shall have no fear, nor shall they grieve. (Qur'ān 2:62)

69 Believers, Jews, Sabians, and Christians—whoever believes in God and the Last Day and does what is right—shall have nothing to fear nor shall they grieve. (Qur'ān 5:69)

Salmān Al-Fārisī (ra) narrated: I asked the Prophet (saws) about the people of religion who had been with me, mentioning their prayers and acts of worship. Then God revealed the verse, "The believers, the Jews, the Christians, and the Sabians—all those who believe in God and the Last Day and do good deeds—will be rewarded by their Lord. They shall have no fear, nor shall they grieve (Qur'ān 2:62)." (Tafsīr Ibn Abū Ḥātim 2:62; Ibn Taymiyyah graded it ṣaḥīḥ.)

(Note that the Sabians were a monotheistic religious group that has become ambiguous to history.) These verses, and this ḥadīth, do not contradict the verses and ḥadīths that mention the notion of Islām being the one true religion:

19The only true religion in God's sight is Islām. And those who were given the Book disagreed only out of rivalry, after knowledge had been given to them. He who denies God's signs should know that God is swift in His reckoning. (Qur'ān 3:19)

85If anyone seeks a religion other than Islām, it will not be accepted from him. He will be among the losers in the Hereafter. (Qur'ān 3:85)

Abū Hurayrah (ra) narrated: The Messenger of God (saws) said, "By the One in Whose Hand is the soul of Muḥammad, none from this nation of Jews and Christians hears of me, and then dies without having faith in my message, but that he will be an inhabitant of Hellfire." (Ṣaḥīḥ Muslim, Ḥadīth 153)

'Umar ibn Al-Khaṭṭāb (ra) narrated: The Messenger of God (saws) said, "O ('Umar) son of Al-Khaṭṭāb, go and call out to the people that no one will enter Paradise except the believers." (Ṣaḥīḥ Muslim, Ḥadīth 114)

The reconciliation between these verses and ḥadīths is that, although the Qur'ān states that Islām is the true religion, the Jews, Christians, and Sabians who practiced their religions with sincerity and did *not* hear about, or properly understand, Islām will be in Paradise, generally speaking. However, once the message of Islām properly reaches an individual, they will be held accountable before God based on their acceptance of it or their rejection of it. As stated above, only believers will enter Paradise, and if a disbeliever hears about, and properly understands, Islām, and then they reject it, they may end up in Hellfire. But the message has to reach them first. The Qur'ān states:

15Whoever chooses to follow the right path, follows it for his own good. And whoever goes astray, goes astray at his own peril. No bearer of burdens shall bear the burdens of another. Nor do We punish until We have sent forth a messenger to forewarn them. (Qur'ān 17:15)

This is because Islām advocates that it must be spread due to the elements of misguidance in, and the incompleteness of, other religions. Previous scriptures applied to their times and places, but the Qur'ān is the final scripture, meant for all of humanity, and it still applies here and now.

[170]Humanity! The Messenger has brought you the truth from your Lord, so believe for your own good. And if you deny the truth, know that to God belongs all that the heavens and the earth contain. God is All-Knowing and Wise. (Qur'ān 4:170)

Chapter 19

Does Hell Contradict God's Mercy and Love?

Is Hell Literally Eternal?

There are those who assert that for disbelievers who die while rejecting Islām, the punishment of Hellfire is literally eternal – that is, forever, unending, never to be cut off. This is the opinion of the majority of Muslim scholars. However, this can be a complicated issue about which there is disagreement, and a minority believe that it may be temporary. Among the minority was the significant scholar Ibn Taymiyyah (1263 – 1328 C.E.).

In three places in the Qur'ān, the Arabic word *abadan*, أَبَدًا, is used to refer to the duration of the punishment in Hell, and abadan literally means "forever":

168 God will not forgive those who deny the truth and act wrongfully, nor will He guide them 169 to any path other than the path of Hell, wherein they shall abide forever. That is easy enough for God. (Qur'ān 4:168-169)

64 God has rejected those who deny the truth and prepared for them a blazing Fire. 65 There they will live forever, and they will find therein neither friend nor helper. (Qur'ān 33:64-65)

23 'My duty is only to convey that which I receive from Him and His messages.' For those who disobey God and His Messenger there is the fire of hell, wherein they will abide forever. (Qur'ān 72:23)

There are other places in the Qur'ān where the word "abadan (forever)" is not used, but the duration of the punishment in Hell is implied to go on perpetually. The word *muqīm* is sometimes used, and although it is sometimes translated as "everlasting," it can also mean "lasting." It appears in places such as in the following verse:

37 They will want to get out of the Fire but they will be unable to do so. Theirs shall be a lasting punishment. (Qur'ān 5:37)

Regarding the word abadan, although it literally means "forever," it can also mean "a long time." This is on the authority of the scholar Ibn Al-Qayyim, who stated in his book Shifā' Al-'Alīl 1/257: "*Rather, the mention of eternity (al-khulūd) and forever (at-ta'bīd) by itself does not necessitate that it is without end, as eternity can mean to remain for a long time.*" Even in English, one may say of a tedious event, "That lasted forever," when in truth it only lasted for a long time. Ibn Al-Qayyim mentions more about God's mercy and the punishment in Hell in his book Ḥādī Al-Arwāḥ.

While abadan is used in the Qur'ān when describing the punishment in Hell for disbelievers *and* the reward for believers in Paradise, the phrase *ghayru mamnūn*, "never to be cut off" or "without end," is only used for the reward in Paradise and not for the punishment in Hell. For example, note the following Qur'ān verses:

106 The wretched ones will be in the Fire, sighing and groaning,
107 remaining in it timelessly, forever, as long as the heavens and earth endure, except as your Lord wills. Your Lord carries out whatever He wills.
108 Those who are blessed shall abide in the Garden; they will dwell therein as long as the heavens and the earth endure, except as your Lord wills. Such bounty shall be unending. (Qur'ān 11:106-108)

Scholars clarify the distinction by saying that only sinful believers will eventually enter Paradise from Hell, but disbelievers who received, understood, and rejected God's evidence will be in Hell for an unending time. That sinful believers will eventually enter Paradise is a known fact in the religion, and the evidence for this notion is provided in certain authentic ḥadīths, which will be quoted later in this chapter. But what about those who knowingly and arrogantly rejected God? Do they truly deserve to be tortured for eternity? Is this just? Is this merciful?

There are those who assert that it is not just to be punished eternally for a finite crime. However, it is not the duration of the crime for which one is punished, but the severity of the crime. For example, if an individual commits murder by shooting someone, the actual shooting takes only a matter of seconds, but the murderer is not punished for only a few seconds. Because of the severity of the crime, the murderer may receive life in prison. So it does not necessarily contradict the concept of justice for eternal Hell to exist because the One Who is being wronged is in this case eternal, and that is God.

However, some say that it might contradict God's infinite mercy to subject even the worst of His creation to literal unending torture. Does it befit the One Who is Ar-Raḥmān, the Most Compassionate (also translated as "the Infinitely Good"), to withhold His mercy from a people for eternity because they were arrogant? Would a human who loves all of humanity wish to subject anyone to eternal torture? God is more merciful than any human, and God is more loving than any human. Do not forget that one of God's names is Al-Wadūd, the Most Loving, or, as Dr. Mustafa Khattab translated it, "All-Loving" (see: the Qur'ān 85:14). Justice is understandable, and temporary torture for the worst of creation may be understood in the light of justice. But is inflicting eternal torture befitting of the One Who is the Most Loving? Would it not be more loving and more merciful for Hell to be a purification, meant to eventually bring one closer to God, even if it took a long time? These are phrased as questions because the author does not have all the answers, and only God knows for certain. Nevertheless, perhaps there is a reason why God simply used *abadan* (a long time) and *muqīm* (lasting) to describe Hell and not *ghayru mamnūn* (without end).

With all of this being said, it may be implied in the authentic ḥadīths that God's mercy will eventually reach even the disbelievers in Hell. Note the following ḥadīths:

Anas (ra) narrated: The Prophet (saws) said, "My intercession will be for those of my nation who have committed major sins." (Sunan Abū Dāwūd, Ḥadīth 4739; Jāmi' At-Tirmidhī, Ḥadīth 2435; Al-Albānī graded it ṣaḥīḥ.)

Abū Hurayrah (ra) narrated: The Messenger of God (saws) said, "The happiest person who will have my intercession on the Day of Resurrection will be the one who said sincerely from the bottom of his heart 'Lā ilāha illallāh (there is no god except for Allāh).'" (Ṣaḥīḥ Al-Bukhārī, Ḥadīth 99)

'Awf ibn Mālik Al-Ashja'ī (ra) narrated: The Messenger of God (saws) said, "A visitor came to me from my Lord and gave me the choice between half of my nation entering Paradise or the intercession in the Hereafter. I chose the intercession, and it is for whoever dies without associating

partners with God." (Jāmi' At-Tirmidhī, Ḥadīth 2441; Al-Albānī graded it ṣaḥīḥ.)

Abū Sa'īd Al-Khudrī (ra) narrated: We said, "O Messenger of God! Shall we see our Lord on the Day of Resurrection?" He said, "Do you have any difficulty in seeing the sun and the moon when the sky is clear?" We said, "No." He said, "So you will have no difficulty in seeing your Lord on that Day as you have no difficulty in seeing the sun and the moon (in a clear sky)."

(The Prophet (saws)) then said, "Somebody will announce, 'Let every nation follow what they used to worship.' So the companions of the cross will go with their cross, and the idolators (will go) with their idols, and the companions of every (false) god (will go) with their (false) gods, until there remain those who used to worship God, both the obedient ones and the mischievous ones, and some of the People of the Book. Then Hell will be presented to them as if it were a mirage.

Then it will be said to the Jews, 'What did you worship?' They will reply, 'We used to worship Ezra, the son of God.' [A note to the reader from the author: this applies only to that sect of Jews in Arabia who worshipped Ezra. The majority of Jews did not and do not.] It will be said to them, 'You are liars, for God has neither a wife nor a son. What do you want (now)?' They will reply, 'We want You to provide us with water.' Then it will be said to them, 'Drink,' and they will fall down in Hell.

Then it will be said to the Christians, 'What did you worship?' They will reply, 'We used to worship the Messiah, the son of God.' It will be said, 'You are liars, for God has neither a wife nor a son. What do you want (now)?' They will say, 'We want You to provide us with water.' It will be said to them, 'Drink,' and they will fall down in Hell.

When there remain only those who used to worship God (alone), both the obedient ones and the mischievous ones, it will be said to them, 'What keeps you here when all the people have gone?' They will say, 'We parted with them (in the world) when we were in greater need of them than we are today. We heard the call of one proclaiming, "Let every nation follow what they used to worship," and now we are waiting for our Lord.' Then the Almighty will come to them in a shape other than the one which they saw the first time, and He will say, 'I am your Lord,' and they will say, 'You are not our Lord.' And none will speak to Him at that time but the prophets. Then it will be said to them, 'Do you know any sign by which you can recognize Him?' They will say, 'The Shin,' and so God will then uncover His Shin, whereupon every believer will prostrate before Him, and there will remain those who used to prostrate before Him just for showing off and for gaining good (worldly) reputation. These people will try to prostrate, but their backs will be rigid like one piece of wood. Then the bridge will be laid across Hell."

We (the companions of the Prophet (saws)) said, "O Messenger of God! What is the bridge?"

He said, "It is a slippery (bridge) on which there are clamps and a thorny seed that is wide at one side and narrow at the other and has thorns with bent ends. Such a thorny seed is found in Najd and is called as-sa'dān. Some of the believers will cross the bridge as quickly as the wink of an eye, some as quick as lightning, a strong wind, fast horses, or she-camels. So some will be safe without any harm. Some will be safe after receiving some scratches, and some will fall down into Hell. The last person will cross by being dragged (over the bridge).

You (Muslims) cannot be more pressing in claiming from me a right that has been clearly proven to be yours than the believers in interceding with the Almighty for their (Muslim) brothers on that Day, when they see themselves safe.

They will say, 'O God! (Save) our brothers (for they) used to pray with us, fast with us, and do good deeds with us.' God will say, 'Go and take out (of Hell) anyone in whose heart you find faith equal to the weight of one (gold) dinar.' God will forbid the Fire to burn the faces of those sinners. They will go to them and find some of them in Hell up to their feet, and some up to the middle of their legs. So they will take out those whom they will recognize, and then they will return. And God will say (to them), 'Go and take out (of Hell) anyone in whose heart you find faith equal to the weight of one half dinar.' They will take out whomever they will recognize and return. And then God will say, 'Go and take out (of Hell) anyone in whose heart you find faith equal to the weight of an atom (i.e., a small ant),' and so they will take out all those whom they will recognize."

Abū Sa'īd said: If you do not believe me then read, "God does not wrong anyone by as much as a grain's weight. If there be a good deed, He will multiply it, and will bestow out of His own bounty an immense reward (Qur'ān 4:40)."

(The Prophet (saws) added), "Then the prophets, the angels, and the believers will intercede, and (last of all) the Almighty will say, 'Now remains My intercession.' He will then hold a handful of the Fire from which He will take out some people whose bodies have been burnt, and they will be thrown into a river at the entrance of Paradise, called the Water of Life.

They will grow on its banks as a seed carried by the torrent grows. You have noticed how it grows beside a rock or beside a tree, and how the side facing the sun is usually green while the side facing the shade is white. Those people will come out (of the Water of Life) like pearls, and they will have (golden) necklaces. Then they will enter Paradise, whereupon the people of Paradise will say, 'These are the people emancipated by the Most Compassionate. He has admitted them into Paradise without them having done any good deeds and without sending forth any good (for themselves).' Then it will be said to them, 'For you is what you have seen and its equivalent as well.'" (Ṣaḥīḥ Al-Bukhārī, Ḥadīth 7439; Ṣaḥīḥ Muslim, Ḥadīth 183)

It is clearly stated that the intercession of the Prophet Muḥammad (saws) will be for those of his ummah, his nation (i.e., all Muslims), that believed in the Oneness of God in their hearts but committed major sins. When one considers what is stated in the long ḥadīth narrated by Abū Sa'īd Al-Khudrī, then one sees that the intercession of the Prophet Muḥammad (saws) is just one out of the intercessions of the other prophets, the angels, and the believers. Now, if all the believers who committed major sins will be taken out of Hell through the intercession of the prophets, the angels, and the believers, even those who only had an atom's weight of good in their hearts, who will be left for God to take out? Indeed, it is stated that those who God will take out of Hell and admit into Paradise will have done no good deeds, and they will not have sent forth any good for themselves. If all the sinful believers will have been taken out by that point through the intercession of the prophets (including Muḥammad (saws)), the angels, and the believers, then it seems that only the disbelievers would be left. However, it may be that God and His Prophet (saws) never stated this explicitly in order to emphasize the severity of disbelief and the punishment associated with it.

Some may quote the verse of the Qur'ān that reads:

48So no intercession will avail them. (Qur'ān 74:48)

But can God really be counted as an intercessor? His intercession is only called that nominally, but in truth, who is there with whom God would intercede? There is no one above God, so He is the *accepter* of intercession, rather than an intercessor Himself. Therefore, considering the verse, the intercession of the prophets, the angels, and the believers will not benefit the disbelievers, but this does not necessarily exclude God's intervention. And God knows best.

Hell Lasts Long and Should Be Avoided

The purpose of this chapter is to point out that Hell does not contradict God's mercy and God's love. However, the purpose of this chapter is *not* to undermine the severity of Hell. According to Islām, Hell certainly exists, and it is a very serious matter. It is a torturous place with suffering beyond the imagination of any human. Hell should be avoided at all costs. And we must not underestimate the duration implied by the word abadan. Even if it means a long, long time, not one of God's creations would want to remain therein even for a second. But one's punishment in Hell could maybe last for one thousand years, one million years, one billion years, one trillion years, or perhaps even beyond that. All of those numbers are finite, so those would all technically be temporary sentences, although they may *feel* like forever. Even a googolplex is a finite number. And this is speculation on the author's part. We ultimately do not know how long Hell will last, so it is best to avoid it altogether. And in the Qur'ān, God condemns those who rely on the temporary nature of Hell as an excuse for rejecting Islām:

80They say, 'The Fire is not going to touch us, and [even if it does], it will only be for a few days!' Say [to them], 'Have you received a promise from God—for God never breaks His promise—or do you attribute something to God which you do not know?' 81Truly, those who do evil and are encompassed by their misdeeds, shall be the inmates of the Fire. Therein they shall abide forever. 82But those who believe and do good works are the heirs of Paradise. There they shall abide forever. (Qur'ān 2:80-82)

23Have you not seen those who received a portion of the Book? When they are invited to accept the judgement of God's Book, a group of them turns away in aversion. 24That is because they say, 'The Fire will touch us only for a limited number of days.' Thus the false beliefs which they have invented have deluded them in the matter of their religion. (Qur'ān 3:23-24)

Chapter 20
Women in Islām

Women are the twin halves of men, originally created from one soul. In Islām, women and men each have their rights and obligations. The religion may enjoin different roles upon them due to differences in biology or psychology, but that does not imply that one is inherently superior to the other. Everything in the Qur'ān and the Sunnah that applies to men applies to women as well, unless otherwise specified, and the different sexes are required to uphold virtues, such as modesty, in their own way. Moreover, Islām explicitly enjoins that women be treated with kindness. Islām gave women rights that they lacked in pre-Islāmic Arabia, such as the right to an inheritance, the right to not be inherited and to choose whether they want to marry someone, and the right to an education. The best man is he who is best to his wife, and his wife, if she is righteous, is so important that she fulfills half of his religion. Raising daughters can bring one close to the Prophet Muḥammad (saws), and Paradise is obtained by tending to one's mother, who is more significant than one's father. In this way, Islām honors wives, daughters, and mothers.

1 *O humanity! Fear your Lord, who created you from a single soul. He created its mate from it and from the two of them spread countless men and women [throughout the earth]. Fear God, in Whose name you appeal to one another, and be mindful of your obligations in respect of ties of kinship. God is always watching over you. (Qur'ān 4:1)*

19 *Believers, it is not lawful for you to inherit women against their will, nor should you detain them wrongfully, so that you may take away a part of what you have given them, unless they are guilty of adultery. Live with them in accordance with what is fair and kind. If you dislike them, it may be that you dislike something which God might make a source of abundant good. (Qur'ān 4:19)*

[21]Another of His signs is that He created for you from among yourselves spouses, so that you might find comfort in them, and He created between you affection and kindness. Truly there are signs in this for people who reflect. (Qur'ān 30:21)

[35]Surely, for men and women who have surrendered [to God], believing men and believing women, obedient men and obedient women, truthful men and truthful women, patient men and patient women, humble men and humble women, charitable men and charitable women, fasting men and fasting women, men and women who guard their chastity, and men and women who are ever mindful of God—God is ready with forgiveness and an immense reward. (Qur'ān 33:35)

'Ā'ishah (ra) narrated: The Messenger of God (saws) said, "The best of you is the best to his wives, and I am the best of you to my wives." (Jāmi' At-Tirmidhī, Ḥadīth 3895; Al-Albānī graded it ṣaḥīḥ.)

Anas (ra) narrated: The Messenger of God (saws) said, "Whoever God provides with a righteous wife, God has assisted him in half of his religion. Let him fear God regarding the second half." (Al-Mu'jam Al-Awsaṭ by Aṭ-Ṭabarānī, Ḥadīth 992; As-Suyūṭī graded it ṣaḥīḥ, and Al-Albānī graded it ḥasan. It is also recorded in Al-Mustadrak by Al-Ḥākim.)

Mālik (ra) narrated: The Messenger of God (saws) said, "Whoever takes care of two girls until they reach puberty, he and I will come like this on the Day of Resurrection" – and he held his two fingers together. (Ṣaḥīḥ Muslim, Ḥadīth 2631)

It was narrated from Mu'āwiyah ibn Jāhimah As-Sulamī that Jāhimah (ra) came to the Prophet (saws) and said, "O Messenger of God! I want to go out and fight (in the cause of God) and I have come to ask your advice." (The Prophet (saws)) said, "Do you have a mother?" He said, "Yes." He said, "Then stay with her, for Paradise is beneath her feet." (Sunan An-Nasa'ī, Ḥadīth 3104; Zubayr 'Alī Za'ī graded it ṣaḥīḥ.)

Abū Hurayrah (ra) narrated: A man came to the Messenger of God (saws) and said, "O Messenger of God! Who is more entitled to be treated with the best companionship by me?" The Prophet (saws) said, "Your mother." The man said, "Who is next?" The Prophet (saws) said, "Your mother." The man further said, "Who is next?" The Prophet (saws) said, "Your mother." The man asked for the fourth time, "Who is next?" The Prophet (saws) said, "Your father." (Ṣaḥīḥ Al-Bukhārī, Ḥadīth 5971)

The Most Righteous Women in History

The four most righteous women in history were Āsiyah (the wife of Pharaoh; she believed in God although her husband did not), Mary (the mother of the Prophet Jesus (as)), Khadījah (the first wife of the Prophet Muḥammad (saws)), and Fāṭimah (the youngest daughter of the Prophet Muḥammad (saws)). 'Ā'ishah, a later wife of the Prophet Muḥammad (saws), was also very significant.

Ibn 'Abbās (ra) narrated: The Messenger of God (saws) said, "The best of women among the people of Paradise are Khadījah bint Khuwaylid, Fāṭimah bint Muḥammad, Maryam bint 'Imrān, and 'Āsiyah bint Muzāḥim, the wife of Pharaoh." (Musnad Aḥmad, Ḥadīth 2896; Al-Albānī graded it ṣaḥīḥ.)

Anas (ra) narrated: The Prophet (saws) said, "Sufficient for you among the women of the worlds are Maryam bint 'Imrān, Khadījah bint Khuwaylid, Fāṭimah bint Muḥammad, and 'Āsiyah the wife of Pharaoh." (Jāmi' At-Tirmidhī, Ḥadīth 3878; Zubayr 'Alī Za'ī graded it ṣaḥīḥ.)

Anas (ra) narrated: The Prophet (saws) said, "The superiority of 'Ā'ishah over other women is like the superiority of tharīd to other kinds of food." (Ṣaḥīḥ Al-Bukhārī, Ḥadīth 5419; Ṣaḥīḥ Muslim, Ḥadīth 2446)

Controversies and Misconceptions regarding Women in Islām

Wife-Beating

It may be noted that some have misunderstood a certain verse in the Qur'ān regarding the treatment of women:

34 Men are protectors of women, because God has made some of them excel others and because they spend their wealth on them. So virtuous women are obedient and guard in the husband's absence what God would have them guard. As for those from whom you apprehend ill conduct, advise them, then refuse to share their beds, and finally hit them [lightly]. Then if they obey you, take no further action against them. For God is High, Great. (Qur'ān 4:34)

The above phrase "discipline them" is often translated as "beat them." The Prophet (saws) taught that if wives behave horribly towards their husbands, "then abandon their beds and beat them with a beating that is not harmful." This is reported in Jāmi' At-Tirmidhī, Ḥadīth 1163. Here are the words used in the last part of the sentence of the ḥadīth:

وَاضْرِبُوهُنَّ ضَرْبًا غَيْرَ مُبَرِّحٍ

waḍribūhunna ḍarban ghayra mubarriḥin

and beat them with a beating that is not severe.

The word *waḍribūhunna* means "and beat them," the word *ḍarban* means "a beating," the word *ghayra* means "other than" and the word *mubarriḥin* means "severe" or "painful." So what is prescribed in extreme cases is a light hitting. Scholars have agreed that the hitting should not cause pain. In fact, Ibn 'Abbās, a young companion of the Prophet (saws) and a significant scholar of the Qur'ān, was asked what was meant by the words "ḍarban ghayra mubarriḥin (a beating that is not severe)." Ibn 'Abbās's response was "bis-siwāki wanaḥwihī (with a toothbrush stick or something similar)." This can be found in the Qur'ān commentary Tafsīr Aṭ-Ṭabarī for sūrah 4, āyah 34. Moreover, if one does lightly beat his wife with a toothbrush stick, he must also avoid her face.

Mu'āwiyah Al-Qushayrī narrated: I said, "O Messenger of God! What is the right of the wife of one of us over him?" The Messenger of God (saws) said, "That you should give her food when you eat, clothe her when you clothe yourself, do not strike her on the face, do not revile her, and do not separate yourself from her except in the house." (Sunan Abū Dāwūd, Ḥadīth 2142; Al-Albānī graded it ḥasan ṣaḥīḥ.)

The beating is therefore symbolic, and even then, it is only to be used as a last resort. The Prophet (saws) himself never beat his wives, and he dissuaded others from doing so.

'Ā'ishah (ra) narrated: The Messenger of God (saws) never hit anyone with his hand, nor any woman or servant, except when fighting in the cause of God. And if he was offended in some way he never took revenge for his own sake, unless one of the sacred limits of God had been transgressed,

then he would take steps to correct it for the sake of God. (Ṣaḥīḥ Muslim, Ḥadīth 2328; Riyāḍ Aṣ-Ṣāliḥīn, Ḥadīth 643)

'Abdullāh ibn Zam'ah (ra) narrated: The Prophet (saws) said, "How does anyone of you beat his wife as he beats the stallion camel, and then embrace her?" (Ṣaḥīḥ Al-Bukhārī, Ḥadīth 6042)

Some say that the Prophet Muḥammad (saws) once beat his wife 'Ā'ishah, but this is a misinterpretation or an exaggeration of what really happened. This was narrated in a long ḥadīth in Ṣaḥīḥ Muslim, Ḥadīth 974, the full extent of which will not be quoted herein for the sake of brevity. Regardless, in the ḥadīth, narrated by 'Ā'ishah herself, the Prophet (saws) thought she was asleep one night, and he took special care to not disturb her as he left the house. She secretly followed him, saw him praying at the cemetery, and then discretely went back to the house before he entered. When he came back, he noticed that she was out of breath, and he asked her about this. When she told him the story, he nudged her on the chest (as he sometimes did when advising male companions of his), and he told her why he went to the cemetery. He did not yell at her or beat her. Sometimes the sentence she spoke is translated as "he gave me a shove in the chest that hurt me," but it has also been translated as "he gave me a nudge on the chest which I felt." The Arabic word *ḍaraba*, "to hit," is not used here. When one looks at the context of the gentle actions of the Prophet (saws) in the ḥadīth, one can gather that any pain 'Ā'ishah may have felt was likely unintentional. Furthermore, in the ḥadīth quoted above, 'Ā'ishah herself stated that the Prophet Muḥammad (saws) never hit a woman.

Wives As Prisoners

The following ḥadīth reads:

Sulaymān ibn 'Amr ibn Al-Aḥwaṣ narrated: My father narrated to me that he witnessed the Farewell Ḥajj with the Messenger of God (saws). So he thanked and praised God, and he reminded and gave admonition. He mentioned a story in his narration, and he (the Prophet (saws)) said: "And indeed I order you to be good to the women, for they are but captives with you over whom you have no power than that, except if they come with manifest evil behavior. If they do that, then abandon their beds and beat them with a beating that is not harmful. And if they obey you then you have no cause against them. Indeed you have rights over your women, and your women have rights over you. As for your rights over your women, they must not allow anyone whom you dislike to tread on your bedding (furniture), nor admit anyone in your home that you dislike. And their rights over you are that you treat them well in clothing them and feeding them." (Jāmi' At-Tirmidhī, Ḥadīth 1163; Zubayr 'Alī Za'ī graded it ṣaḥīḥ.)

Some may take issue with the wording that the Prophet (saws) used in saying that wives are "captives" (also translated as "prisoners"). However, the Arabic word he used was عَوَانٌ (*'awānun*), and it is derived from the root عان, ع و ن ('āna: to assist, to help), and in various places in the Qur'ān forms of this verb are used to convey the meaning of helping or seeking help. Therefore, the word 'awānun may be translated as "helpers" or "assistants." If one insists on using the term "captives," then understand that the wife is captive to the husband's rights over her, but it may be understood that the husband is also captive to the rights of the wife over him. Lastly, the Qur'ān says:

71The believers, both men and women, are guardians of each other. (Qur'ān 9:71)

And the following ḥadīth reads:

'Ā'ishah (ra) narrated: The Messenger of God (saws) said, "Verily, women are the counterparts of men." (Jāmi' At-Tirmidhī, Ḥadīth 113; Al-Albānī graded it ṣaḥīḥ.)

A Woman's Inheritance

The Qur'ān states:

11Concerning your children, God enjoins you that a male shall receive a share equivalent to that of two females. (Qur'ān 4:11)

In verses 11, 12, and 176 of chapter 4 of the Qur'ān, there are instances in which the share of inheritance that a female receives is equal to half of the share of inheritance that a male receives. The reason for males receiving twice as much is simply because the Qur'ān designates men to be the providers of women:

[34]Men are protectors of women, because God has made some of them excel others and because they spend their wealth on them. (Qur'ān 4:34)

In Islām, a husband is obligated to spend on his wife, but a wife is not obligated to spend on her husband. Women can provide if there is consent on their part to do so, but they do not have to. Rather, it is the man's responsibility to provide for the woman. For this reason, males receive twice the share of females when it comes to inheritance because they are obligated to provide for their families whereas a woman's money is her own.

A Woman's Ability to Bear Witness

The longest verse in the Qur'ān is 2:282, and it is about making a contract for a debt. Part of the verse states:

Call in two of your men as witnesses. But if two men cannot be found, then call one man and two women out of those you approve of as witnesses, so that if one of the two women should forget the other can remind her.

Some object to the fact that two women must be called to witness in place of one man. However, one must bear in mind the sociological context in which this verse was revealed. In that setting, centuries ago in Arabia, women did not normally take part in matters of business, so there might have been aspects of a business contract that a woman would forget or misunderstand. In other words, the cultural norms of the pre-Islamic period of ignorance caused women to be financially illiterate. It should be noted that Islām does not forbid a woman from taking part in business, but due to the societal norms of that time, many women did not. So this Qur'ānic verse is a product of its setting, and only in this instance of a debt transaction is the bearing witness by two women equal to that of one man. In other instances, the testimony of a woman is equal to that of a man.

Note also that in attributing ḥadīths to the Prophet (saws) there is supposed to be a reliable chain of transmitters, and one of the top transmitters of ḥadīth from the time of the companions of the Prophet (saws) was his wife 'Ā'ishah. She did not require the testimony of another woman or that of a man in order to relate ḥadīths. Rather, her testimony by itself was considered trustworthy enough. This is just one example of one woman's testimony being considered acceptable.

Polygyny

Polygamy is the practice of marrying more than one person. Polygyny is the practice of one man marrying more than one woman. Polyandry is the practice of one woman marrying more than one man. In Islām, polygyny is permissible, whereas polyandry is forbidden. Although the explanation behind this is not explicitly elaborated upon in the Qur'ān and the Sunnah, there may be several reasons behind this. One could be that this allows for a man, who can afford to, to take care of widows or needy women, as Islām designated men to be the providers of women. Another reason could be to increase one's offspring, thereby multiplying their family and the Islāmic community at large. And another reason could be to allow a man of influence to strengthen ties between tribes and families.

Polyandry, however, is forbidden because if a woman was to marry more than one husband, a child's lineage would not be known, and there would be dispute as to which man would have the responsibility of raising the child. This could lead to the breaking of the family structure. While in modern times there exist paternity tests, the older principle still stands, as it is unthinkable Islāmically that there should be a test to determine to whom a child belongs. In pre-Islāmic Arabia, there would sometimes exist a marriage that resulted from a woman having intercourse with multiple men. If a child was born from that, a seeress would supposedly determine who the father was, and he would marry the mother. Islām abolished that practice, solidified the family structure, and aims to protect one's lineage, thereby strengthening the ties among relatives.

It should also be noted that there are conditions to a man taking multiple wives. A Muslim man is not permitted to marry more than four wives, and he must be able to provide for them all on an equal basis in terms of finance, food, and clothing. If he cannot do that, then he should only marry one woman. Only the Prophet Muḥammad (saws) was permitted to marry more than four wives because God gave him the strength and financial ability to do that, and in doing so he was able to help more widows. As has been stated in another chapter, the Prophet's (saws) first wife from the age of 25 was Khadījah, and she remained his only wife until she passed away when he was in his 50's. Although Muḥammad (saws) did have several wives at once further on in his life, all of the marriages were to support widows and/or to cement political ties, with the exception of his marriage to 'Ā'ishah bint Abū Bakr, who was his only virgin wife. It is unlikely that a man of such high integrity and piety, who had been monogamous from the age of 25, and who was in his 50's, would marry multiple women out of mere lust.

Lastly, if one has a background with the Jewish scriptures, then it may be noted that a few righteous men in the Hebrew Bible took more than one wife at a time, including Abraham (as), Jacob (as), David (as), and Solomon (as).

Women in Hell

There exists a ḥadīth that reads as follows:

Ibn 'Abbās (ra) narrated: The Prophet (saws) said, "I looked into Paradise and saw that most of its people are the poor, and I looked into the Fire and saw that most of its people are women." (Ṣaḥīḥ Muslim, Ḥadīth 2737)

Some people are shocked to read that the Prophet Muḥammad (saws) said that the majority of the people of Hell are women. However, this does not at all imply that women are inferior to men.

Firstly, this is only an instance of the Prophet (saws) reporting numerical estimates. It is not a commentary on the character of women.

Secondly, there is another ḥadīth that reads:

Abū Hurayrah (ra) narrated: Abū Al-Qāsim (a nickname for the Prophet Muḥammad (saws), meaning "Father of Al-Qāsim") said, "Verily, the first group to enter Paradise will have faces as bright as the full moon at night. The next group will have faces as bright as shining stars in the sky. Every man will have two wives and the marrow of their shanks would glimmer beneath their skin and there will be no one in Paradise without a wife." (Ṣaḥīḥ Muslim, Ḥadīth 2834)

Some scholars have figured that if every man in Paradise will have two wives, that means there will be twice as many women in Paradise as men. In other words, women may be the majority in Paradise too. So if women are the majority in Hellfire and the majority in Paradise, then it follows that women are simply the majority of humankind. This may be corroborated by the following ḥadīth, which predicts the ratio of the genders in the last days:

Anas ibn Mālik (ra) narrated: The Prophet (saws) said, "There will be an abundance of women and a scarcity of men such that fifty women will be maintained by a single man." (Ṣaḥīḥ Al-Bukhārī, Ḥadīth 81; Ṣaḥīḥ Muslim, Ḥadīth 2671)

Chapter 21

Marriage and Divorce in Islām

Marriage

The Arabic word for marriage is *nikāḥ*, and marriage is highly recommended in Islām.

[32]Marry those among you who are single, and those of your male and female slaves who are righteous. If they are poor, God will provide for them from His bounty, for God is All-Bountiful, All-Knowing. (Qur'ān 24:32)

[21]Another of His signs is that He created for you from among yourselves spouses, so that you might find comfort in them, and He created between you affection and kindness. Truly there are signs in this for people who reflect. (Qur'ān 30:21)

'Abdullāh ibn Mas'ūd (ra) narrated: The Messenger of God (saws) said, "O young people! Whoever among you can marry should marry because it helps him lower his gaze and guard his modesty. And whoever is not able to marry should fast as fasting diminishes his sexual desire." (Ṣaḥīḥ Al-Bukhārī, Ḥadīth 5066; Ṣaḥīḥ Muslim, Ḥadīth 1400)

Anas (ra) narrated: The Messenger of God (saws) said, "Whoever God provides with a righteous wife, God has assisted him in half of his religion. Let him fear God regarding the second half." (Al-Mu'jam Al-Awsaṭ by Aṭ-Ṭabarānī, Ḥadīth 992; As-Suyūṭī graded it ṣaḥīḥ, and Al-Albānī graded it ḥasan. It is also recorded in Al-Mustadrak by Al-Ḥākim.)

Abū Hurayrah (ra) narrated: The Prophet (saws) said, "A woman is married for four things: her wealth, her family status, her beauty, and her religion. So marry the religious woman and prosper." (Ṣaḥīḥ Al-Bukhārī, Ḥadīth 5090; Ṣaḥīḥ Muslim, Ḥadīth 1466)

As stated above, spouses are supposed to find comfort in each other, not anxiety, fear, or dread. They must not harm one another because in Islām there exists the principle of not harming and not reciprocating harm. And the best of the Muslims are those who are the best to their wives.

'Ā'ishah (ra) narrated: The Messenger of God (saws) said, "The best of you is the best to his wives, and I am the best of you to my wives." (Jāmi' At-Tirmidhī, Ḥadīth 3895; Al-Albānī graded it ṣaḥīḥ.)

Each spouse has rights over the other spouse. The husband is designated to be the provider for his wife and children. Women are allowed to earn money too, but the wife is not obligated to share any of her money with her husband, and he may not take any of it without her permission. It is the right of the wife over the husband to be provided for in the sense that she is fed and clothed in kindness, and she must also be accommodated with a suitable dwelling. The rights of the husband over the wife are that she must take care of the household; she must not allow into their home anyone that the husband dislikes; and she must respond to the husband's call of desire, as long as she is not on her period or sick, and as long as she will not be harmed in some way.

In order to get married, a woman must consent to the marriage, and she must have a *walī*, a guardian, to give her in marriage. A walī must be a sane man, of the same religion as the bride, and he may be a close relative that she is not allowed to marry. This includes fathers, grandfathers, sons who have reached puberty, brothers, uncles, nephews, etc. A Muslim leader serves as the walī for a woman that does not have one.

If a man and a woman are serious about marrying each other, then the man may look at the woman's face and hands in order to know the manner of her appearance. This applies even if the woman normally chooses to wear gloves and a face veil (*niqāb*). In order for the marriage to take place, the man must give the woman a *mahr* (dowry), which is a gift for the bride. This gift can be anything, including money, but it does not have to be extravagant. It can be something as simple as some dates, which are a type of fruit, or it can be some sort of clothing, or it can be teaching her a part of the Qur'ān that he knows and she does not know. These are just examples, and there is no set minimum or maximum for a mahr. The mahr may be paid immediately at the marriage or it can be delayed if both parties agree to that.

When the marriage takes place, an imām or a judge may guide the ceremony, although this is technically not required. The mahr is mentioned, and the walī says to the groom something along the lines of "I marry you to so-and-so," and the groom says, "I accept," or something similar. One essential condition for the marriage is that it must take place in the presence of two witnesses. If all of these qualifications are met, then the marriage is valid. There is also nothing wrong with having a written marriage contract with stipulations from both the bride and the groom.

Any time soon after the marriage contract has been made, the husband must host a *walīmah*, which is a wedding feast. There are no stipulations regarding the size of the walīmah, how many guests to invite, or the specific time for it, but it should be held regardless. Furthermore, those invited to a walīmah should accept the invitation.

Anas (ra) narrated: The Prophet (saws) saw traces of yellow perfume on 'Abdur-Raḥmān ibn 'Awf, and he said, "What is this?" 'Abdur-Raḥmān said, "I have married a woman and have paid gold equal to the weight of a datestone (as her mahr). The Prophet (saws) said to him, "May God bless you. Offer a wedding banquet, even with one sheep." (Ṣaḥīḥ Al-Bukhārī, Ḥadīth 5155; Ṣaḥīḥ Muslim, Ḥadīth 1427)

Abū Hurayrah (ra) narrated: The Messenger of God (saws) said, "When any of you is invited, he should accept the invitation. If he is fasting, he should pray (for the betterment of the host), and if he is not fasting, he should eat." (Ṣaḥīḥ Muslim, Ḥadīth 1431; Riyāḍ Aṣ-Ṣāliḥīn, Ḥadīth 737)

Divorce

The Arabic word for divorce is *ṭalāq*, and it should be avoided if there is a way to reconcile a couple. However, if reconciliation is not possible, then there is a specific time to divorce a wife in Islām. A man may not divorce his wife while she is on her period, and he may not divorce her if he has recently had sexual intercourse with her until she gets her period and finishes it. In order to divorce a wife, a husband simply has to state clearly, with clear intention, something along the lines of, "I divorce you." The husband should only say this *once*; although there is a misconception that he may say it three times at once. Additionally, the husband may *not* take back any of her mahr if he was the one to initiate the divorce.

From the time the husband makes the statement of divorce, a waiting period begins, called an *'iddah.* The 'iddah lasts for the time it takes the woman to go through three menstrual cycles. However, if she has reached menopause, or for some medical reason does not have a menstrual cycle, then the 'iddah is for three Hijrī months. During the 'iddah, the couple is still married, they are supposed to live in the same home, the wife still has rights over her husband, and the husband may take her back if he wishes. Once the three months are over, if they have not had sexual intercourse or the divorce has not been retracted, then the husband and the wife are officially divorced, and they no longer have spousal rights over each other.

If a woman is clearly pregnant, then the husband may divorce her any time during the pregnancy, and her 'iddah is until she gives birth.

If the husband and the wife have never consummated their marriage, then there is no 'iddah for the divorce. However, if the ex-husband had specified the mahr and not given it yet, he must give the ex-wife half of the mahr. If the ex-wife allows the ex-husband to not pay, that is permissible, and if the ex-husband pays the full mahr, then that is permissible too.

If a woman wishes to divorce her husband, then she must give him back her mahr, or some payment that is agreed upon between the two of them, and he may agree to divorce her. Some scholars say that the husband may let her go without any payment, if he wishes, but there is a difference of opinion on this matter. This type of divorce is called *khul'* (also spelled: *khul'a*) , and it can take place even during the woman's period, and the 'iddah after divorce through khul' is her having one menstrual cycle. However, divorce is technically in the hands of the husband, and he may refuse to divorce her. If she is in danger or in dire need of divorce, she may seek refuge with the authorities, and she should go to a Muslim judge or leader and explain the situation. Once both parties are heard, the judge or leader may order a divorce for the woman.

A husband and a wife may divorce and get back together twice, if they wish to try and reconcile differences. However, if the husband divorces his wife a third time, then it is not permissible for them to get back together until she has *sincerely* married another man. If the woman married another man, truly intending to make things work, but he divorces her, only then may she remarry the first man, who divorced her three times.

Interfaith Marriage

In Islām, it is permissible for Muslim men to marry women from the People of Book (i.e., Jews and Christians). In such a circumstance, the Muslim husband and the Jewish or Christian wife must allow each other to practice their religions in peace, and any children they have should be raised as Muslims. Therefore, if a man embraces Islām, and he is married to a Jew or a Christian, he may keep his wife.

5Today, all good things have been made lawful to you. The food of the People of the Book is lawful to you, and your food is lawful to them. The chaste believing women and the chaste women of the people who were given the Book before you, are lawful to you, provided that you give them their dowries, and marry them, neither committing fornication nor taking them as mistresses. The deeds of anyone who rejects the faith will come to nothing, and in the Hereafter he will be among the losers. (Qur'ān 5:5)

However, it is not permissible for Muslim men to marry any woman who is not a Muslim, a Jew, or a Christian.

Additionally, a Muslim woman can only marry a Muslim man, and she may not even marry a Jewish man or a Christian man. This may be to protect a Muslim woman from oppression or discrimination she may face in practicing her religion, however subtle such oppression or discrimination might be. If a woman who is married to a non-Muslim embraces Islām, then the marriage is suspended, and she should separate from her non-Muslim husband, she should not have sexual intercourse with him, and it is better that she covers herself fully around him, except for her face and hands. However, if he accepts Islām during her 'iddah (waiting period), then their marriage becomes valid again. The Qur'ān states:

10Believers! When believing women come to you as refugees, submit them to a test. Their faith is best known to God. Then if you find them to be true believers, do not send them back to those who deny the truth. These [women] are not lawful for them, nor are those who deny the truth lawful for these women. But hand back to those who deny the truth the dowries they gave them. And it is not an offence for you to marry such women, provided you give them their dowries. Do not maintain your marriages with those women who deny the truth. Demand repayment of the dowries you have given them, and let the disbelievers ask for the return of what they have spent. Such is God's judgement. He judges with justice between you. God is All-Knowing, All-Wise. [11] *If any of your wives desert you to go over to the disbelievers, and you subsequently take spoils from them, give to those who have been deserted by their wives the equivalent of the dowries they gave them. Fear God in whom you believe. (Qur'ān 60:10-11)*

Chapter 22

Reproductive Practices and Islām

Contraception

It is permissible to use temporary means of contraception in Islām because some of the companions of the Prophet (saws) practiced coitus interruptus (i.e., pulling out before ejaculation), and the Prophet (saws) did not forbid them from doing that.

Jābir ibn 'Abdullāh (ra) narrated: We used to practice coitus interruptus during the lifetime of the Messenger of God (saws). This (news) reached the Messenger of God (saws), and he did not forbid us (this practice). (Ṣaḥīḥ Al-Bukhārī, Ḥadīth 5207; Ṣaḥīḥ Muslim, Ḥadīth 1440)

Based on this ḥadīth, many view contraception as analogous to coitus interruptus. However, permanent sterilization of the reproductive system is forbidden in Islām because Muslims are encouraged to have children, as having children is in alignment with the example of the Prophet Muḥammad (saws) as well as the examples of the prophets before him. And the following ḥadīth states:

Ma'qil ibn Yasār (ra) narrated: The Prophet (saws) said, "Marry those who are loving and fertile, for I shall outnumber the nations by you." (Sunan Abū Dāwūd, Ḥadīth 2050; Al-Albānī graded it ḥasan ṣaḥīḥ.)

Abortion

Abortion is a complicated issue that often depends upon the circumstance, and an Islāmic scholar should be consulted for each case. However, generally speaking, abortion is forbidden in Islām unless there is a serious risk to the mother's health or life. The Qur'ān states:

[31]You shall not kill your offspring for fear of poverty. It is We who provide for them and for you. Indeed, killing them is a great sin. (Qur'ān 17:31)

[32]Whoever kills a human being—except as a punishment for murder or for spreading corruption in the land— shall be regarded as having killed all of humanity, and whoever saves a human being shall be regarded as having saved all of humanity. (Qur'ān 5:32)

And the following ḥadīth states:

'Abdullāh ibn Mas'ūd (ra) narrated: The Messenger of God (saws), and he is truthful and trusted, said, "Indeed, the creation of each one of you is brought together in his mother's womb for forty days as a drop, then he is a clot for a similar period, then a morsel for a similar period, then there is sent to him the angel who blows the spirit into him, and he is commanded regarding four matters: to write down his provision, his life span, his deeds, and whether he is blessed or damned. By Allāh, other than Whom there is no god, one of you acts like the people of Paradise until he is but an arm's length from it, and what is written overtakes him, so he acts like the people of Hellfire, and he enters it. Indeed, one of you acts like the people of Hellfire until he is but an arm's length from it, and what is written overtakes him, so he acts like the people of Paradise, and he enters it." (Ṣaḥīḥ Al-Bukhārī, Ḥadīth 3332; Ṣaḥīḥ Muslim, Ḥadīth 2643)

This ḥadīth informs us that a fetus starts out as a drop for 40 days, then a clot for 40 days, then a morsel for 40 days. That is a total time of 120 days, and *then* the spirit is breathed into the fetus. 120 days is about 4 months, a little over the first trimester.

[Note: The second part of the ḥadīth quoted above is regarding the matters of the decree (qadar) of God and a human's free will. The phrase "what is written" refers to a person's freely made choices, all of which God knew about beforehand. God's prior knowledge of a choice does not cancel out the free will a human used in making that choice."]

Scholars say that abortion out of necessity should only be performed within the first 40 days, while it is still a drop and therefore like an inanimate object. This is because once it transitions from a drop to a clot, it begins to take on human features even though it has no soul yet. However, if abortion is not necessary, then it should not be performed, and fear of the socio-economic status of the potential child and mother is not a valid reason for abortion. In other words, one cannot have an abortion if they are afraid of poverty or social estrangement. This is according to the Permanent Committee for Scholarly Research and Ifta, which is an organization of senior scholars in Saudi Arabia, and the reference for this ruling is in Fatāwā Al-Lajnah Ad-Dā'imah 21/450.

After the first 40 days, if there is a pressing need to abort the fetus, such as extreme fetal deformity or a pregnancy resulting from rape, then it is permissible to terminate the pregnancy any time before the 120th day because the fetus still does not have a soul. However, once the soul has been breathed into the fetus, then it is absolutely forbidden to abort it unless one or more trusted medical doctors confirm that the mother will die unless it is aborted.

The reason that early abortion is discouraged, even within the first 40 days, is that the fetus is potential life, and needlessly altering its course of growth is a breach of trust in God and His ability to provide, both financially and emotionally.

Chapter 23
The LGBTQ+ Community and Islām

Islām discourages sexual relations that are not between a married man and woman. God says in the Qur'ān:

[80]We sent Lot, who said to his people, 'How can you commit an abomination such as no one in the world has ever done before you? [81]You lust after men rather than women! You transgress all bounds!' (Qur'ān 7:80-81)

[54]And tell of Lot. He said to his people, 'Will you commit evil knowingly? [55]Must you go lustfully to men instead of women? Indeed, you are a people who are deeply ignorant.' (Qur'ān 27:54-55)

And the following ḥadīth states:

'Abdullāh ibn 'Abbās (ra) narrated: The Prophet (saws) said, " "The curse of God is upon the one who engages in the act of the people of Lot. The curse of God is upon the one who engages in the act of the people of Lot. The curse of God is upon the one who engages in the act of the people of Lot." (Musnad Aḥmad, Ḥadīth 2816; Al-Albānī graded it ṣaḥīḥ.)

It is important to note that individuals with homosexual inclinations are not condemned, but the act itself is condemned, and it is a personal test for such individuals. Muslims believe in putting the desires of God before their own desires in the hopes that it will lead to a better life in this world and the next. Homosexual acts are clearly forbidden in the religion. However, part of submitting to God is to treat everyone with kindness and gentle manners, regardless of their background. In the Qur'ān, when God was about to destroy the people of Lot (as), Abraham (as) prayed for those people.

[74]When the fear had left Abraham, and the glad tidings had been conveyed to him, he began to plead with Us for Lot's people, [75]for Abraham was forbearing, tender-hearted and oft-returning to God. (Qur'ān 11:74-75)

And the Prophet Muḥammad (saws) said: "God is Gentle and loves gentleness in all things." (Ṣaḥīḥ Al-Bukhārī, Ḥadīth 6927; Riyāḍ Aṣ-Ṣāliḥīn, Ḥadīth 632)

Cross-Dressing

Cross-dressing, transvestite practices, and transgender practices are also forbidden in Islām, as the following ḥadīths state:

Ibn 'Abbās (ra) narrated: The Messenger of God (saws) cursed men who imitate women and women who imitate men. (Ṣaḥīḥ Al-Bukhārī, Ḥadīth 5885)

Abū Hurayrah (ra) narrated: The Messenger of God (saws) cursed the man who dressed like a woman and the woman who dressed like a man. (Sunan Abū Dāwūd, Ḥadīth 4098; Al-Albānī graded it ṣaḥīḥ.)

Did the Prophet (saws) cross-dress?

There are some who misread certain ḥadīths, and they claim that the Prophet Muḥammad (saws) himself cross-dressed. The ḥadīths in question are Ṣaḥīḥ Al-Bukhārī, Ḥadīth 3775 and Ṣaḥīḥ Muslim, Ḥadīth 2402. These are two separate ḥadīths, and as they are long, they will not be quoted herein. However, for each ḥadīth, some mistranslate them to say that the Prophet (saws) was wearing 'Ā'ishah's garment. However, in the ḥadīth recorded in Ṣaḥīḥ Al-Bukhārī, the word used is *liḥāf*, which literally means "blanket" or "bedspread." So the Prophet (saws) was simply in 'Ā'ishah's blanket. In the ḥadīth recorded in Ṣaḥīḥ Muslim, the word used is *mirṭ*, which can be any garment that is not sewed. Although a woman may sometimes cover her head with a mirṭ, it can also be worn in different ways by anyone, so it is essentially a large piece of cloth that can be unisex. In the context of the ḥadīth, the Prophet (saws) was lying on their bed, covered with the mirṭ, so he was simply covered with a large piece of cloth that belonged to 'Ā'ishah.

Moreover, Ṣaḥīḥ Muslim, Ḥadīth 2424 states that the Prophet (saws) was one morning wearing a mirṭ, and his grandsons, Al-Ḥasan and Al-Ḥusayn came to him. Then his daughter, Fāṭimah, came to him. Then 'Alī, Fāṭimah's husband and the Prophet's (saws) son-in-law, came to him. And the Prophet (saws) wrapped them all under the mirṭ. This shows just how large a mirṭ can be and that it is not just a piece of clothing for a woman.

Chapter 24

War and Jihād

Islām is a religion of peace. The Qur'ān and the Sunnah teach us to forgive when we are angry; to treat others with justice and respect, regardless of their race, ethnicity, gender, or even religion; and to not be aggressive. It is forbidden in Islām to force others to adhere to the religion. War is not enjoined upon Muslims except out of defense, security, and the upholding of justice, and, contrary to popular misconception, the Arabic word *jihād* does not mean "holy war." Jihād means "struggle," and it refers to struggling for the sake of God, both inwardly and outwardly – a concept that is shared in other religions. Any who commit despicable atrocities in the name of Islām have no true basis on which to do so. On the contrary, Muslims are obliged to respect all. Furthermore, non-combatants, women, children, the elderly, and monks are not to be killed in war.

[39]Permission to fight is granted to those who are attacked, because they have been wronged. God indeed has the power to help them. [40]They are those who have been driven out of their homes unjustly, only because they said, 'Our Lord is God.' If God did not repel the aggression of some people by means of others, monasteries and churches and synagogues and mosques, wherein the name of God is much invoked, would surely be destroyed. God will surely help him who helps His cause—God is indeed Powerful and Mighty. (Qur'ān 22:39-40)

[190]And fight in God's cause against those who wage war against you, but do not commit aggression, for surely, God does not love aggressors.
[191]Slay them wherever you find them. Drive them out of the places from which they drove you, for persecution is worse than killing. Do not fight them at the Sacred Mosque unless they fight you there. If they do fight you, slay them. Such is the recompense for those who deny the truth.
[192]But if they desist, then surely God is Most Forgiving and Most Merciful. [193]Fight them until there is no more persecution and religion

belongs to God alone. If they desist, then let there be no hostility, except towards aggressors. [194][There will be retaliation in] a sacred month for [an offence in] a sacred month; violation of sanctity calls for fair retribution. Thus you may exact retribution from whoever transgresses against you, in proportion to his transgression. Fear God and know that God is with those who are mindful of Him. (Qur'ān 2:190-194)

[75]And how should you not fight for the cause of God, and for the oppressed men, women, and children who say, 'Deliver us, Lord, from this city of wrongdoers. Grant us a protector out of Your grace, and grant us a supporter out of Your grace'? (Qur'ān 4:75)

[256]There shall be no compulsion in religion. True guidance has become distinct from error. Whoever refuses to be led by false gods and believes in God has grasped the strong handhold that will never break. God is All-Hearing and All-Knowing. (Qur'ān 2:256)

Faḍālah ibn 'Ubayd narrated: The Messenger of God (saws) said, "The one who strives in jihād is the one who strives against himself." (Jāmi' At-Tirmidhī, Ḥadīth 1621; Zubayr 'Alī Za'ī graded it ṣaḥīḥ.)

'Abdullāh ibn Yazīd (ra) narrated: The Prophet (saws) prohibited plundering and mutilation. (Ṣaḥīḥ Al-Bukhārī, Ḥadīth 5516)

'Abdullāh ibn 'Umar (ra) narrated: A woman was found killed in one of the battles of the Prophet (saws), so the Messenger of God (saws) condemned the killing of women and children. (Ṣaḥīḥ Al-Bukhārī, Ḥadīth 3014)

Rabāḥ ibn Rabī' (ra) narrated: The Messenger of God (saws) said, "Do not kill women or workers!" (Sunan Abū Dāwūd, Ḥadīth 2669; Al-Albānī graded it ḥasan ṣaḥīḥ.)

'Abdullāh ibn 'Amr (ra) narrated: The Messenger of God (saws) said, "Verily, the worst transgressors to God are those who kill in the Sacred Mosque, those who kill whoever did not fight him, or those who kill with the vindictiveness of ignorance." (Musnad Aḥmad, Ḥadīth 6681; Aḥmad Shākir graded it ṣaḥīḥ.)

Ibn 'Abbās (ra) narrated: When the Messenger of God (saws) dispatched his armies, he would say, "Go forth in the name of God, and fight in the way of God those who deny God. Do not be treacherous, do not embezzle the spoils, do not mutilate, and do not kill children, nor the monks in their monasteries." (Musnad Aḥmad, Ḥadīth 2728; Al-Arnā'ūṭ graded it ḥasan.)

Abū Hurayrah (ra) narrated: The Prophet (saws) said, "Do not wish to meet the enemy in battle, but if you meet them, be steadfast." (Ṣaḥīḥ Al-Bukhārī, Ḥadīth 3026; Ṣaḥīḥ Muslim, Ḥadīth 1741)

Yaḥyā ibn Sa'īd narrated: Abū Bakr (ra) dispatched armies to Syria, and he said, "I give you ten instructions: Do not kill a woman, nor a child, nor an infirm elder. Do not cut down fruit-bearing trees, nor tear down inhabited buildings. Do not slaughter sheep or camels, except for food. Do not burn or drown bees nests. Do not steal from the spoils, and do not act cowardly." (Al-Muwaṭṭa' by Mālik ibn Anas, Ḥadīth 918 [Book 21, Ḥadīth 10])

Suicide

Suicide is considered a major sin in Islām. It is strictly forbidden not only in instances of war but also under any circumstance. The Qur'ān states:

29 And do not kill yourselves. (Qur'ān 4:29)

And the following ḥadīths state:

Abū Hurayrah (ra) narrated: The Prophet (saws) said, "He who commits suicide by throttling shall keep on throttling himself in Hellfire and he who commits suicide by stabbing himself shall keep on stabbing himself in Hellfire." (Ṣaḥīḥ Al-Bukhārī, Ḥadīth 1365)

Abū Hurayrah (ra) narrated: The Prophet (saws) said, "Whoever purposely throws himself from a mountain and kills himself will be in Hellfire falling down into it and abiding therein perpetually. And whoever drinks poison and kills himself with it, he will be carrying his poison in his hand and drinking it in Hellfire wherein he will abide perpetually. And whoever kills himself with an iron weapon will be carrying that weapon in his hand and stabbing his abdomen with it in Hellfire wherein he will abide perpetually. (Ṣaḥīḥ Al-Bukhārī, Ḥadīth 5778; Ṣaḥīḥ Muslim, Ḥadīth 109)

Thābit ibn Aḍ-Ḍaḥḥāk (ra) narrated: The Messenger of God (saws) said, "If somebody commits suicide with anything in this world, he will be tortured with that very thing on the Day of Resurrection." (Ṣaḥīḥ Al-Bukhārī, Ḥadīth 6047; Ṣaḥīḥ Muslim, Ḥadīth 110)

Jundub ibn 'Abdullāh (ra) narrated: The Messenger of God (saws) said, "Amongst the nations before you there was a man who got a wound, and, growing impatient (with its pain), he took a knife and cut his hand with it, and the blood did not stop till he died. God said, 'My slave hurried to bring death upon himself, so I have forbidden him (to enter) Paradise.'" (Ṣaḥīḥ Al-Bukhārī, Ḥadīth 3463)

Chapter 25
Slavery and Islām

The Qur'ān and the Sunnah do not enjoin enslaving people, but in many places the Qur'ān and the Sunnah promote the freeing of slaves. Slavery is now officially outlawed in the Muslim world, and Islām established the pathway for this to happen through its rulings, even if many so-called Muslims throughout history did not follow those rulings and mistreated slaves. The only way that one could become a slave, according to Islām, was if they were a captive of war, and even then, they had to be treated with kindness. It was forbidden to sell a free person. If a slave desired to set up a contract to earn their freedom, then their owner had to oblige them. A slave had to be fed and clothed in the same way that their owner was, and it was forbidden to overburden a slave with work unless the owner helped the slave out with the work. If one abused their slave, then the atonement was to free them. A slave woman could not be separated from her child. A slave could not be raped or forced into prostitution. And overall, it was emphasized that freeing a slave was a good deed and would save the person who freed them from Hellfire. Furthermore, when one looks at slavery through the context of the commands of the Prophet Muḥammad (saws) to be merciful, to be gentle, to not cause harm, and to do unto others what one would have done unto them, then one would not be able to justify abusing a slave.

The Qur'ān states:

11 But he has not attempted the challenging path. 12 What will explain to you what the challenging path is? 13 ***It is the freeing of a slave****; 14 or the feeding in times of famine 15 of an orphaned relative 16 or some needy person in distress, 17 and to be one of those who believe and urge one another to steadfastness and compassion. (Qur'ān 90:11-17)*

177 Virtue does not consist in whether you face towards the East or the West. Virtue means believing in God, the Last Day, the angels, the Book and the prophets. The virtuous are those who, despite their love for it, give away their wealth to their relatives and to orphans and the very poor, and to travelers and those who ask [for charity], ***and to set slaves free****, and who attend to their prayers and pay the alms, and who keep their pledges when they make them, and show patience in hardship and adversity, and in times of distress. Such are the true believers, and such are the God-fearing. (Qur'ān 2:177)*

[60]*Alms are only for: the poor, the needy, those employed to administer alms, conciliating people's hearts,* ***freeing slaves****, those in debt, spending for God's cause, and for travelers in need. It is a legal obligation enjoined by God. God is All-Knowing and Wise. (Qur'ān 9:60)*

[92]*No believer should kill another believer, unless it be by mistake. Anyone who kills a believer by mistake* ***should free a believing slave*** *and pay blood money to the victim's relatives unless they forego it as an act of charity. If the victim belongs to a people at war with you, but is a believer, then the compensation is to* ***free a believing slave****. If he belongs to a people with whom you have a treaty, then blood-money should be handed over to his relatives and* ***a believing slave set free****. Anyone who lacks the means must fast for two consecutive months. Such is the penance imposed by God. God is All-Knowing and Wise. (Qur'ān 4:92)*

[89]*God will not call you to account for your meaningless oaths, but He will call you to account for the oaths which you swear in earnest. The expiation for a broken oath is the feeding of ten poor people with such food as you normally offer to your own people; or the clothing of ten poor people; or* ***the freeing of one slave****. Anyone who lacks the means shall fast for three days. That is the expiation of your breaking the oaths that you have sworn. Do keep your oaths. Thus God explains to you His commandments, so that you may be grateful. (Qur'ān 5:89)*

[36]*Worship God, and do not associate partners with Him. Be good to your parents, to relatives, to orphans, to the needy, and the neighbor who is a kinsman, and the neighbor who is not related to you and your companions and the travelers* ***and those whom you rightfully possess****. God does not like arrogant, boastful people. (Qur'ān 4:36)*

[33]*Those who do not have the means to marry should keep themselves chaste until God grants them enough out of His bounty. If any of your slaves desire a deed of freedom, write it out for them, if you find any goodness in them, and give them some of the wealth God has given you.*

Do not force your [slave] maids into prostitution, in order to enrich yourself, when they wish to preserve their chastity. Yet if anyone forces them, once they have been forced, God will be Forgiving and Merciful to them. (Qur'ān 24:33)

The following ḥadīths state:

Ibn 'Umar (ra) narrated: The Prophet (saws) said, "If anyone beats his slave for an offence he did not commit, or slaps him, the atonement due from him (i.e., the free person) is to set him (i.e., the slave) free." (Ṣaḥīḥ Muslim, Ḥadīth 1657; Riyāḍ Aṣ-Ṣāliḥīn, Ḥadīth 1605)

Abū Dharr (ra) narrated: The Prophet (saws) said, "They (i.e., slaves) are your brothers whom God has placed under your control, so feed them what you eat, clothe them with what you wear, and do not burden them with more than they can bear. If you do burden them, then help them." (Ṣaḥīḥ Al-Bukhārī, Ḥadīth 30; Ṣaḥīḥ Muslim, Ḥadīth 1661)

Abū Hurayrah (ra) narrated: The Prophet (saws) said, "God said, 'I will be against three people on the Day of Resurrection: one who makes a covenant in My name, but he proves treacherous; one who sells a free person (as a slave) and eats the price; and one who employs a laborer and gets the full work done by him but does not pay him his wages.'" (Ṣaḥīḥ Al-Bukhārī, Ḥadīth 2227)

Abū Hurayrah (ra) narrated: The Messenger of God (saws) said, "Whoever frees a believing slave, God will ransom each of his limbs from the Fire for each of his (the slave's) limbs, until He ransoms his private part for his private part." (Ṣaḥīḥ Al-Bukhārī, Ḥadīth 6715; Ṣaḥīḥ Muslim, Ḥadīth 1509; Riyāḍ Aṣ-Ṣāliḥīn, Ḥadīth 1358)

Suwayd ibn Muqarrin Al-Muzanī (ra) narrated: We were seven brothers without a servant except one, and one of us slapped her, so the Prophet (saws) ordered us to free her. (Jāmi' At-Tirmidhī, Ḥadīth 1542; Zubayr 'Alī Za'ī graded it ṣaḥīḥ.)

Abū Bakr (ra) narrated: The Messenger of God (saws) said, "The evil custodian (of a slave) will not enter Paradise." (Jāmi' At-Tirmidhī, Ḥadīth 1946; Al-Albānī graded it ḥasan.)

Ibn 'Abbās (ra) narrated: When the Messenger of God (saws) besieged the people of Aṭ-Ṭā'if, he freed their slaves who came out to him. (Musnad Aḥmad, Ḥadīth 3257; Aḥmad Shākir graded it ṣaḥīḥ.)

Salamah ibn Al-Muḥabbiq (ra) narrated: A man had intercourse with the servant girl of his wife, so the matter was referred to the Prophet (saws). He (i.e., the Prophet (saws)) said, "If she had done so willingly, then she belongs to him, and he must pay the likes of her price. If he had forced her, then she is free, and he must pay the likes of her price." (Musnad Aḥmad, Ḥadīth 20060; Ibn Al-Qayyim graded it ḥasan.)

Abū Ayyūb (ra) narrated: The Messenger of God (saws) said, "Whoever separates a mother from her child, God will separate him from his loved ones on the Day of Resurrection." (Jāmi' At-Tirmidhī, Ḥadīth 1566; Al-Albānī graded it ḥasan.)

Abū Hurayrah (ra) narrated: The Prophet (saws) told a man who broke his fast in Ramaḍān to free a slave, or to fast for two (consecutive) months, or to feed sixty poor people. (Ṣaḥīḥ Muslim, Ḥadīth 1111)

'Alī ibn Abū Ṭālib (ra) narrated: The last words which the Messenger of God (saws) spoke were: "The prayer, the prayer. Fear God regarding those whom your right hands possess." (Sunan Abū Dāwūd, Ḥadīth 5156; Al-Albānī graded it ṣaḥīḥ.)

Chapter 26

Apostasy and Islām

Apostasy means to leave a religion. Apostatizing from Islām is considered a major sin in the religion.

85 If anyone seeks a religion other than Islām, it will not be accepted from him. He will be among the losers in the Hereafter. 86 How would God bestow His guidance upon people who have opted for unbelief after having embraced the faith and having borne witness that this Messenger is true and [after] all evidence of the truth has come to them? For God does not guide such wrongdoers. 87 Such people will be recompensed with rejection by God, by the angels, by all humanity. 88 In this state they shall abide forever; their punishment shall not be lightened nor shall they be granted respite. 89 Except for those who afterwards repent and reform. God is Forgiving and Merciful. (Qur'ān 3:85-89)

There are those people, both Muslims and non-Muslims, who assert that the legal punishment for apostasy in Islām is death. It is easy for one to state this and to bring as evidence certain ḥadīths that may initially appear to prove a point, but everything has its context, and, upon deeper examination of what Islām teaches, one finds that apostasy is not necessarily punishable by death.

Firstly, there is the famous statement in the Qur'ān:

256 There shall be no compulsion in religion. True guidance has become distinct from error. Whoever refuses to be led by false gods and believes in God has grasped the strong handhold that will never break. God is All-Hearing and All-Knowing. (Qur'ān 2:256)

"No compulsion in religion" means that you cannot compel, or force, someone to adhere to the religion. This statement seems to clearly end the issue of compulsion in religion, and the sentiment is echoed in other verses of the Qur'ān, such as:

[40]Whether We show you part of what We have promised them or cause you to pass away [before that], your mission is only to give warning. It is for Us to do the reckoning. (Qur'ān 13:40)

[45]We know best what those who deny the truth say. You are not there to force them. So remind, with this Quran, those who fear My warning. (Qur'ān 50:45)

[22]You are not their keeper. (Qur'ān 88:22)

It would not be logical for the Qur'ān to repeat a concept, not only in the above verses but in other places as well, and then for the religion to give a command to do the opposite. However, there exist the following ḥadīths:

Ibn 'Abbās (ra) narrated: The Messenger of God (saws) said, "Whoever changed his religion, kill him." (Ṣaḥīḥ Al-Bukhārī, Ḥadīth 6922; Bulūgh Al-Marām, Ḥadīth 1032)

Mu'ādh ibn Jabal narrated regarding a man who had accepted Islām then became a Jew: "I will not sit down till he is killed. That is the judgement of God and His Messenger." Hence, an order was given, and he was killed. (Ṣaḥīḥ Al-Bukhārī, Ḥadīth 6923; Ṣaḥīḥ Muslim, Ḥadīth 1733; Bulūgh Al-Marām, Ḥadīth 1031)

Ibn 'Abbās (ra) narrated: A blind man had a slave woman who gave birth to his child, and she was reviling the Prophet (saws) and speaking evil of him. He forbade her, but she did not desist. One night, he took a pickax, put it on her belly, and leaned on it, killing her. The Prophet (saws) was informed about that and said, "Be witness that the spilling of her blood is lawful (with impunity)." (Sunan Abū Dāwūd, Ḥadīth 4361; Bulūgh Al-Marām, Ḥadīth 1033; Ibn Ḥajar Al-'Asqalānī said its narrators are reliable, and Al-Albānī graded it ṣaḥīḥ.)

So what is the reconciliation between "no compulsion in religion" and "whoever changed his religion, kill him"? One may look to the following ḥadīth:

'Ā'ishah (ra) narrated: The Messenger of God (saws) said, "It is not permissible to shed the blood of a Muslim except in three cases: an adulterer who had been married, who should be stoned to death; or a man who killed another man intentionally, who should be killed; or a man who left Islām and waged war against God, Mighty and Sublime,

and His Messenger, who should be killed, or crucified, or banished from the land. (Sunan Abū Dāwūd, Ḥadīth 4353; Al-Albānī graded it ṣaḥīḥ; Sunan An-Nasā'ī, Ḥadīth 4048; Zubayr 'Alī Za'ī graded it ṣaḥīḥ; Bulūgh Al-Marām, Ḥadīth 994)

In this ḥadīth, the Prophet (saws) joined together the action of leaving Islām ("yakhruju minal-Islām") with waging war against God, mighty and sublime, and His Messenger ("yuḥāribullāha, 'azza wa jalla, wa rasūlahū"). In other words, if someone leaves Islām to wage war on the Muslims, then their penalty is death, and this is what was understood by early Muslims. During the time of the Prophet (saws), he and his companions were under constant threat of war from the disbelievers among Quraysh, the Jewish tribes of Al-Madīnah, and other Arab tribes. For them, leaving Islām was often tantamount to high treason because it entailed not only a change in faith but also a change in moral leaning and political standing. This is what is known as "major apostasy" or "political apostasy." However, "minor apostasy" or "religious apostasy" is a simple change in faith, and it should not be requited with death.

So whoever changed their religion and sided with the disbelievers against the Muslims, seeking to destroy Islām and the Muslim community, was to be sentenced to death. This is what was meant by "whoever changed his religion, kill him." And this is why Mu'ādh ibn Jabal had the man who reverted from Islām killed. That man had to have been waging war against the Muslims.

As for the blind man who killed his concubine for insulting the Prophet (saws), Abu Amina Elias, a well-read Muslim, states the following in his blog post entitled "Blind man kills his concubine for blasphemy?" (published on September 21, 2019, on abuaminaelias.com):

"The Prophet (ṣ) did not kill people just for insulting him. Many people insulted him, cursed him, and harmed him, yet he was forgiving, patient, and forbearing. The legal maxim of no-harm requires that one can only harm others if it is necessary to avoid a greater harm.

The Prophet (ṣ) also would not have allowed a man to designate himself as judge, jury, and executioner. If the Prophet (ṣ) did in fact pardon the man for killing his concubine, it could only have been in such a case that she was aiding or inciting the enemy. No one needs permission from authorities to fight or kill someone who is waging war against them."

Taking this into account, the concubine must have sided in some way with those who were seeking to destroy the Muslims, thereby committing treason, and that context is likely missing from the narration.

The following ḥadīths state:

Jābir ibn 'Abdullāh As-Salamī narrated: A Bedouin gave the pledge of allegiance for embracing Islām to the Messenger of God (saws), and then he got an attack of fever in Al-Madīnah and came to the Messenger of God (saws) and said, "O Messenger of God! Cancel my pledge." The Messenger of God (saws) refused to do so. The Bedouin came to him again and said, "Cancel my pledge," but he refused again. Then again, the Bedouin came to him and said, "Cancel my pledge," and the Messenger of God (saws) refused. The Bedouin finally went away, and the Messenger of God (saws) said, "Al-Madīnah is like a pair of bellows. It expels its impurities while it brightens and clears its good." (Ṣaḥīḥ Al-Bukhārī, Ḥadīth 7322; Ṣaḥīḥ Muslim, Ḥadīth 1383)

Anas ibn Mālik narrated: I said (to 'Umar), "O Commander of the Faithful, some people have turned renegade against Islām and joined the idolaters. What is to be done to them other than killing?" 'Umar ibn Al-Khaṭṭāb (ra) said, "That I take hold of them on peaceful terms is more beloved to me than everything over which the sun rises, from the horizon to the zenith." I said, "O Commander of the Faithful, what would you do if you took hold of them?" 'Umar said, "I would offer them the door through which they exited, that they would enter it again. If they did so, I would accept it from them. Otherwise I would keep them in prison." (Al-Muṣannaf by 'Abdur-Razzāq Aṣ-Ṣan'ānī, Ḥadīth 18696; Ibn Kathīr graded it ṣaḥīḥ in Musnad Al-Fārūq 2/458.)

The ḥadīth about the Bedouin shows us that the Prophet (saws) did not have the man killed simply for wanting to leave Islām. And the ḥadīth about the conversation between 'Umar and Anas shows us that even 'Umar, one of the strictest companions of the Prophet (saws), was willing to spare the lives of apostates who sided with the enemy even if they did not come back to Islām. In Islām, one cannot be forced to adhere to the religion. If one simply rejects the religion, even after accepting it, their judgment is with God.

Chapter 27
Legal Punishments in Islām

As stated earlier in the book, the word Sharī'ah is used to encompass all rulings of the religion of Islām. The word Sharī'ah literally refers to "a path to a flowing spring of water." However, it is usually used as a synonym for "law." One small aspect of the Islāmic Sharī'ah are the *ḥudūd.* It is a plural word in Arabic, and its singular form is *ḥadd.* The word ḥadd means "limit" or "boundary," but it can also be taken to mean "penalty" or "punishment." Thus, ḥudūd can refer to legal punishments.

Islāmic legal punishments are often described by non-Muslims as barbaric or extreme. Indeed, the punishments for certain major sins in Islām are severe, but this is meant to be a deterrent for criminals. Moreover, each ḥadd has so many conditions for a criminal to meet that the penalties are very difficult to justly apply. For example, adulterers are supposed to be stoned to death. However, the qualifications for this penalty actually being carried out include either a confession from a perpetrator, if they are sane, or the testimonies of four reliable witnesses who are proven to have good character. Furthermore, each of the four witnesses had to have seen the act of penetration taking place between the adulterers. In practice, this can make it very difficult to apply the legal punishment.

Another example is theft, for which the punishment is amputation of the thief's hand. However, in order for this punishment to be applied, the stolen property must have worth, it must match a certain value (a quarter of an Islāmic dīnār, which is equal to 1.0625 grams of gold), it must have been taken from a secure place, the theft has to be proven either through a confession or the testimonies of two eyewitnesses who are proven to be reliable and of good character, the thief has to be sane, the thief must not have been forced to steal, the thief must not have stolen out of dire need, and the owner has to claim the stolen property. And there may be more conditions that have not been listed here.

Adultery and theft are just two examples, but each legal punishment in Islām has conditions that make it difficult to implement, so they mainly serve as deterrents. Here is a list of certain crimes and their Islāmic punishments:

- Murder: execution. However, the victim's family may choose to forgive the murderer and accept monetary compensation. (source: Qur'ān 2:178)
- Manslaughter: monetary compensation to the victim's family or fasting for two consecutive months from dawn to sunset each day (source: Qur'ān 4:92)
- Piracy, terrorism, and rape: execution, or crucifixion, or amputation of alternate hands and feet, or exile (source: Qur'ān 5:33)
- Theft: amputation of one hand (source: Qur'ān 5:38)
- Fornication: flogging (source: Qur'ān 24:2)
- Adultery: stoning to death (source: Ṣaḥīḥ Al-Bukhārī, Ḥadīth 6829; Ṣaḥīḥ Muslim, Ḥadīth 1691 | Ṣaḥīḥ Muslim, Ḥadīth 1690)
- Slandering a person regarding their chastity: flogging (source: Qur'ān 24:4)
- Homosexual intercourse: execution (source: Sunan Abū Dāwūd, Ḥadīth 4462; Al-Albānī graded it ḥasan ṣaḥīḥ.)
- Consuming alcohol: flogging (source: Ṣaḥīḥ Al-Bukhārī, Ḥadīth 6773 | Ṣaḥīḥ Muslim, Ḥadīth 1707)

These are all considered crimes because they are Islāmically considered a threat to society at some level, even if it is only a threat to the family structure, as in the cases of sexual crimes. If there is any doubt (Arabic: *shubhah*; Arabic plural: *shubuhāt*) regarding a crime, then the legal punishment cannot be applied. If there is no prescribed legal punishment for a crime in the Qur'ān and the Sunnah, then the judge will give a *ta'zīr*, which is a verdict decided by the judge. Furthermore, only a well-informed Islāmic judge can call for a legal punishment to be implemented after sufficient evidence for a crime is provided. Anyone who is not a judge cannot act as a vigilante and implement legal punishments, whether alone or in a group. And Islāmic legal punishments only apply in lands with an Islāmic government, not in lands in which Muslims are a minority or in lands which have a secular government. Lastly, the concept of "innocent until proven guilty" firmly applies in Islām, and it is better to avoid applying the legal punishments if one can find a way out of them. The concept of leniency is proven from the statements of the Prophet (saws), his companions, and Muslim scholars.

Abū Hurayrah (ra) narrated: The Messenger of God (saws) said, "He who removes from a believer one of his difficulties of this world, God will remove one of his troubles on the Day of Resurrection. And he who finds relief for a hard-pressed person, God will make things easy for him on the Day of Resurrection. He who covers up (the faults and sins) of a Muslim, God will cover up (his faults and sins) in this world and in the Hereafter. God supports His slave as long as the slave is supportive of his brother." (Ṣaḥīḥ Muslim, Ḥadīth 2699; Riyāḍ Aṣ-Ṣāliḥīn, Ḥadīth 245)

Anas ibn Mālik (ra) narrated: I never saw a case involving legal retaliation being referred to the Prophet (saws), but that he would command pardoning the criminal. (Sunan Abū Dāwūd, Ḥadīth 4497; Al-Albānī graded it ṣaḥīḥ.)

Abū Wā'il narrated: 'Abdullāh ibn Mas'ūd (ra) said, "Avoid flogging and applying the death penalty upon Muslims as much as you can." (As-Sunan Al-Kubrā by Al-Bayhaqī, Ḥadīth 15686; Al-Albānī graded it ṣaḥīḥ.)

The scholar Ibn Taymiyyah said, "Indeed, the matter of benevolence and forgiveness towards people takes precedence over the matter of vengeance and revenge." (Minhāj As-Sunnah 4/372)

The scholar Ibn Al-Qayyim said, "Indeed, the Sharī'ah is founded upon wisdom and welfare for the servants in this life and the afterlife. In its entirety it is justice, mercy, benefit, and wisdom. Every matter which abandons justice for tyranny, mercy for cruelty, benefit for corruption, and wisdom for foolishness is not a part of the Sharī'ah even if it was introduced therein by an interpretation." (I'lām Al-Muwaqqi'īn 3/11)

Chapter 28

Selected Portions of the Qur'ān and Their Merits

It is highly recommended for a Muslim to memorize these portions of the Qur'ān in Arabic if they are able to. A Muslim should also understand their meanings and recite them regularly. Transliteration is a method used to present the sounds of a language into another language. Transliterating Arabic into English can be helpful for those who do not speak Arabic or even know its alphabet. However, if one puts their mind to it, one can learn Arabic enough to understand the Qur'ān. Everyone learns at their own pace, so do not take on too much at once, but know that it can be done.

Transliterations

A'ūdhu billāhi minash-Shayṭānir-rajīm.

Sūratul-Fātiḥah (The Opening; Chapter 1)

Bismillāhir-Raḥmānir-Raḥīm.

1. Al-ḥamdu lillāhi Rabbil-'ālamīn,
2. Ar-Raḥmānir-Rahīm,
3. Māliki Yawmid-dīn,
4. Iyyāka na'budu wa iyyāka nasta'īn.
5. Ihdinaṣ-Ṣirāṭal-Mustaqīm,
6. Ṣirātalladhīna an'amta 'alayhim
7. Ghayril-maghḍūbi 'alayhim walaḍ-ḍāllīn.

Sūratul-Kāfirūn (The Disbelievers; Chapter 109)

Bismillāhir-Raḥmānir-Raḥīm.

1. Qul yā ayyuhal-kāfirūn.
2. Lā a'budu mā ta'budūn.
3. Walā antum 'ābidūna mā a'bud.
4. Walā ana 'ābidum-mā 'abattum.
5. Walā antum 'ābidūna mā a'bud.
6. Lakum dīnukum waliya dīn.

Sūratul-Ikhlāṣ (The Sincerity; Chapter 112)

Bismillāhir-Raḥmānir-Raḥīm.

1. Qul huwallāhu aḥad.
2. Allāhuṣ-Ṣamad.
3. Lam yalid walam yūlad.
4. Walam yakullahū kufuwan aḥad.

Sūratul-Falaq (The Daybreak; Chapter 113)

Bismillāhir-Raḥmānir-Raḥīm.

1. Qul a'ūdhu biRabbil-falaq.
2. Min sharri mā khalaq.
3. Wa min sharri ghāsiqin idhā waqab.
4. Wa min sharrin-naffāthāti fil-'uqad.
5. Wa min sharri ḥāsidin idhā ḥasad.

Sūratun-Nās (Mankind; Chapter 114)

Bismillāhir-Raḥmānir-Raḥīm.

1. Qul a'ūdhu biRabbin-nās.
2. Malikin-nās.
3. Ilāhin-nās.
4. Min sharril-waswāsil-khannās.
5. Alladhī yuwaswisu fī ṣudūrin-nās.
6. Minal-jinnati wan-nās.

Āyatul-Kursī (The Verse of the Seat; Verse 255 from Chapter 2 [Sūratul-Baqarah])

Allāhu lā ilāha illā huwal-Ḥayyul-Qayyūm. Lā ta'khudhuhū sinatun walā nawm. Lahū mā fis-samāwāti wamā fil-arḍ. Man dhalladhī yashfa'u 'indahū illā bi idhnih. Ya'lamu mā bayna aydīhim wamā khalfahum. Walā yuḥīṭūna bishay-im-min 'ilmihī illā bimā shā'. Wasi'a kursīy-yuhus-samāwāti wal-arḍ. Walā ya'ūduhū ḥifẓuhumā. Wa huwal-'Alīy-yul-'Aẓīm.

The Last Three Āyāt (Verses) of Sūratul-Baqarah (Verses 284-286)

Lillāhi mā fis-samāwāti wamā fil-arḍ. Wa in tubdū mā fī anfusikum aw tukhfūhu yuḥāsibkum bihillāh. Fa yaghfiru liman yashā'u wa yu'adh-dhibu man yashā'. Wallāhu 'alā kulli shay'in qadīr.

Āmanar-rasūlu bimā unzila ilayhi mir-Rabbihī wal-mu'minūn. Kullun āmana billāhi wamalā'ikatihī wakutubihī warusulihī lā nufarriqu bayna aḥadim-mir-rusulih. Wa qālū sami'nā wa aṭa'nā. Ghufrānaka Rabbanā wa ilaykal-maṣīr.

Lā yukalliful-lāhu nafsan illā wus'ahā. Lahā mā kasabat wa 'alayhā maktasabat. Rabbanā lā tu'ākhidhnā in-nasīnā aw akhṭa'nā. Rabbanā walā taḥmil 'alaynā iṣran kamā ḥamaltahū 'alal-ladhīna min qablinā. Rabbanā walā tuḥammilnā mā lā ṭāqata lanā bih. Wa'fu 'annā waghfir lanā warḥamnā. Anta mawlānā fanṣurnā 'alal-qawmil-kāfirīn.

English Translations

I seek refuge in God from Satan, the accursed.

Sūratul-Fātiḥah (The Opening; Chapter 1)

In the name of God, the Most Compassionate, the Most Merciful.

1. All praise is due to God, the Lord of all worlds,
2. the Most Compassionate, the Most Merciful,

3. Master of the Day of Judgement.
4. You alone we worship, and to You alone we turn for help.
5. Guide us to the straight path,
6. the path of those You have blessed,
7. not of those who have incurred wrath, nor of those who have gone astray.

Sūratul-Kāfirūn (The Disbelievers; Chapter 109)

In the name of God, the Most Compassionate, the Most Merciful.

1. Say [O Prophet], 'O disbelievers,
2. I do not worship what you worship.
3. You do not worship what I worship.
4. I will never worship what you worship.
5. You will never worship what I worship.
6. You have your religion and I have mine.'

Sūratul-Ikhlāṣ (The Sincerity; Chapter 112)

In the name of God, the Most Compassionate, the Most Merciful.

1. Say [O Prophet], 'He is God, the One,
2. God, the Self-Sufficient, needed by all.
3. He does not have offspring, nor was He born,
4. and there is nothing like Him.

Sūratul-Falaq (The Daybreak; Chapter 113)

In the name of God, the Most Compassionate, the Most Merciful.

1. Say [O Prophet], 'I seek refuge in the Lord of the daybreak
2. from the evil of what He has created,
3. from the evil of darkness as it descends,
4. from the evil of those [witches casting spells by] blowing on knots
5. and from the evil of the envier when he envies.'

Sūratun-Nās (Mankind; Chapter 114)

In the name of God, the Most Compassionate, the Most Merciful.

1. Say [O Prophet], 'I seek refuge in the Lord of humankind,
2. the King of humankind,
3. the God of humankind,
4. from the mischief of the sneaking whisperer,
5. who whispers into the hearts of humankind,
6. from jinn and humankind.'

Āyatul-Kursī (The Verse of the Seat; Verse 255 from Chapter 2 [Sūratul-Baqarah])

God: there is no deity except for Him, the Ever-Living, the Eternal. Neither drowsiness nor sleep overtakes Him. To Him belong whatsoever is in the heavens and whatsoever is on the earth. Who can intercede with Him except by His permission? He knows all that is before them and all that is behind them. They can grasp only that part of His knowledge which He wills. His seat extends over the heavens and the earth, and their upholding does not weary Him. And He is the Most Exalted, the Absolute Greatest.

The Last Three Āyāt (Verses) of Sūratul-Baqarah (Verses 284-286)

All that the heavens and the earth contain belongs to God. Whether you disclose what is in your minds or keep it hidden, God will bring you to account for it. He will forgive whom He pleases and punish whom He pleases. And God has power over all things.

The Messenger believes in what has been sent down to him from his Lord, and [so do] the believers. They all believe in God, His angels, His books, and His messengers. They say, 'We do not differentiate between any of His messengers. We hear and obey. Grant us Your forgiveness, Lord. To You we shall all return!'

God does not charge a soul with more than it can bear. It shall be requited for whatever good and whatever evil it has done. [They pray], 'Our Lord, do not take us to task if we forget or make a mistake! Our Lord, do not place on us a burden like the one You placed on those before us! Our

Lord, do not place on us a burden we have not the strength to bear! Pardon us, and forgive us, and have mercy on us. You are our Guardian, so help us against the disbelievers.'

Significance and Merits of These Selected Portions

Because there are many ḥadīths that explain the significance and merits of certain portions of the Qur'ān, these ḥadīths will not be quoted herein, but the references to books that contain them, as well as the ḥadīths' authenticity, will be quoted herein. This is to maintain brevity and ease for the reader.

Significance and Merits of Sūratul-Fātiḥah

It is the first sūrah in the Qur'ān.

It is also known as Umm Al-Qur'ān (the Mother of the Qur'ān) and As-Sab' Al-Mathānī (the Seven Often-Repeated Verses).

It is a summary of the entire Qur'ān, as the Prophet (saws) said it is the Magnificent Qur'ān that was given to him. (Ṣaḥīḥ Al-Bukhārī, Ḥadīth 4474; Riyāḍ Aṣ-Ṣāliḥīn, Ḥadīth 1009| Jāmi' At-Tirmidhī, Ḥadīth 2875)

It is the greatest sūrah in the Qur'ān. (Ṣaḥīḥ Al-Bukhārī, Ḥadīth 4474; Riyāḍ Aṣ-Ṣāliḥīn, Ḥadīth 1009| Jāmi' At-Tirmidhī, Ḥadīth 2875; Zubayr 'Alī Za'ī graded it ṣaḥīḥ.| Ṣaḥīḥ Ibn Ḥibbān, Ḥadīth 774; Al-Albānī graded it ṣaḥīḥ.)

No unit (rak'ah) of any prayer is complete without it. (Ṣaḥīḥ Al-Bukhārī, Ḥadīth 756; Ṣaḥīḥ Muslim, Ḥadīth 394, 395)

God responds to every verse of it. (Ṣaḥīḥ Muslim, Ḥadīth 395)

Nothing like it has been revealed in the Torah, the Zabūr (said to be the Psalms), the Gospel, or the rest of the Furqān (i.e., the Criterion, another name for the Qur'ān). (Jāmi' At-Tirmidhī, Ḥadīth 2875, 3125; Zubayr 'Alī Za'ī graded them ṣaḥīḥ.)

No prophet was given it before Muḥammad (saws). (Ṣaḥīḥ Muslim, Ḥadīth 806; Riyāḍ Aṣ-Ṣāliḥīn, Ḥadīth 1022)

It was mentioned as a light. (Ṣaḥīḥ Muslim, Ḥadīth 806; Riyāḍ Aṣ-Ṣāliḥīn, Ḥadīth 1022)

You will not recite a letter of it, except that you will get its benefit. (Ṣaḥīḥ Muslim, Ḥadīth 806; Riyāḍ Aṣ-Ṣāliḥīn, Ḥadīth 1022)

It is used as ruqyah (healing). (Ṣaḥīḥ Al-Bukhārī, Ḥadīth 5007, 5749)

Significance and Merits of Sūratul-Kāfirūn

It is recommended to recite it before going to sleep. (Jāmi‘ At-Tirmidhī, Ḥadīth 3403; Zubayr ‘Alī Za’ī graded it ṣaḥīḥ; Sunan Abū Dāwūd, Ḥadīth 5055; Al-Albānī graded it ṣaḥīḥ.)

It is equal to one fourth of the Qur’ān. (Al-Mu‘jam Al-Kabīr by Aṭ-Ṭabarānī, Ḥadīth 13319; Al-Albānī graded it ṣaḥīḥ in Ṣaḥīḥ At-Targhīb 583)

The Prophet would recite Al-Kāfirūn and Al-Ikhlāṣ in the two rak‘ahs before Fajr. (Ṣaḥīḥ Muslim, Ḥadīth 726)

Significance and Merits of Sūratul-Ikhlāṣ

It is a summary of the Oneness of God.

It is equal to one third of the Qur’ān. (Ṣaḥīḥ Al-Bukhārī, Ḥadīth 5013; Riyāḍ Aṣ-Ṣāliḥīn, Ḥadīth 1011| Ṣaḥīḥ Al-Bukhārī, Ḥadīth 5015; Riyāḍ Aṣ-Ṣāliḥīn, Ḥadīth 1010| Ṣaḥīḥ Muslim, Ḥadīth 812; Riyāḍ Aṣ-Ṣāliḥīn, Ḥadīth 1012| Jāmi‘ At-Tirmidhī, Ḥadīth 2896; Zubayr ‘Alī Za’ī graded it ṣaḥīḥ.| Al-Mu‘jam Al-Kabīr by Aṭ-Ṭabarānī, Ḥadīth 13319; Al-Albānī graded it ṣaḥīḥ in Ṣaḥīḥ At-Targhīb 583.)

Love for it leads to Paradise. (Jāmi‘ At-Tirmidhī, Ḥadīth 2901; Zubayr ‘Alī Za’ī graded it ṣaḥīḥ; Riyāḍ Aṣ-Ṣāliḥīn, Ḥadīth 1013| Jāmi‘ At-Tirmidhī, Ḥadīth 2901; Zubayr ‘Alī Za’ī graded it ḥasan.| Ṣaḥīḥ Muslim, Ḥadīth 813)

Whoever recites it 10 times will have a palace in Paradise. (Al-Mu‘jam Al-Awsaṭ by Aṭ-Ṭabarānī, Ḥadīth 281; Al-Albānī graded it ṣaḥīḥ in As-Silsilah Aṣ-Ṣaḥīḥah 2/136.)

Whoever recites it, along with Āyatul-Kursī, after every obligatory prayer, nothing will stop him from entering Paradise except death. (Bulūgh Al-Marām, Ḥadīth 258)

The Prophet would recite Al-Kāfirūn and Al-Ikhlāṣ in the two rak'ahs before Fajr. (Ṣaḥīḥ Muslim, Ḥadīth 726)

Significance and Merits of Sūratul-Falaq and Sūratun-Nās

Together, these two sūrahs are known as Al-Mu'awwidhatayn (the Two Refuges).

Their like was not seen before they were revealed. (Ṣaḥīḥ Muslim, Ḥadīth 814; Riyāḍ Aṣ-Ṣāliḥīn, Ḥadīth 1014)

They are the best way of seeking refuge with God. (Sunan An-Nasā'ī, Ḥadīth 5432; Al-Albānī graded it ṣaḥīḥ.| Sunan An-Nasā'ī, Ḥadīth 953; Zubayr 'Alī Za'ī graded it ṣaḥīḥ.| Jāmi' At-Tirmidhī, Ḥadīth 2058; Al-Albānī graded it ṣaḥīḥ.)

It is recommended to recite them after every prayer. (Jāmi' At-Tirmidhī, Ḥadīth 2903; Al-Albānī graded it ṣaḥīḥ.)

It is recommended to recite them before going to sleep. This can be done by blowing into one's hands, reciting the sūrahs, and then wiping the hands over the body. (Ṣaḥīḥ Al-Bukhārī, Ḥadīth 6319| Sunan Abū Dāwūd, Ḥadīth 1523; Al-Albānī graded it ṣaḥīḥ.)

They can be used as ruqyah (healing) by reciting them and then blowing one's breath over the body. (Ṣaḥīḥ Al-Bukhārī, Ḥadīth 5016; Ṣaḥīḥ Muslim, Ḥadīth 2192)

Significance and Merits of Sūratul-Ikhlāṣ, Sūratul-Falaq, and Sūratun-Nās – All Three Together

If one recites these three sūrahs three times every evening and every morning, they will suffice that person against everything. (Jāmi' At-Tirmidhī, Ḥadīth 3575; An-Nawawī graded it ṣaḥīḥ; Zubayr 'Alī Za'ī graded it ḥasan.)

When the Prophet (saws) went to bed every night, he used to cup his hands together and blow over them, recite these three sūrahs, and then rub his hands over whatever parts of his body he was able to rub, starting with his head, face and front of his body. He used to do that three times. (Ṣaḥīḥ Al-Bukhārī, Ḥadīth 5017)

Their like was not revealed in the Torah, the Zabūr, the Gospel, or the rest of the Qur'ān. (Musnad Aḥmad, Ḥadīth 16810; Al-Albānī graded it ṣaḥīḥ in As-Silsilah Aṣ-Ṣaḥīḥah 2861.)

Significance and Merits of Āyatul-Kursī

It is the greatest verse in the Qur'ān. (Ṣaḥīḥ Muslim, Ḥadīth 810; Riyāḍ Aṣ-Ṣāliḥīn, Ḥadīth 1019| Jāmi' At-Tirmidhī, Ḥadīth 2878; Al-Albānī graded it ḥasan.)

Whoever recites it at night before bed will have a guardian appointed over them by God, and Satan will not be able to come near them until morning. (Ṣaḥīḥ Al-Bukhārī, Ḥadīth 5010; Riyāḍ Aṣ-Ṣāliḥīn, Ḥadīth 1020)

Whoever recites it, along with Sūratul-Ikhlāṣ, after every obligatory prayer, nothing will stop him from entering Paradise except death. (Al-Mu'jam Al-Awsaṭ by Aṭ-Ṭabarānī, Ḥadīth 8060; Al-Albānī graded it ṣaḥīḥ in Ṣaḥīḥ Al- Jāmi'; Bulūgh Al-Marām, Ḥadīth 258)

Significance and Merits of The Last Two Verses of Sūratul-Baqarah

God revealed them directly to the Prophet Muḥammad (saws) in Heaven, during Al-Isrā' wal-Mi'rāj (the Night Journey and the Ascension). (Ṣaḥīḥ Muslim, Ḥadīth 173)

Whoever recites them in the night, it is enough for him. (Ṣaḥīḥ Al-Bukhārī, Ḥadīth 5051; Ṣaḥīḥ Muslim, Ḥadīth 807; ; Riyāḍ Aṣ-Ṣāliḥīn, Ḥadīth 1017)

They are from a book that God wrote 2,000 years before He created the heavens and the earth. (Jāmi' At-Tirmidhī, Ḥadīth 2882; Zubayr 'Alī Za'ī graded it ḥasan; Al-Albānī graded it ṣaḥīḥ in Ṣaḥīḥ Al- Jāmi'.)

If they are recited in a home for three nights, no devil will come near it. (Jāmi' At-Tirmidhī, Ḥadīth 2882; Zubayr 'Alī Za'ī graded it ḥasan; Al-Albānī graded it ṣaḥīḥ in Ṣaḥīḥ Al- Jāmi'.)

No prophet was given them before Muḥammad (saws). (Ṣaḥīḥ Muslim, Ḥadīth 806; Riyāḍ Aṣ-Ṣāliḥīn, Ḥadīth 1022| Musnad Aḥmad, Ḥadīth 23251; Al-Arnā'ūṭ graded it ṣaḥīḥ.)

They were mentioned as a light. (Ṣaḥīḥ Muslim, Ḥadīth 806; Riyāḍ Aṣ-Ṣāliḥīn, Ḥadīth 1022)

You will not recite a letter of them, except that you will get their benefit. (Ṣaḥīḥ Muslim, Ḥadīth 806; Riyāḍ Aṣ-Ṣāliḥīn, Ḥadīth 1022)

'Alī recommended that a person should recite the last <u>three</u> verses of Sūratul-Baqarah before going to sleep. (Sunan Ad-Dārimī, Ḥadīth 3289; An-Nawawī graded it ṣaḥīḥ.)

Appendix A
The Gabriel Ḥadīth

'Umar ibn Al-Khaṭṭāb (ra) narrated:

One day we were sitting with the Messenger of God (saws) when there appeared before us a man dressed in exceedingly white clothes, his hair exceedingly black. There were no signs of travel on him, and none of us recognized him. He sat down knee to knee opposite the Prophet (saws), upon whose thighs he placed his palms. And he said, "O Muḥammad, inform me about Islām (Submission)." The Messenger of God (saws) said, "Islām is that you testify that there is no god except for Allāh (God) and that Muḥammad is the Messenger of God, and that you establish the ṣalāh (prayer), pay the zakāh (obligatory charity), fast in Ramaḍān, and perform Ḥajj (the major pilgrimage) to the House (i.e., the Ka'bah) if you are able to." He (the questioner) said, "You have spoken the truth."

He ('Umar ibn Al-Khaṭṭāb) said, "We were amazed that having questioned him he should corroborate him."

He (the questioner) said, "Inform me about Īmān (Faith)." He (the Prophet (saws)) said, "That you believe in God and His angels and His books and His messengers and the Last Day, and that you believe in the Decree (of God), both its positive and its negative." He (the questioner) said, "You have spoken the truth."

He (the questioner) said, "Inform me about Iḥsān (Excellence)." He (the Prophet (saws)) said, "That you worship God as if you are seeing Him, for if you do not see Him, then He indeed sees you."

He (the questioner) said, "Inform me about the (Last) Hour." He (the Prophet (saws)) said, "The one who is questioned about it knows no better than the questioner."

He (the questioner) said, "Tell me about its signs." He (the Prophet (saws)) said, "That the slave-girl will give birth to her mistress; and that you will find barefoot, destitute herdsmen constructing buildings higher and higher."

He ('Umar ibn Al-Khaṭṭāb) said, "Then he (the questioner) went away, and I stayed a while. Then he (the Prophet (saws)) said to me, "O 'Umar, do you know who the questioner was?"

I said, "God and His Messenger know best." He (the Prophet (saws)) said, "He indeed was Gabriel. He came to you to teach you your religion."

(Ṣaḥīḥ Muslim, Ḥadīth 8)

Appendix B
Ḥadīths about Hygiene

Abū Hurayrah [(ra)] narrated: The Prophet [(saws)] said, "Five acts are a part of natural instinct: circumcision, shaving pubic hair, shortening the moustache, clipping the nails, and plucking hair from the armpits." (Ṣaḥīḥ Al-Bukhārī, Ḥadīth 5891; Ṣaḥīḥ Muslim, Ḥadīth 257)

Yūnus ibn 'Abdul-A'lā narrated: I entered the home of Ash-Shāfi'ī, may God have mercy on him, and with him was a barber shaving his armpits. Ash-Shāfi'ī said, "I know the Sunnah is to pluck them, but I am not strong enough to endure the pain." (Sharḥ of An-Nawawī on Ṣaḥīḥ Muslim 257)

Anas [(ra)] narrated: A time limit was set for us for trimming the moustache, clipping the nails, plucking the armpit hairs, and shaving the pubes: that was not to be left for more than forty days. (Ṣaḥīḥ Muslim, Ḥadīth 258)

Nāfi' narrated: Ibn 'Umar [(ra)] narrated: The Prophet [(saws)] said, "Do the opposite of what the pagans do. Keep the beards and cut the moustaches short." Whenever Ibn 'Umar performed Ḥajj or 'Umrah, he used to hold his beard with his hand and cut whatever remained outside his grasp. (Ṣaḥīḥ Al-Bukhārī, Ḥadīth 5892; Ṣaḥīḥ Muslim, Ḥadīth 259)

Acknowledgements

I would like to thank my parents (Paula and Ayub), Imam Adam, Imam Atif, Rashad I, Rashad II, Abdul Salaam, Andy, and Jeremy for their helpful reviews, suggestions, discussions, and encouragements.

Glossary

'Abd: slave, servant

Adhān: the call to prayer

Ahlus-Sunnah wal-Jamā'ah: the People of the Sunnah and the Community; the proper name of the Sunnī sect

Ākhirah: the afterlife

Al-Anṣār: the Helpers; those native to Al-Madīnah

'Alayhis-Salām: "Peace be upon him"

Al-Fātiḥah: The Opening; the first sūrah of the Qur'ān

Al-Ḥajar Al-Aswad: the Black Stone; a special stone that descended from Paradise

Alhamdulillāh: "All praise is for God"

Al-Iḍṭibā': uncovering one's right shoulder

Al-Islām: the proper name of the religion of Islām

Al-Jannah: the Garden, Paradise, Heaven

Al-Kutub Al-Ar'ba'ah: the Four Books (of Shī'ah ḥadīths)

Al-Kutub As-Sittah: the Six Books (of ḥadīths)

Allāh: the name of the One God; God with a capital "G"

Allāhu Akbar: "God is Greater"

Al-Madīnah: the second holiest city in Islām

Al-Masīḥ: the Christ, the Messiah

Al-Masīḥ Ad-Dajjāl: the Antichrist

Al-Masjid Al-Aqṣā: the third holiest masjid in Islām, located in Jerusalem

Al-Masjid Al-Ḥarām: the holiest masjid in Islām, located in Makkah

Al-Masjid Al-Nabawī: the second holiest masjid in Islām, located in Al-Madīnah

Al-Muhājirūn: the Emigrants; those who emigrated to Al-Madīnah

Al-Quds: Jerusalem, the third holiest city in Islām

'Amal: deed, work; plural: a'māl

An-Nār: the Fire (of Hell)

'Aqīdah: creed

'Arafāt: a large plain to the southeast of Makkah, where pilgrims go during Ḥajj

Arkān: pillars; singular: rukn

'Aṣr: the late afternoon prayer

As-Sā'ah: the Hour; the (Last) Hour

As-Salām: The Ultimate Peace, a name of God

As-Salāmu 'alaykum: "Peace be upon you"; the standard Muslim greeting

Astaghfirullāh: "I seek God's forgiveness"

A'ūdhu billāhi minash-Shayṭānir-rajīm: "I seek refuge in God from Satan the accursed"

'Awrah: the part of the body that is not permissible to be exposed to the public and while praying

Āyah: sign; a verse of the Qur'ān; plural: āyāt

Ayyām Al-Bīḍ: "the White Days"; the three days in the middle of a lunar month when the moon is most full

Ayyām At-Tashrīq: "the Days of Drying Meat"; the fourth, fifth, and sixth days of Ḥajj; the 11th, 12th, and 13th of Dhūl-Ḥijjah

'Azza wa jall: "Mighty and Sublime"

Bayyinah: evidence

Bint: "daughter of"

Bismillāh: "in the name of God"

Bismillāhir-Raḥmānir-Raḥīm: "in the name of God, the Infinitely Good, the Most Merciful"

Caliph: the ruler of the Muslim community after the Prophet (saws)

Ḍa'īf: weak, in reference to ḥadīth terminology

Deen: an alternate, and common, spelling of dīn

Dhikr: remembrance (of God); plural: adhkār

Dhūl-Ḥijjah: the 12th month in the Hijrī calendar; the month in which the Ḥajj pilgrimage takes place

Dīn: religion; judgment

Du'ā': supplication (to God)

Ḍuḥā: an optional prayer performed in the morning after sunrise

Dunyā: this world

'Eid: an alternate spelling of 'Īd

'Eid Mubārak: "Blessed 'Eid"; a common greeting on 'Eid

Fajr: the dawn prayer

Faqīr: a poor person; one who is destitute or possesses at most half of their minimum needs; plural: fuqarā'

Farḍ: mandatory; plural: farā'iḍ

Fidyah: a compensation

Fiqh: jurisprudence

Ghā'ib: absent

Ghusl: a full bath

Ḥadd: boundary, limit, legal punishment; plural: ḥudūd

Hadī: a sacrificial animal

Ḥadīth: narration; a narration of a saying, action, or approval of the Prophet Muḥammad (saws); plural: aḥādīth

Ḥāfiẓ: preserver; one who has memorized the entire Qur'ān

Ḥajj: the obligatory pilgrimage; a pillar of Islām

Ḥalāl: lawful, permissible

Ḥaqq: Truth

Ḥaram: a sanctuary

Ḥarām: unlawful, impermissible

Ḥasan: good, in reference to ḥadīth terminology

Ḥawḍ: fountain tank

Hidāyah: guidance

Ḥijāb: a veil; a partition; a woman's head covering

Hijrah: the migration of the Prophet (saws) from Mecca to Medina

Hijrī: the Islāmic calendar

Ḥikmah: wisdom

Ḥirā': the cave in Jabal An-Nūr, where the Qur'ān was first revealed on Earth

Hudā: guidance

'Ibādah: worship

Ibn: "son of"

'Īd: the Muslim holiday; a day of celebration

'Īd Al-Aḍḥā: the holiday towards the end of the days of Ḥajj

'Īd Al-Fiṭr: the holiday after Ramaḍān

'Iddah: a waiting period

Ifrād: Ḥajj by itself, with no 'Umrah

Ifṭār: breaking the fast

Iḥrām: a spiritual state of being in which one intends to perform 'Umrah and/or Ḥajj, and in which certain things become forbidden to an individual

Iḥsān: excellence

Ijmā': consensus

Ilāh: god with a lowercase "g"

'Ilm: knowledge

Imām: the person who leads Muslims in prayer; the spiritual leader of a Muslim community; a scholar; (for Shī‘ahs:) a Muslim leader descended from Muḥammad (saws) through ‘Alī

Imāmiyyah: the largest Shī‘ah denomination; also known as the Twelver denomination

Īmān: faith

Injīl: Gospel

Innā lillāhi wa innā ilayhi rāji‘ūn: "indeed, we belong to God, and indeed, to Him we shall return"

In shā Allāh: "if God wills," "God-willing"

Iqāmah: the call that establishes that the prayer is about to begin

‘Ishā’: the early night prayer

Ishrāq: Ḍuḥā prayed in the early part of its time, immediately after sunrise

Islām: "submission (to the will of God)"; the religion that was revealed to Muḥammad (saws)

Isnād: a chain of narrators, in reference to ḥadīth terminology

Istighfār: to ask forgiveness (from God)

Istinjā’: cleansing one's private parts with water

I‘tikāf: staying in the mosque for a period of time

Izār: the lower iḥrām garment for a man

Jabal Ar-Raḥmah: the Mount of Mercy; the hill in Arafāt

Jabal An-Nūr: the Mountain of Light

Jahannam: Hell

Jamā‘ah: congregation

Jamrah: pillar; plural: jamarāt

Janāzah: funeral

Jazākallāhu khayran: "May God reward you with good"

Jerusalem: the third holiest city in Islām

Jibrīl: Angel Gabriel

Jihād: struggle

Jinn: a type of being generally not perceptible to humans, originally created from a smokeless flame of fire

Jumu'ah: Friday, the 6th day of the week

Kaaba: an alternate spelling of "Ka'bah"

Ka'bah: the first house of worship that God appointed

Kāfir: disbeliever; plural: kāfirūn or kuffār

Khalīfah: the Arabic word for caliph

Khaṭīb: one who gives a sermon

Khaṭmul-Qur'ān: the finishing of the recitation of the entire Qur'ān

Khul': divorce initiated by a wife

Khul'a: an alternate spelling of khul'

Khulafā' Ar-Rāshidūn: the Rightly Guided Caliphs

Khuṭbah: sermon

Khuṭbah Al-Ḥājah: the Sermon of Necessity

Kitāb: book; plural: kutub

Koran: an alternate spelling of "Qur'ān"

Kusūf: eclipse

Lā ḥawla walā quwwata illā billāh: "There is no might and no strength except with God"

Lā ilāha illallāh: "There is no god except for Allāh"

Laylah Al-Qadr: the Night of Power, on one of the odd nights of the last ten nights of Ramaḍān

Madhhab: a school of thought; plural: madhāhib

Maghrib: the sunset prayer

Mahr: dowry; a gift from a groom to a bride

Makkah: the holiest city in Islām

Malak: angel; plural: malā'ikah

Manārah: the Arabic word for "minaret"

Maqām Ibrāhīm: the Standing Place of Abraham (as)

Marwah: a hill in Makkah, near the Ka'bah

Mas'ā: the path between the hills of Ṣafā and Marwah; the place where sa'ī is done

Mā shā Allāh: "what God willed"

Masjid: the Arabic word for "mosque"; plural: masājid

Masjid Qubā': a special mosque in Al-Madīnah

Maṭāf: the flat, wide circle around the Ka'bah, where pilgrims circle the Ka'bah

Matn: text, in reference to ḥadīth terminology

Mawḍū': fabricated, in reference to ḥadīth terminology

Mecca: an alternate spelling of "Makkah"

Medina: an alternate spelling of "Al-Madīnah"

Minā: a place near Makkah where pilgrims go during Ḥajj

Minaret: a tower from which the adhān is called

Minbar: pulpit

Mīqāt: a place from which one assumes iḥrām; plural: mawāqīt

Miskīn: a needy person; one who has financial difficulty but is better off than a faqīr (poor person); plural: masākīn

Mosque: the place of worship for Muslims

Muezzin: one who calls people to prayer

Muḥammad: the last prophet in Islām and the one to whom the Qur'ān was revealed

Mu'min: believer; plural: mu'minūn

Munāfiq: hypocrite; one who outwardly professes Islām but inwardly disbelieves; plural: munāfiqūn

Muṣallā: an area for prayer; a sanctuary

Muṣḥaf: a copy of the Qur'ān written in its original Arabic

Muslim: one who submits to God; an adherent of the religion of Islām; plural: Muslimūn

Muzdalifah: a place where pilgrims stop at during Ḥajj

Nabī: prophet; plural: nabiyyūn or anbiyā'

Nafl: a voluntary action; plural: nawāfil

Nafs: soul; self

Namirah: a place where pilgrims stop at during Ḥajj

Nikāḥ: marriage

Niqāb: a face covering

Niṣāb: the minimum amount of wealth that one must have in order to pay zakāh

Niyyah: intention

Qabr: grave

Qadar: decree

Qiblah: the direction to be faced while praying

Qirān: 'Umrah and Ḥajj with no gap in the middle

Qiyām Al-Layl: worship performed at night

Qiyās: analogy

Qur'ān: the holy book of Islām

Qurbāni: a sacrifice

Rabb: Lord

Raḍiyallāhu 'anhu: "may God be pleased with him"

Rak'ah: a unit of prayer

Ramaḍān: the 9th month of the Hijrī calendar; the month in which Muslims fast

Ramī: stoning

Raml: A light jog

Rasūl: messenger; plural: rusul

Rasūlullāh: Messenger of God

Rawātib: the 12 optional rak'ahs prayed in a day

Rawḍah: a garden; the part of Masjid An-Nabawī that is a garden of Paradise; plural: riyāḍ

Ridā': the upper iḥrām garment for a man

Rūḥ: spirit

Rūḥ Al-Qudus: the Holy Spirit

Ruqyah: a method of healing

Ṣā': four complete scoops as scooped up with two hands; it is approximately equal to 3 kilograms or 6.5 pounds

Ṣadaqah: general charity

Ṣadaqat Al-Fiṭr: another term for zakāt al-fiṭr

Ṣafā: a hill in Makkah, near the Ka'bah

Ṣaḥābī: companion; plural: ṣaḥābah or aṣḥāb

Ṣaḥīḥ: authentic, in reference to ḥadīth terminology

Ṣaḥīḥ Al-Bukhārī: the most authentic book of ḥadīths

Ṣaḥīḥ Muslim: the second most authentic book of ḥadīths

Saḥūr: the meal before dawn that is eaten by one about to fast

Sa'ī: a ritual in 'Umrah and Ḥajj in which one goes back and forth in between the hills of Ṣafā and Marwah

Salām: peace

Ṣalāh: the formal prayer; a pillar of Islām; plural: ṣalawāt

Ṣallallāhu ‘alayhi wa sallam: “commendations and peace from God be upon him”

Ṣawm: fasting; the obligatory fasting is the one in Ramaḍān; a pillar of Islām

Shahādah: testimony (of faith); a pillar of Islām

Sharī‘ah: law; all of the rulings derived from the Qur’ān and the Sunnah that are to be implemented in a believer’s life

Shayṭān: Satan

Shī‘ah: the second largest sect in Islām; its proper name is Shī‘atu ‘Alī

Shī‘atu ‘Alī: the Partisans of ‘Alī; the proper name of the Shī‘ah sect

Shifā’: healing

Shirk: associating partners with God

Shubhah: doubt; plural: shubuhāt

Shurūq: sunrise

Sīrah: a genre of literature about the biography of the Prophet Muḥammad (saws)

Ṣiyām: another word for “ṣawm”

Subḥānahū wa ta‘ālā: “Glorified and Exalted is He”

Subḥānallāh: “Glory be to God”

Suḥūr: an alternate spelling of saḥūr

Sunnah: example; the example of the Prophet Muḥammad (saws)

Sunnah Mu’akkadah: an optional act that the Prophet (saws) always performed

Sunnī: the largest sect in Islām; its proper name is Ahlus-Sunnah wal-Jamā‘ah

Sūrah: a chapter of the Qur’ān

Sutrah: a barrier in front of a praying person

Tābi': a successor or follower; one from the generation following the ṣaḥābah; plural: tābi'ūn

Tābi'ut-tābi'īn: one from the generation following the tābi'ūn; plural: tābi'ūt-tābi'īn

Tafsīr: a type of literature that explains the Qur'ān

Tahajjud: the optional prayer at night

Taḥiyyah: greeting; used in the phrase "Taḥiyyatul-Masjid," which means, "Greeting of the Mosque"

Tahlīl: to say "Lā ilāha illallāh"

Taḥmīd: to say "Alḥamdulillāh"

Takbīr: to say "Allāhu Akbar"

Ṭalāq: divorce

Talbiyah: a group of phrases praising God that are chanted after one assumes iḥrām

Tamattu': 'Umrah and Ḥajj with a gap in the middle

Taqwā: righteousness, piety

Tarāwīḥ: the optional night prayer during Ramaḍān

Tasbīḥ: to say "Subḥānallāh"

Ṭawāf: circumambulation; circling around the Ka'bah

Ṭawāf Al-Ifāḍah: a ṭawāf performed during Ḥajj

Ṭawāf Al-Qudūm: the ṭawāf of arrival

Ṭawāf Al-Wadā': the farewell ṭawāf

Ṭawāf Az-Ziyārah: another name for ṭawāf al-ifāḍah

Tawakkul: reliance; reliance on God

Tawbah: repentance

Tawfīq: the internal and external means to do acts that please God

Tawḥīd: the Oneness of God; monotheism

Tawrāh: Torah

Tayammum: purification with clean dust

Ta'zīr: a legal punishment decided by a judge

Twelver: a term for the Imāmiyyah denomination in the Shī'ah sect

Uḍḥiyah: a sacrifice

Ummah: nation; a very large number of people

'Umrah: the lesser pilgrimage that is not obligatory

'Uranah: a place where pilgrims stop at during Ḥajj

Wa 'alaykum As-Salām: "and upon you be Peace"; the reply to As-Salāmu 'alaykum

Waḥy: revelation

Wa iyyāk: "and you"; the response to "Jazākallāhu khayran"

Walī: a guardian

Walīmah: a wedding feast

Witr: an odd number; the optional prayer that has one extra rak'ah, to be performed at night between 'Ishā' and Fajr

Wuḍū': ablution, washing

Yaqīn: certainty

Yawm: a 24-hour day; in the Hijrī calendar it begins at sunset (Maghrib), as opposed to midnight

Yawm 'Arafah: the best day of the year; the second day of Ḥajj; the 9th of Dhul-Ḥijjah

Yawm 'Āshūrā': the day on which God saved Moses and his people from Pharaoh, on the 10th of Muḥarram

Yawm Ad-Dīn: the Day of Judgement

Yawm Al-Ākhir: the Last Day

Yawm Al-Qiyāmah: the Day of Resurrection

Yawm An-Naḥr: the third day of Ḥajj; the 10th of Dhūl-Ḥijjah

Yawm At-Tarwiyah: the first day of Ḥajj; the 8th of Dhūl-Ḥijjah

Zabihah: an alternate spelling of dhabīḥah

Zakāh: a type of annual charity; a pillar of Islām

Zakāt Al-Fiṭr: a certain charity to be paid at the end of Ramaḍān

Zamzam: the sacred well in Makkah, near the Ka‘bah

Ẓuhr: the early afternoon prayer

Recommended Resources

Textual Resources

1. **The Qur'an** with translation and commentary by 'Abdullah Yusuf 'Ali
2. **The Qur'an** with translation and commentary by M.A.S. Abdel Haleem
3. **The Clear Qur'an** with translation and commentary by Dr. Mustafa Khattab
4. **Muhammad: His Life Based on the Earliest Sources** by Martin Lings
5. **The Sīrah of the Prophet** by Dr. Yasir Qadhi
6. **Atlas on the Prophet's Biography** by Dr. Shawqi Abu Khalil
7. **The History of the Four Caliphs** by Shaykh Muhammad Al-Khudari Bak Al-Bajuri
8. **Scholars of Hadith** by Syed Bashir Ali
9. **In the Company of Scholars** by Furhan Zubairi
10. **Riyad-us-Saliheen** by Imam An-Nawawi (published in two volumes with commentary by Darussalam)
11. **Bulugh Al-Maram** by Imam Ibn Hajar Al-'Asqalani (published with commentary by Darussalam)
12. **Fortress of the Muslim** by Sa'id ibn Ali Al-Qahtani (published by Darussalam)
13. **The Prophet's Prayer Described** by Imam Nasiruddin Al-Albani
14. **The Everything Understanding Islam Book** by Christine Huda Dodge

Online Resources

www.whyislam.org

This is a site that introduces Islām.

www.letmeturnthetables.com

This is a site that debunks slanders and misconceptions against Islām.

This book is not affiliated in any way with the resources mentioned above.

Bibliography

The Qur'an. Translated by Maulana Wahiduddin Khan, Goodword Books, 2009. 2019.

Abdul-Aziz bin Abdullah bin Baz. *Explanation of Important Lessons*. Compiled by Muhammad bin Ali bin Ibrahim Al-Arfaj, Maktaba Dar-us-Salam, 2002. 2003.

'Abdullah ibn 'Abdur-Rahman Ad-Darimi. *Sunan Ad-Darimi*.

Abu Dawud Sulayman ibn Ash'ath. *Sunan Abu Dawud*. Translated by Yaser Qadhi, Darussalam, 2008.

Ahmad ibn Nuruddin 'Ali ibn Muhammad ibn Hajar Al-'Asqalani. *Bulugh Al-Maram*. Translated by Darussalam, Darussalam, 2002.

Ahmad ibn Shu'ayb An-Nasa'i. *Sunan An-Nasa'i*. Translated by Nasiruddin al-Khattab, Darussalam, 2007.

Ali, Syed Bashir. *Scholars of Hadith*. IQRA' Educational Foundation, 2003.

"Allaah decrees disasters for children – why?" *Islamqa*, 11 April 2009, https://islamqa.info/en/answers/13610/allaah-decrees-disasters-for-children-why. Accessed 17 August 2024.

Al-Mubarakpuri, Safi-ur-Rahman. *Ar-Raheeq Al-Makhtum*. Darussalam, 1979. 1996.

"Conditions of the Validity of Prayer." *Islamqa*, 21 April 2008, https://islamqa.info/en/answers/107701/conditions-of-the-validity-of-prayer. Accessed 12 June 2022.

"Different Types of Fidyah in Hajj." *Islamqa*. 9 May 2011, https://islamqa.info/en/answers/49027/different-types-of-fidyah-in-hajj#:~:text=It%20is%20prohibited%20for%20the,game%2C%20to%20enter%20into%20a. Accessed 17 August 2024.

Elias, Abu Amina. *abuaminaelias.com*. Accessed 2024.

Isma'il ibn 'Umar ibn Kathir. *Tafsir Ibn Kathir (Abridged)*. Darussalam, 2003.

Jalaluddin Abdur-Rahman ibn Abu Bakr As-Suyuti. *Ad-Durr Al-Manthur*.

Lings, Martin. *Muhammad: His Life Based on the Earliest Sources*. Inner Traditions, 1983. 2006.

Muhammad ibn 'Abdullah ibn Al-Khatib At-Tibrizi. *Mishkat Al-Masabih*. Translated by James Robson, Sh. Muhammad Ashraf, Publishers, 1990. 1991.

Muhammad ibn 'Isa At-Tirmidhi. *Jami' At-Tirmidhi*. Translated by Abu Khallyl, Darussalam, 2007.

Muhammad ibn Ishaq and 'Abdul-Malik ibn Hisham. *The Prophetic Sirah (The Life of Muhammad)*. Translated by Alfred Guillaume, Oxford University Press, 1955. 2004.

Muhammad ibn Isma'il Al-Bukhari. *Sahih Al-Bukhari*. Translated by Muhammad Muhsin Khan, Darussalam, 1997.

Muhammad ibn Nuh Al-Albani. *Khutbat-ul-Haajah*. Translated by Isma'eel Alarcon, Al-Ibaanah Book Publishing, USA, 2006.

Muhammad ibn Nuh Al-Albani. *The Prophet's Prayer Described*. Translated by Usama ibn Suhaib Hasan, Jam'iat Ihyaa Minhaaj Al-Sunnah, 2007.

Muhammad ibn Yazid ibn Majah. *Sunan Ibn Majah*. Translated by Nasiruddin al-Khattab, Darussalam, 2007.

Muslim ibn Al-Ḥajjāj. *Sahih Muslim*. Translated by Nasiruddin al-Khattab, Darussalam, 2007.

Qadhi, Yasir. *The Sīrah of the Prophet*. Kube Publishing Ltd., 2023.

Sulayman ibn Ahmad At-Tabarani. *Al-Mu'jam Al-Kabir*.

"The fate of kuffaar who did not hear the message of Islam." *Islamqa*, 10 July 1998, https://islamqa.info/en/answers/1244/the-fate-of-kuffaar-who-did-not-hear-the-message-of-islam. Accessed 11 June 2022.

"When to Read Surat al-Kahf on Friday?." *Islamqa*, 03 March 2010, https://islamqa.info/en/answers/10700/when-to-read-surat-al-kahf-on-friday. Accessed 28 August 2023.

Yahya ibn Sharaf An-Nawawi. *Riyad As-Salihin.* Translated by Muhammad Amin Abu Usamah Al-Arabi bin Razduq, Darussalam, 2003.

Zeno, Muhammad bin Jamil. *The Pillars of Islam and Iman.* Dar-us-Salam Publications, 1996.

www.ingramcontent.com/pod-product-compliance
Lightning Source LLC
Chambersburg PA
CBHW060904120626
46553CB00001B/202
* 9 7 9 8 9 9 1 4 7 6 8 0 5 *